# A Little History of

# MY FOREST LIFE

A Little History of My Forest Life
First edition, ©2002
Preface, introduction, interpretation, notes, glossaries, index copyright Victoria Brehm 2002

Printed in the United States of America

ISBN 0-9702606-2-8

Cover photographs courtesy of Northwest Architectural Archives and the editor
Design and Production: Clarity, Duluth, Minnesota

Library of Congress Cataloging-in-Publication Data
A Little History of My Forest Life / by Eliza Morrison / edited by Victoria Brehm

Includes bibliographical references.
ISBN 0-9702606-2-8
1. Indian women—Great Lakes Region—autobiography.
2. Indians—Great Lakes Region—social life and customs.
3. Racially mixed people—United States—autobiography.
4. Frontier and pioneer life—Great Lakes Region

Ladyslipper Press
15075 County Line Road
Tustin, Michigan 49688 USA
Phone/Fax 231-775-9455
ladyslipperpress.com

# A Little History of

# MY FOREST LIFE

## AN INDIAN-WHITE AUTOBIOGRAPHY

*Eliza Morrison*

✺※✺

### EDITED BY VICTORIA BREHM

*Eliza Morrison about 1894*
*Photograph by William Gray Purcell*

*He will triumph who understands how to conciliate and combine with the greatest skill the benefits of the past with the demands of the future.*

Joseph N. Nicollet
Journal of 1836

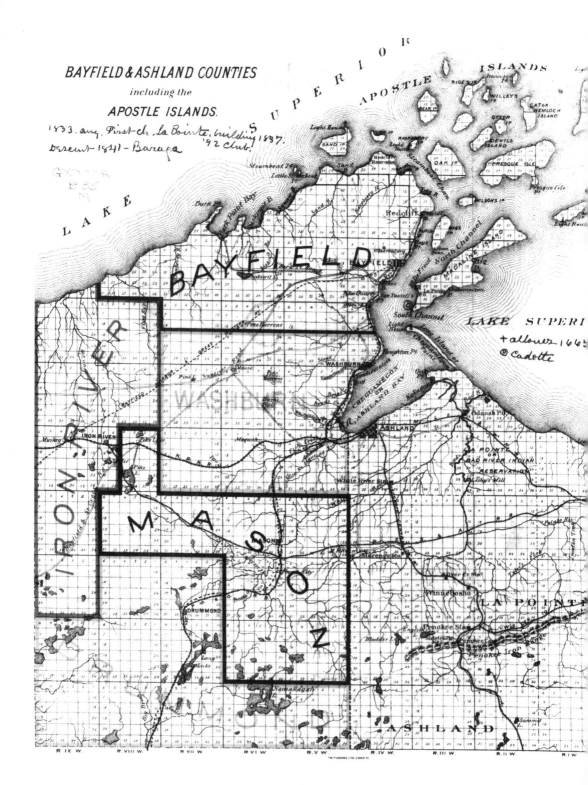

BAYFIELD & ASHLAND COUNTIES

*including the*

APOSTLE ISLANDS.

# CONTENTS

# ILLUSTRATIONS

Illustration credits begin on page 196

# PREFACE

I FIRST KNEW ELIZA MORRISON'S autobiography as a citation in a computerized data base that listed it as being available at the Minnesota Historical Society in St. Paul. When other business brought me to the Twin Cities, I looked it up and was presented with a small, elegant, letterpress volume, the work of a printing aficionado, that appeared to be only a part of a longer manuscript. Intrigued, I approached the reference librarian on duty, Mark Green, and asked if he knew where the entire manuscript was. He frowned in quizzical frustration and said that yes, it was part of a longer manuscript and he vaguely remembered where that manuscript was, but it would take him a while to find it. I should be patient. A few hours later he returned and directed me to the Northwest Architectural Archives, which at that point was in temporary quarters in a old building in another section of the Cities. I followed his hand-drawn map through the by-ways and found it, then was ushered into an old, cramped, badly lighted building with makeshift tables and handed a copy of a typescript made sometime in the 1960s. People around me were rolling out large drawings and blueprints. The pipes overhead clanked. But as soon as I started to read the original, or as close to the original as the typescript came, I was transported back to the world of the late nineteenth century and into the midst of a love story, told in the unique voice of a wonderful storyteller who had a fascinating story to tell.

Eliza Morrison's autobiography had been written as a series of letters to Catherine Gray, the grandmother of William Gray Purcell, a Prairie School architect in the Twin Cities. When he died and left his papers to the University of Minnesota, Mrs. Morrison's manuscript had come along with everything else, including all his drawings, publications, a lifetime of professional correspondence, decades of letters between himself and his grandparents, and their correspondence as well. Purcell's grandfather, William Cunningham Gray, had edited a religious newspaper in Chicago, the *Interior*, and wrote weekly columns about the north woods during his summers there. The Morrisons had worked as hired help at the Gray camp. Purcell had written a memoir about his childhood experiences in northern Wisconsin with his grandparents, *St. Croix Trail Country*, mining part of Eliza Morrison's narrative and parts of his grandfather's newspaper columns for his book. He had planned to edit and publish Eliza Morrison's narrative, but age and ill-health prevented it. After he died, Austin J. McLean, Curator of Special Collections at the University of Minnesota, took brief sections of the manuscript and edited them to conform to standard English, then hand-printed a small volume in a run of a few dozen copies. This was the book that was listed in contemporary computerized data bases. The original manuscript lay unknown even to Eliza Morrison's descendants, many of whom still live on the Bad River Reservation at Odanah, Wisconsin, a few hours' drive away.

When I found *A Little History of My Forest Life* I was working on a long anthology of Great Lakes American Indian literatures, which is what had brought me to the Minnesota Historical Society. Once I read Eliza Morrison's narrative, I decided to stop work on the anthology and edit her autobiography instead. It would, I thought serenely, only take a few months, and I would learn about northern Wisconsin in the process, which would help with the *Great Lakes Indian Reader*. After all, I'd studied autobiography and Great Lakes American Indian narratives, so this should not be difficult. Let me also say the history of literature is replete with books that writers began while escaping from huge projects and that turned into projects of their own; Mark Twain's *Life on the Mississippi* comes to mind.

Three years later, as I was *still* editing *A Little History of My Forest Life*, I was a chastened, although wiser, editor. But I had also spent numerous hours in the company of a charming, kind, generous, unfailingly entertaining companion who was not only highly intelligent but a gifted raconteur as well. Eliza Morrison was everything William Gray Purcell had described her as being: a wonderful woman. No matter how many times I went back into her text, I never failed to be interested, and I never failed to learn something. If her initial impulse in writing her autobiography was

to teach others about her way of life, she succeeded. My only hope now is that I have managed to bring her story to light so that others may experience what I did, and what "Young Willie" Purcell, the boy she and her friend Mrs. Bousky nicknamed *deen de sa*, "bluejay," apparently for his raucous inquisitiveness, experienced in the 1880s and 1890s. In June 1941, when he was collecting information and photographs he had taken decades before prefatory to writing *St. Croix Trail Country*, Purcell wrote to Daniel Russell "Danny" Morrison, one of Eliza's sons who was living in Milwaukee:

"I ran across this picture of your mother the other day so I send it along. I think it is a very good one it must have been taken about 1896. There in the old North Woods I was a busy kid—into everything—always lining up people to take their pictures. That was my hobby—developed them down in the root house, and if Georgie [Morrison] or Old Mr. Ramsdel stomped down to the lake to get two pails of water, sand would jar down through the cracks in the roof logs and make spots on my pictures. I hope you don't mind it too much—living in the city.

"Beside me as I write, are a pair of moccasins that were made for me by your mother with nice embroidery on them and which I have always cherished. If we could draw up to the old oil cloth covered table in the little old cabin at Spider Lake, have a venison stew with a few onions and some pork in it, a cup of Arbuckles coffee and some blueberry pie—that wouldn't be hard to take! We can be thankful that we had these simple and good experiences—contact with the virgin forest and natural men and women. . . .”

Danny Morrison may have had other ideas about that cabin, since he had grown up poor and suffering prejudice in a way William Gray Purcell never could have imagined. But Purcell's memory of the woman who had mothered him when his own mother was absent was no less valid despite his comfortable city childhood and his privileged summers in the north. We are wiser readers now; we understand the complications of race and prejudice and class in ways neither the Grays nor Purcell did, but that has no effect on the artistry of Eliza Morrison's story. She entertains us all, just as she did a rambunctious boy from Chicago over a hundred years ago.

## Editing *A Little History of My Forest Life*

MY AIM IN EDITING MRS. MORRISON'S autobiography has been to preserve her original manuscript as closely possible while making changes that increase the enjoyment of contemporary readers. Trained as a scholar, initially I was loathe to make any changes at all, since close textual interpretation depends on the nuances of a writer's exact wording. But Mrs. Morrison was writing in her second language, English, and she struggled with spelling and grammar, since both are inconsistent, as is her punctuation. Some punctuation marks she never uses and likely never learned to use them. As the sample pages I have included here demonstrate, Mrs. Morrison's main

concern appears to have been setting down her story in a reasonably readable format using as little paper as possible: paragraphing, punctuation, and regularity of grammar were items Kitty Gray probably had volunteered to change as necessary if selections from the letters were ever printed as part of an *Interior* editorial. In addition, there are some unavoidable repetitions, since Mrs. Morrison seems to have sent the manuscript off in sections, which would preclude rereading for consistency. While she may have sent rewritten copies of some portions of the manuscript to Oak Park, she also may have written some sections without revision, mailing the letters off by attaching them to a stick alongside the railroad tracks for the train to pick up as she did her usual letters to Kitty Gray, a correspondence that sometimes included items such as plum trees.

The changes I have made are designed to preserve Eliza Morrison's unique voice while attempting to avoid confusing readers. The original manuscript does not use capital letters at the beginning of sentences, runs sentences together, does not use quotation marks for direct discourse, and rarely signals paragraph breaks. In the original, it resembles the diaries of Lewis and Clark. To read the entire manuscript exactly as it is written often involves translation as well as comprehension, a task contemporary, non-scholarly readers find burdensome. Therefore, at the risk of alienating everyone—scholars who want an exact replication of the original and non-scholars who want easily readable, standard English—I have

added some punctuation and created paragraphs and broken up run-on sentences
when necessary for clarity. I have, however,
done this with a light hand, so readers
accustomed to finding apostrophes in con-
junctions such as "don't," for example, will
find few here because Mrs. Morrison seldom used them. I have added commas
when necessary, and I have added quotation marks to signify direct discourse,
although she never used these either. I have
broken long, run-on sentences into shorter
sentences. Mrs. Morrison never used question marks, which I have added when
necessary. When I have added words or
phrases for clarity, I have enclosed them in
brackets. Mrs. Morrison's underlining has
been converted to italics.

The result is, I hope, a reasonable and
happy compromise between an exact transcription of the original, which can be
difficult and confusing to read since sentences can continue for pages, and a
rewritten version that reflects an editor's
rigid and high-handed imposition of standard English on the text of a writer who
can't argue, and worse, that ends up sound-
ing like Standard Ethnologist Speak, which
is a good deal more boring than Mrs. Morrison. Purists on both sides of the
textual-change debate will be dissatisfied,
but most readers will benefit, since Mrs.
Morrison's lovely, lilting voice and her
unique syntax, a product of two languages
and two cultures, remain intact and yet the
readability of her narrative is enhanced.
Those who wish to read the original in its
entirety can order copies from the North-

west Architectural Archives, Elmer Ander-
son Library, University of Minnesota,
222-21st Avenue South, Minneapolis, MN
55455.

To further aid readers I have included
several glossaries. The Glossary of
Chippewa Words and Phrases lists all the
Chippewa Mrs. Morrison uses in *A Little
History of My Forest Life*. Readers should
note that Chippewa/Ojibwe is one of the
more difficult languages in the world; after
years of trying to learn it, Henry Rowe
Schoolcraft gave up and said Greek was easier. Chippewa also has numerous dialects,
and these are different enough to provide a
basis for jokes among the Chippewa. Trans-
lators are less amused, especially since Mrs.
Morrison's Chippewa does not always
appear in Chippewa dictionaries. The Glossary of Places attempts to locate each place
and gives a brief enough description so that
it can be found on the enclosed maps. The
French explorer Joseph N. Nicollet, whose
observation on change opens this book,
noted that "the geologic language of the
Chippewa is richer than ours," as readers
will realize when they look carefully at this
glossary. The Glossary of Personal Names
lists all the names, both Chippewa and
white, mentioned in the text, and identifies
them whenever possible. The Chronology
lists the major events of Eliza Morrison's
life, although I have included a number of
events, including the births and deaths of
two children, she does not mention. I have
also included side bars throughout the text
describing cultural customs and historical
events related to her narrative that readers

may find necessary in order to understand more fully what she describes.

No book is ever written by one person and *A Little History of My Forest Life* is the product not only of Eliza Morrison's devoted hours in the winters of 1894 and 1895, but also of her husband, John Morrison, and of William Gray Purcell, who saved her manuscript and collected many of the photographs that illustrate it. As I have continued Purcell's work, I have been aided by numerous friends and professionals who deserve heartfelt thanks for their continued support. Mark Green, formerly of the Minnesota Historical Society and now of the Michigan Historical Collections in Ann Arbor, first located the manuscript for me. Without him, this book would never have been. Barbara Bezat of the Northwest Architectural Archives routinely furnished information, read the completed manuscript and, because of her twenty-year's experience with the Purcell Archive, kept me from making many mistakes; to her I owe as large a debt of thanks as I owe to Mark Green. Bob Mackreth, of the National Park Service, Apostle Islands National Park, not only kept me from making mistakes, but cheerfully crawled around Madeline Island with me to replicate Eliza's sugar-camp clamber up a cliff, although we did it in summer not winter. Bob unfailingly provided information and photographs, and he and his wife, Sue, and their dogs, opened their home in Washburn, Wisconsin, to me and my peripatetic family while I did research. They made northern Wisconsin home. Patty J. Bigboy,

of the Bad River Reservation, took time after a long day of running the tribal casino to tromp around old graveyards looking for tombstones when she surely would have preferred to be home with her feet up. Liz Arbuckle, Eliza and John Morrisons's great-great granddaughter, cheerfully answered questions and kept me current on terminology. John "Doug" Morrison, Eliza and John's great-grandson, provided me with a valuable genealogy and answered a number of stupid questions with patient goodwill. His brother, Earl "Toby" Morrison, told me stories of the Morrison's life on the reservation after they left Spider Lake. George Morrison, Eliza and John's great-great-grandson, answered my questions with an attorney's care and attention. He also sent me to Paul DeMain who gave me more genealogy and a great deal of help as well. Laura J. Corbine, of the Bureau of Indian Affairs in Ashland, helped with enrollments at Bad River and with genealogy. Jim Zorn, Bad River Reservation attorney, helped me understand the State v. Morrin case. Linda Long, at the Division of Special collections, University of Oregon-Eugene, looked through the large Purcell archive housed there, then sent copies of the Morrison manuscript and of Eliza Morrison's later letters to Catherine Gray. The Oak Park Historical Society cheerfully furnished clippings and biographical data on William Gray Purcell. Jennifer and Drew Harrison helped create maps and kept my computer functional, no small effort. A number of friends read drafts of the manuscript and made comments that helped it become a better book: Barbara Chrenka, Diana VanAntwerp, Jane Everhart, Betsy Erickson, and Don Boggs made excellent suggestions that led me to understand how I needed to rewrite the introduction and interpretation. Otto Korpela, Bayfield County Register of Deeds, helped me trace the history of Island Lake Camp and the Morrison homestead. Karen Miller, Ashland County Register of Deeds, helped me check deeds and death certificates. Theresa Schenck patiently answered my questions about Cadotte genealogy and searched her records until she found John Morrison's mother's name. Cheri Cornell's cleverness helped solve a puzzle. Professor Anton Treuer of Bemidji State University translated the Ojibwa for John Morrison's family totem, confirming that it did indeed look like an alligator. Finally, the interlibrary loan librarians at Grand Valley State University—Laurel Balkema, Millie Holtvluwer, Yvonne Williams, and Jill Reyers—requested dozens of books for me and, when I wasn't on campus, mailed them to me and said nothing when they became long overdue.

To these and to many others who helped and whose names I have mistakenly omitted, I ask that you please consider this your book too.

*Victoria Brehm, Ph.D*
*Tustin, Michigan*

# Introduction

## Eliza Morrison's World

LATE OCTOBER IN NORTHERN WISCONSIN
is cool and the nights come early, portend-
ing the deep cold and darkness of *biboon*,
what Chippewa call winter, that will soon
begin. When the clouds are heavy, Lake
Superior is sullen, heaving slowly at the
shore as if it were already thick with ice; on
sunny days it shines like hammered silver,
refusing to turn blue. At night, the "falling
leaves moon" rides the sky with the wind
keening through bare branches. It is the
time of waiting, of preparing for the long
darkness, of the beginning of "winter
work," those tasks that were set aside during the busy summer and that now can be
taken up again to pass the hours until
spring.

In a raw, treeless frontier town a few
miles south of the lakeshore, one the whites
call Iron River and the Chippewa knew as
*pikwabiku sibi*, river of iron, the harvest
chores are nearly complete. The songbirds
have flown and only the ravens are left,
arguing over some spilled corn in the gardens before sunset. Soon they too will leave
and the snow will come, melt, come again,
and finally stick. Then the horses' breath
will freeze in the air and coat their whiskers
with rime as they stand blowing and stamp-
ing with their wagons outside the stores
along the single main street. Inside a small,
rented house on the edge of town it is
quiet, the only sound the snap of a burning

log in the iron cookstove as the gray-haired
woman sits down at the table after wiping
the supper dishes and carefully aligns a
stack of ruled paper in the pool of yellow
light made by the kerosene lamp. One of
the geraniums she potted up in coffee cans
before she left the farm sits cheerfully on
the table next to her and it makes her
happy to have it there. She picks up the pen
to begin, but then pauses, as if listening.

It is so still now, too quiet with all the
older the boys off working. Now there is
only her husband dozing in his chair and
their daughter and son doing homework
beside the stove, not like when everyone
was home at the farm where the room was
always noisy until bedtime, filled with talking and Charlie playing his harmonica.
There had seldom been any time to write
long letters then! She would get off a few
lines maybe when there was a break in the
work, just enough to let her friend Mrs.
Gray know how things were going with her
summer camp, with the children and the
farm. But then everyone grew up so fast,
and now they will leave the farm forever
next spring. Her husband says that's good.
He says if they're going to take up an allotment on the reservation, they must do it
now.

The wood settles noisily in the stove
and she pulls herself back to the stack of
paper. Mrs. Gray's letter, written nearly a

month ago, is on the table in front of her but she doesn't need to read it again. She promised she would write down her stories and she will. The Grays will go through at least a bushel of moccasins again next summer, so she needs to get started on them pretty soon, but first there are the stories to write. Dipping the pen Dr. Gray gave her in the ink, she takes a sheet of paper from the top of the stack and moves the lamp a bit closer for better light. Then, in the careful penmanship she learned from the young woman with the strange accent at the mission school on Madeline Island so many years before, Eliza Morrison writes the date, October 23, 1894, precisely in the upper-right corner of the page.

SO MAY HAVE BEGUN ONE OF THE MOST remarkable autobiographies created by a woman in the nineteenth century, one of a scant handful created by mixed-race, or métis, writers, and wholly unlike those of the white American industrialists, frontiersmen, and ministers who were writing at the same time. That it was not lost is a small miracle. Only because a man once called Willie fondly remembered his childhood summers in the Wisconsin woods with his grandparents, where a part-Indian woman who called him deen de se, bluejay, cheerfully posed for his new camera, made birchbark baskets, and told stories, was *A Little History of My Forest Life* preserved. William Gray Purcell grew up to become a Prairie School architect in Minneapolis who had

trained with Louis Sullivan in Chicago, but he never forgot his time in the St. Croix River country near Lake Superior. When his grandmother died, he preserved among his papers the manuscript Eliza Morrison had written for her. Mrs. Morrison, as she was known to him in an era of more formality when even husbands and wives did not always address each other by their first names, had not created a manufacturing dynasty in Chicago, or conquered souls for Christ on the frontier, or founded a town or a city, or tamed anything except a brood of energetic sons. Other than a few short trips, she had never been far from the island in Lake Superior where she was born, which she still missed and still visited to see the house where she'd grown up and the cemetery where her people were buried. She may not have thought about writing anything until she agreed to cook and help out for the family from Oak Park, Illinois, who had built a primitive summer camp a few miles from the farm. The Grays had a big campfire every night to which everyone was invited and where everyone told stories. They'd heard all Mrs. Morrison's stories before, but when the Morrisons decided to sell their farm and move to the Bad River Indian Reservation and might no longer be working at the camp in summer, Mrs. Morrison remembered the Grays had asked her to write down her stories. Because Mrs. Gray, her "most dearest friend," had been so kind—every winter there were barrels of clothes and food—Eliza Morrison felt obligated to repay, and writing her stories was a way to do that.

*Campfire Gathering*
*Front row: William Cunningham Gray, Everett Sisson, Margarette Bousky, Ralph Purcell, Willie Purcell*
*Second row: Albert Muther, Jonathon Gray, John Norton, Kitty Gray, Annie Zeigler, Eliza Morrison*
*Top row: C. A. Purcell, Will Gray, Eunice Morrison*

She did not tell the entire truth about her life, few autobiographers do. The long years when she had to care for her invalid mother, forced to leave her beloved mission school to do so, the births and deaths of two babies she never mentions, the hardening prejudices against Indians and mixed-race people she surely experienced, the sadness she felt when she had to sell her childhood home to move to the woods to homestead: these the reader must piece together from government records or imagine. What writers write about themselves for others to read is notoriously unreliable, not the "truth," but the creation of an image the writer holds, or believes the reader holds. Autobiography is always part wish-fulfillment, a chance to create in narrative a better or more coherent reality than the writer lived, and memory, never perfect, can often play tricks. Legal documents may be a bit more truthful, but baptismal records, marriage licenses, deeds, and death certificates are frequently completed by relatives with something to hide or who never knew the truth. Even if these records are accurate, that does not mean they allow for complexities either.

# TERMINOLOGY

THE CHIPPEWA AND OJIBWE (Ojibwa or Ojibway) peoples are the same, today calling themselves *Anishinaabeg*, meaning "spontaneous people." The words "Chippewa" and "Ojibwe" come from the same root, which may mean "puckered up" and refer to how moccasins were made or how enemies were treated, or which may come from an ancient word for "crane," one of the early Ojibwe/Chippewa totems. Anishinaabeg historians believe their ancestors migrated to the Great Lakes from the Atlantic, stopping at Sault Ste. Marie, where they were called Saulteurs, meaning people of the rapids, by the French. Numerous other names would follow. Eventually they split into three different groups that became the Odawa, the Pottawatomi, and the Ojibwe/Chippewa that together came to be known as the People of the Three Fires. The Odawa traveled south into Michigan, the Pottawatomi moved southwest into southern Michigan and Wisconsin, and the Ojibwe/Chippewa continued north and west. Confused British and US government agents (including George Washington) initially called the Anishinaabeg who lived south of Lake Superior Chippewa and those who lived north of it Ojibwe, not realizing they belonged to the same group.

Until the end of the fur trade and the beginning of reservations in the nineteenth century, the Anishinaabeg were organized into independent migratory bands, which made them ideal partners with European, Canadian, and American fur traders. Many traders married into Anishinaabeg families, creating a unique mixed-race, or métis, culture in the Great Lakes region that lasted for more than a century and developed into wealthy, proud communities at Detroit, Green Bay, Mackinac, Sault Ste. Marie, La Pointe, and other places. When Yankees and European immigrants began moving into the Great Lakes after 1815, however, they denigrated métis culture with racist disdain, forcing persons of mixed race to choose between assimilating into either white or Indian cultures. Canadian Métis began a colony at Red River (present-day Winnipeg) for themselves, but communities of métis around the Great Lakes disappeared. Anyone of mixed race can be considered métis; Canadians of mixed race are referred to as Métis (with a capital) because they consider themselves a separate people. Indians now refer to mixed-race peoples as *wiisaakodewininiwag* or half-burnt wood, although this term does not appear in older dictionaries. Older terms used by the voyageurs meaning the same thing are *chicot* and *bois brulé*. "Half-breed" was coined in the southern United States before 1800, then picked up by the fur companies. "Mixed-blood" was a term developed by the pseudo-intellectual field of scientific racism in the latter half of the nineteenth century. Before the treaty era, race was seldom an issue for Indian peoples: anyone could be adopted as a full member of the band. It is wise, therefore, to consider pre-twentieth-century "Indian" and "métis" as cultural categories as well as racial ones.[1]

Eliza Morrison's death certificate lists her race as "Indian," although she suggests she was French and Scots with one Chippewa grandmother. The death certificate of her husband, John, lists his race as "white" although he was at least half Chippewa. Ultimately they would both live on the Bad River Reservation at Odanah, Wisconsin, as Indians. But governmental records have no spaces long enough for nuances, for accommodations, for stories about negotiating a Great Lakes frontier, where divergent cultures had met and mingled, as a mixed-race person in the nineteenth century, and that is what Mrs. Morrison portrays.[2] Although she seldom writes directly of prejudice, she is well aware of the complicated ironies of race, and she wields a dry wit to poke fun at peo-ple's preconceptions. She relates her father's judgment that her new husband is "liked by the whites," a nod to the racism that was beginning to affect everyone. But when she and John are first married and visit her sister, who had married a locally well-known white man and was clearly proud of it, Mrs. Morrison pretends that John can't speak English, thus forcing her sister to speak the Chippewa of their mother. She relates stories about presumptuous white men, including a city attorney, but then counters with stories about murderous Indian women. She speaks Chippewa as a first language but writes dramatically and well in English, all the while protesting that she isn't very good at this and occasionally complaining that English doesn't have enough words to describe emotions. (Com-

*Bird's-Eye View of Chequamegon Bay and Apostle Islands*

pared to Chippewa, it doesn't.) In the manner of traditional Indian storytellers, she conveys knowledge and belief with tales, relating them with little editorial comment to allow readers to figure out the point. But because this method requires extensive prior knowledge to understand the implications of a story, of Mrs. Morrison's history as she calls it, it is helpful to begin where she did: with Madeline Island, known to the Indians for thousands of years, and to the Europeans nearly as long as they had known any other place in North America.

Eliza Morrison's Madeline is the largest of the Apostle Group, twenty-two islands that lie like rough-cut emeralds scattered on turquoise silk over an area nearly six hundred miles square off the southwestern shore of Lake Superior. Today the Apostles are a national park and a tourist mecca, but when she knew them in the nineteenth century they were entering their long, quiet twilight at the end of the fur trade. La Pointe, the village on Madeline Island where she was born in 1837, had been a fur company headquarters since the late 1600s, but by the time she wrote in 1894 it was nearly empty and would remain so until summer people began building cottages there in the early part of the twentieth century. By the twenty-first century, the church she attended and the mission school where she had learned to write were gone; the land where Mrs. Morrison's childhood home stood became a golf course. The Protestant cemetery where she buried her parents and perhaps a baby is overgrown

and abandoned. Now the ungainly rusting hulk of a water tower, built to supply the summer houses nearby, pushes its supply pipe through her father's grave. La Pointe may be filled with people once more, but they are not mixed-race, they earn their livings in the cities to the south rather than in the woods and streams of the surrounding countryside, and they speak English, not Chippewa, as a first language.

These summer folk are much like William and Catherine Gray, Mrs. Morrison's employers from Oak Park, Illinois, for whom she wrote *A Little History of My Forest Life*. The Grays had established a primitive summer camp at Island Lake near Iron River in 1887, forty miles west of the Apostle Islands, in one of the last remaining stands of virgin white pine in Wisconsin. There they found John and Eliza Morrison on the homestead they had begun in 1879. The meeting of the Grays and the Morrisons is emblematic, one symbol of the region's change from the Old Northwest of the fur trade to the new Midwest of resource extraction, homesteading, and tourism, from Indian and métis to white, from people who spoke Chippewa and English and often French as well to people who spoke northern European languages or English, from a livelihood earned by making a semi-nomadic yearly journey between sugaring, fishing, berrying, and ricing camps and working in the fur trade to one dependant on precarious revenues from a fledgling homestead or on a salary determined by a supervisor in a factory.

Both the Morrisons and the Grays were connected to men who had influenced the history of the Great Lakes region. John and Eliza Morrison were descended from fur traders, and John from warriors who had fought with Tecumseh against American colonization on the Ohio frontier in the War of 1812. When Tecumseh was killed and his warriors scattered after his British allies lost their second war with the new United States, squatters and homesteaders pushed farther into the region to displace the Indians as he had feared. William Gray's parents had been among those who homesteaded in Ohio. Later, Gray worked with Cyrus McCormick, another newcomer to the Great Lakes, who invented the mechanical grain reaper, a machine that revolutionized farming and so increased the pace of colonization even more. The history John and Eliza Morrison had known was being overwritten by forces set in motion by men like Gray and McCormick as a clamorous tide of immigrant homesteaders, lumbermen, and miners began drowning the Indian and métis cultures that had occupied the northern Great Lakes for centuries. The Grays recognized there would be no more storytellers like the Morrisons; consequently, when Eliza Morrison reciprocated for a gift with a gift in turn, in the traditional Indian manner, there was born a project of recording what the Morrisons

knew about Chippewa culture for posterity. What the Grays wanted and what they got, however, may have been two different things.

The Morrisons were descended from French and Scots men who worked in the fur trade and their Chippewa or Chippewa/French wives. Like many métis, the Morrisons were bi-lingual, with the Chippewa of their mothers serving as the language of home and the French and/or English of their fathers as the language used with the outside world. They were educated mem-

*William Cunningham Gray*

*Catherine Gray*

Theirs was an interesting love story. Mrs. Morrison notes that she had heard "a young man" was coming to Bayfield and so she decided to take a boat and go and see him. What she does not say, but what the census records reveal, is that he was five years younger than she, and that they had grown up down the street from each other. She does not mention that at twenty-seven and still unmarried, she had taken care of her invalid mother for fifteen long years and would now be considered an old maid. La Pointe was a neglected relic of the fur trade; there would be few men there she would be willing to marry. John Morrison, while not her last hope for a good marriage with someone who was her equal, may have been close to it. Thus she was willing to take a large fishing boat, which would have been hard for her to handle under the best of circumstances, and row three miles across the channel separating Madeline Island from Bayfield in hope of seeing the person she had first known as a young boy and may have seen only briefly after they were grown. He had led a difficult life, his mother dying when he was very young, his father while he was a teen-ager, and he had been adopted by—perhaps after being packed off to—his Indian relatives near St. Croix. The boy the Indians named *Ma Danse* had made his own way. But Eliza

bers of the old, unique, Great Lakes métis culture, choosing to live in white or mixed-race communities rather than in traditional Indian bands in the remote woods. Mrs. Morrison declares she knows little of those traditional Indian life-ways, and while she says John knows more, apparently John was not always willing to share. Although the manuscript she sent Mrs. Gray describes some Indian customs, it records the life she and John had lived as métis on the frontier in much greater detail and this may have been a conscious choice.

Morrin had not forgotten him and made the effort to see him, even though he had spent years living as a traditional, a situation her relatives would have understood but may have not welcomed when marriage was considered. Apparently John shared Eliza's fond memories, since her presence convinced him to give up what was most likely a timber cruising or prospecting or fur collecting trip to marry her when, as she notes, he had not planned on getting married so soon. Marrying her also meant he would give up forever the possibility of continuing to live in traditional Indian culture in the deep woods, since her father would never permit it even if Eliza had been willing, and she clearly wasn't.

At the time Mrs. Morrison wrote prejudice against Indians and mixed-race peoples and their chosen ways of life was intense. The United States had been waging an expensive and bloody war against the Plains and Western tribes since the mid-1870s, abetted by sensationally negative journalism. Governmental and religious programs designed to strip non-white and non-English-speaking peoples of their cultural identities were popular. Those who resisted melding into white American society, whatever their ethnicity, were considered ignorant and perhaps mentally deficient. Describing traditional life-ways, including Indian religions, unless the people who practiced them were dead or dying, would have been considered evidence of what was termed "Indian savagery." "Civilization" was its opposite, comprised of a constellation of characteristics—dress, language, personal habits, religion—that had probably been drummed into Mrs. Morrison since her childhood at the mission school at La Pointe. When she began to write, she may have found herself in the uncomfortable situation familiar to many Indians and métis, that of being requested for cultural information from one white person while enduring prejudice from others. In addition, although Mrs. Morrison did try to oblige her friends, her story took on a life of its own as autobiography is wont to do, and she keeps pulling herself back to her task, saying on several occasions "Since I am required to write about the Indians...."

She was interested in matters other than race and other than historic Indian life-ways. Left to her own devices she preferred to write primarily about the journeys she had taken, about that "quite peculiar charm" of the business of making maple sugar, about the places she had lived, about her marriage, and about the interesting people she had known, some of whom were Indian. These subjects were a good deal more compelling to her than interpreting ancient Indian religious rituals like the *Midéwiwin*, or Medicine Rite, that were not only dying out but were practiced in an antique dialect few still understood. The result of her attempts to fulfill the Grays' ethnographic curiosity while getting her own story told as well is that she writes a métis autobiography.

As she describes what it means to have two identities, two languages, and two life-ways, she creates a narrative that is, paradoxically, more representative of an

American life than a purely Indian autobiography would have been because few Americans are "pure" anything. By persisting in describing métis choices, Mrs. Morrison allows readers to experience life in a threatened but still-comfortable space comprised of two cultures, just before métis peoples were forced to choose between attempting acculturation into white society or life on a reservation, a choice that foreshadowed their predicament for much of the twentieth century. She may have been asked to write about historic Indian customs, but she replied with an American story of what it meant to belong to two cultures at once during an era when scientific racism was being used to justify manifest destiny in a region where, fifty years before, so few people had spoken English the census taker hadn't bothered visit.[3]

To appreciate the nuances of Eliza Morrison's métis story, it is necessary to understand the history of the northern Great Lakes. Native peoples arrived in the region ten millennia ago—some of the copper workings on nearby Isle Royale date to at least 3000 BCE and other sites are older—but the Late Woodland peoples who would become the Chippewa and the Ojibwe emigrated to western Lake Superior sometime after the 1400s. William Whipple Warren, historian and author of *History of the Ojibway People* (1885) who was born into another mixed-race family at La Pointe shortly before Mrs. Morrison, describes his Indian ancestors as migrating west in small bands from the confluence of the St. Lawrence River and the Atlantic Ocean following a sacred shell. They stopped for an undetermined number of decades at Sault Ste. Marie, and then moved on west along the southern shore of Lake Superior to the area surrounding *Shagawaumikong*, the long sand spit that reaches into the lake to form a bay and gives the region its name: Chequamegon. Others moved farther west near the headwaters of the Mississippi River where they fought with the Santee branch of the Dakota for control of the rich food and fur resources of the area. They spent their summers on the largest of the islands off Shagawaumikong for many generations, fishing, gathering, and refining the sacred Midéwiwin ceremonies, until some confluence of events—cannibalistic sorcery or pestilence or war—caused them to abandon the island beach they called *Moningwu-nakauning*, Golden-Breasted Woodpecker Point, and return to the Sault. They would not come back for over a century, until they accompanied a fur trader to establish a new trading post, although other Indians, notably the Hurons who were fleeing the Iroquois wars, made the island home.

Initially, the French had come in the seventeenth century, to the region they named La Pointe, which included the village around their fort as well as the entire western end of Lake Superior and the surrounding countryside. The first to record their stay there were two self-styled "Caesars of the wilderness," Radisson and Groseilliers, unlicensed fur traders who camped at Chequamegon Bay in 1659.[4]

# The Fur Trade

"Fur trade" is a portmanteau term for a number of commercial activities that employed natives, métis, and whites, beginning in the 1500s. The Puritans of New England, among others, paid their debts with fur. The trade opened up the Great Lakes in the 1600s, earlier than most other places in North America, and preserved their northern reaches unspoiled until the mid 1800s. But profit margins were often slim and cut-throat competition was frequent. Native women who did much of the piece work of preparing skins saw their workload increase, and traders' demands often helped inflame intertribal wars.

The trade was usually dominated by governments or businesses, despite the romantic mythology of *couriers des bois*, or wood runners, the unlicensed traders who paddled and portaged deep into the wilderness. The Hudson's Bay Company, begun in 1670, controlled the trade north of the Great Lakes. The Northwest Company was the most powerful company in the Great Lakes region until 1815, when John Jacob Astor convinced the United States Congress to forbid foreign companies from doing business in the US. This protected Astor's American Fur Company, which could then embark on a campaign to consolidate the independent traders, many of whom were French or métis, and force everyone to do business as American citizens. Ultimately ninety percent of métis traders would work for Astor or suffer the consequences. Traders bought goods from the company at a small discount, gave them to the Indians in the fall in exchange for a promise to deliver furs in spring. If the furs were not delivered, the company would take title to the land holdings of either the Indians or traders. In this way much of the land owned by métis traders passed to

the American Fur Company by the 1840s when it was resold to speculators, immigrants, and timber companies.

The fur trade post at La Pointe was controlled by French commanders from 1693 to 1762. The British came into the region in 1765 and stayed until 1815 when, at the close of the War of 1812, John Jacob Astor took control. Furs came to the La Pointe trading post from the east, west, and south: from the Keeweenaw Peninsula of Michigan, from the upper reaches of the Mississippi, and from the areas drained by the rivers of northern Wisconsin. In the spring the thirty-foot *canot du maitre*, paddled by *voyageurs* or *mangeurs du lard* ("lard eaters," or summer workers), arrived with their tons of trade goods, including guns, ammunition, beads, cloth, liquor, and tobacco. They were met by the *hivernants*, the winterers, men who had traded for furs and lived with the Indians in the interior, and by the Indians themselves. The exchange was controlled by the *bourgeois*, or factor, who assumed responsibility for the returns of an entire district, often spending the winter at a remote site, and the clerks, or *commis*.

During the time of the French, voyageurs had been considered traders, but after the British and Americans assumed control, they were demoted to laborers. The voyageurs were paid virtually the same for decades: one hundred pounds of beaver skins per year and "found," which consisted of one bushel of corn and two pounds of fat per man per month, supplemented by whatever they could hunt or catch. For this they were expected to rise before daybreak, paddle up to a hundred miles a day broken only by short rests or "pipes" (time enough to smoke a pipe), and portage each canoe's load of four tons or more whenever necessary.[5]

*Canoe Shooting the Rapids*

These two Caesars were the vanguard of the fur trade in the Great Lakes region, part of the economic engine that drove North America for over two centuries. Of the three countries that engaged in it, the French were by far the most benign, largely because the Indians still exerted control. The French were not particularly interested in colonization or in controlling land except for fur-trading rights. Their traders, men like the Morrison's ancestors, married into the Native populations who supplied them with furs, some becoming acculturated Indians, others creating a "new people" and a new culture, the métis. The vigilant French priests who regulated trading licenses and insisted on accompanying the traders kept the trade in whiskey under as much control as possible. When the French lost North America in 1763, they were replaced by the British who were less concerned for Native souls, more concerned about peddling cheap whiskey, and most concerned about profitability. Eventually the Indians were able to co-exist with the British nearly as well as with the French, especially since the Scots who worked for the British married Indians and métis, but the Americans who followed after 1814 were a disaster for one major reason: they wanted not just furs, but land as well. The middle ground of negotiation and accommodation, of a balance of power established between the Europeans and the Indians, vanished before American racism and economic ruthlessness.[6]

By the mid-nineteenth century, commercial fur trading between Indian trappers and métis traders had become a casualty of the industrial revolution, which made possible the invention of the mechanical reaper to increase grain harvests and the development of rail and ship transportation in the Great Lakes region, including the Erie Canal, to transport the grain to urban markets and haul settlers back to the prairies. Mechanization and easy access to markets, combined with cheap and abundant land, was encouraging unprecedented immigration from the Eastern United States and Europe. Wisconsin had become a Territory in 1836 and a state in 1848, developments that brought not only white settlers, but governmental control of land and an economic incentive, disguised as a lofty cultural mission, to remake the wilderness into small farms. Less than fifty years after Americans had assumed control of the upper Great Lakes, the fur trade was finished and, as a direct consequence, Native peoples had lost ninety percent of their land through a series of treaties designed to allow whites to lumber, mine, and homestead. It is of this period, from the 1850s to the turn of the twentieth century, that Mrs. Morrison writes.

She was a child of the fur trade and the mixed-race world the fur trade helped create. Her mother was *Wabegieah* (Flower), daughter of a Chippewa woman who was probably descended from those Indians who had first colonized La Pointe and a French fur trader. Mrs. Morrison's father, Robert Morrin, was Scots, as she is careful to point out. Scots had entered the fur trade with the Hudson's Bay Company and the North West Company when the British discovered young men from Scotland, particularly the Highlands, could handle the difficult work and deprivation required at fur company posts far better than Londoners. The Scots were willing to come to North America for the same reason they went to India after 1755; life in Scotland was hard, and it was easier to make one's way in a place more free of British prejudice. Because of nearly universal literacy in Scotland, the Scots quickly moved into positions of responsibility in the fur trade, consigning the French to the heavy physical work. Within a few decades a class system of sorts developed: the English or Americans and a few Scots controlled the most important positions, Scots did the clerical work and controlled minor posts, the French did the heavy work of paddling and portaging. When Mrs. Morrison documents her Scots heritage, she is calling attention to the old class system of the fur trade and noting her place in it.[7]

John Morrison's father, also named John, had married Agathe Cadotte, the daughter of Jean-Baptiste, a métis trader who was killed by the Santee, and *Kakinoacassi*, a Chippewa. The Morrisons were an old, distinguished, Great Lakes fur-trading family, begun when Allan Morrison emigrated from Scotland to Canada in 1766. John Morrison's grandfather was one of the sons of Allan Morrison, men who eventually became chief factors for the North West and American Fur Companies, positions of enormous influence. Indian women like John and Eliza's grandmothers married European and Canadian men for several reasons: intertribal wars had left many women without suitable marriage partners and, if they were Christian and did not believe in polygyny, they were condemned to spinsterhood or widowdom, a difficult situation in an environment where it took a partnership to survive. In addition, traders had ready access to desirable goods, and in a few tribes it was considered a mark of status to marry a trader, particularly one with power and prestige. Sometimes these men abandoned their native wives when they returned to Europe or Lower Canada; some sent their sons east to be educated; others stayed in the fur country. Generally, the richer and more powerful whites returned east alone, leaving their mixed-race descendants behind. If a child grew up at a trading post, as both John Morrison and his father apparently did, he would have thought of himself as métis; if he were raised in an Indian band,

he would be Indian. Many considered themselves both. The result was the métis world where John Morrison and Eliza Morrin had both grown up, a world where most people spoke at least two languages fluently, fortunes made in the fur trade rather than one's race determined status, and women assumed an egalitarian position in their marriages and their communities unheard of in the United States again until the late twentieth century. The Morrisons' childhood society had been an old and accepting one, which may be one reason Mrs. Morrison preferred to live at La Pointe where race was less of an issue.[8] Even the name of the island was a result of the marriage between a mixed-race trader, Michel Cadotte, and *Equaysayway*, a chief's daughter, who was given the name Madeline at her baptism. In her honor, her father promptly changed the name of the island from La Pointe to Madeline and, since he was chief of the Crane clan, the most powerful clan of the Chippewa, no one succeeded in changing the island's name again.

*La Pointe in 1852 : Catholic church is to the left; Protestant church is to the right*

European religions had come to La Pointe with the Jesuits, and although Mrs. Morrison makes much of her Protestant history for the benefit of the Grays, who were active in the Presbyterian church, the Presbyterian mission on La Pointe never reckoned itself a great success. Most métis peoples were Catholic, and even though the Protestant school and mission were established 1830 and 1831, and the Catholic in 1835, Father Baraga, the Catholic priest, was tireless. His church required only a simple baptism for admission, but the Presbyterian required a formal period of study and confession of faith. In addition, it was a morally severe, Puritan-inspired, evangelical, New England-style faith that encouraged a public declaration of the believer's "conversion experience." This was the exact opposite of the traditional Indian requirement that spiritual visions remain personal secrets throughout life.[9] The Presbyterian mission eventually closed, despite its founder having written some of the first books in the Ojibwe language, including the complete New Testament that Father Baraga used for years.

*Old Mission Church and Cemetery*

The legacy of the mission endured in the person of Reverend Leonard Wheeler, who had come to the mission to encourage its efforts. He helped the Indians establish a permanent settlement at the mouth of the Bad River south of La Pointe on the Wisconsin mainland in 1845, at a place the Indians called the Old Gardens, their traditional summer gardening spot. Odanah, the new "town," which is what the word *odena* means in Chippewa, was Wheeler's project to help the Indians become self-supporting as the fur trade ended. It became a reservation as part of the 1854 treaty, and Wheeler's efforts prevented the Chippewa there from being removed west of the Mississippi River, the fate of many tribes during this era. Catholic Indians were sent to the reservation established at Red Cliff, north on the Wisconsin shore, because the US government allowed only one denomination per reservation. Once these reservations were in place, much of the population of La Pointe left and the Presbyterian mission closed, which is why Mrs. Morrison speaks of rowing across the channel from the island to go to church on the mainland.

Although no one realized it at the time, a far greater threat than denominational squabbling had begun to affect the Lake Superior region: the fur trade was becoming much less important. The mother lode of peltry that had supplied everyone's needs and wants for two centuries was no longer as lucrative as speculating in land or timber, and the pressure to open Indian lands to white development was intense. The American Fur Company, the last in a long line of companies that had operated at La Pointe since the 1600s, declared bankruptcy in 1842 when Mrs. Morrison was a child. It had earlier tried diversifying into shipping salted fish in addition to furs, but was caught oversupplied with both in a recession and could no longer pay its creditors. Fish would be its salvation when business picked up again, but fur was finished forever. The beaver hat was no longer fashionable in Europe, and fur companies found it more profitable to diversify into banking, mining, lumbering, shipping, and land speculation. To buy the companies' help in coercing the Indians to sign away their lands in treaties, the government gave them generous subsidies to cover the outstanding debts of Indian trappers. Once they were given this financial boon, the fur companies abandoned their former partners to the new reservations and retired to more urban areas to tally their profits.

Trading fur would continue in a loosely organized fashion as many new immigrants gleaned a second income trapping in winter. Indeed, years later Mrs. Morrison notes how John made a tidy sum trapping fisher, a type of weasel, one spring after they homesteaded. But those fur company men like Eliza's father who had stayed on in La Pointe in the 1840s and 1850s were only granted land in the village for a nominal payment and survived as best they could: fishing, working in the woods, carpentering. Bayfield, Wisconsin, had been founded on the mainland to the west in 1856, which drew even more people from the island, and Ashland, Wisconsin, would soon follow on the shore to the south. By the 1870s, when the Morrisons were still living at La Pointe before they moved to the woods to homestead, the village was practically a ghost town, described by the nascent Bayfield paper as "the poor little village of the island [that] looks sadly enough at present. Every thing around bears the marks of neglect, decay, and deso-

feed, he needed more dependable work than carrying the mail for a dying village, fishing, and trying to garden. He had followed the old Chippewa custom of moving to his wife's family home after their marriage, but after eight years of attempting to survive there, he insisted they move. Unfortunately, Ashland, Wisconsin, south across Chequamegon Bay, was not a particularly good alternative. Mr. Morrison did not

ASHLAND, WIS.
COUNTY SEAT OF ASHLAND CO.
1886

lation. . . . But the island is lovely still."[10] By the early 1890s, when the Morrisons left their homestead and moved to the reservation at Odanah, La Pointe had been reduced to scarcely seventy-five people, a figure that would not change dramatically until the advent of summer tourism a few years later.

John Morrison had little love for La Pointe. It was nearly impossible for him to earn a decent living there, and as a man who would soon have eight children to

exaggerate when he suggested that living in the woods on a raw wilderness farm was preferable to living in Ashland because the children would not be exposed to drunkenness and rough language. At the time the Morrisons moved to their homestead in the woods near Spider Lake in 1879, Ashland was a wide-open, frontier boom town, complete with twenty-four-hour bars and brothels, land speculation, and every variety of unregulated greed, lust, and corruption that most boom towns experienced. The lumber mills ran night and day and the shrieks of their saws could be heard for miles.[11] When the lumberjacks came out of the "swamps," or woods, at the end of the spring drives, their peavy hooks would be lined up on the board sidewalks outside the saloons for blocks. Sailors off Great Lakes ships roamed the streets, along with timber cruisers, railroad workers, and every variety of grifter, speculator, and shark. Ashland was no worse than other frontier towns, where many a woman's club was begun when the wives of the town leaders found themselves stepping over the prone bodies of drunken "jacks" on their way to church and decided something needed to be done to bring culture, and control, to town. While Bayfield was becoming a placidly charming tourist retreat, and La Pointe continued to shrink, Ashland, with fifty-three saloons, was competing with nearby Hurley, Wisconsin, for the dubious distinction of Sodom on Lake Superior. And not only because of the timber industry.

Mrs. Morrison reacts to being uprooted from La Pointe by mocking her husband's dreams of finding silver deposits near where they built their farm, but John was not as daft as she makes him out to be. The Precambrian Shield—the bedrock of the earth—is rich in minerals, and it outcrops in the western Lake Superior region. Mineralogists had discovered a huge deposit of

pure silver at the "Silver Isle" off present-day Thunder Bay, Ontario, in 1868, not far up the shore from what Mrs. Morrison calls Fondulac, or Fond du Lac, the present-day Duluth, and other silver deposits had been discovered earlier nearby. Raphael Pumphelly, an Eastern geologist who was hired to locate copper and iron deposits in the Lake Superior region, bought hundreds of acres of land near the Morrison homestead in the 1880s, and he certainly wasn't interested in raising hay. The prospecting fever created by these discoveries, and the founding of Superior, Wisconsin, in 1853 and Duluth, Minnesota, in 1854, effected what the treaties had not: the nearly complete evacuation of La Pointe.

Although Mrs. Morrison initially hated the idea of a homestead in the woods, she came to value the time they had spent there. Writing to Mrs. Gray from the reservation years later, she notes that she is lonesome for the old place. She began *A Little History of My Forest Life* when they still owned the farm, even though they were living in town for the winter so the two youngest children could attend school, and she finished it in the spring of 1895, after they moved to Odanah. This may not have been a move they chose freely. There were undoubtedly problems of age and health that affected how well they could run their homestead, but there were other, more negative forces operating.

# MAJOR CHIPPEWA-U.S. LAND USE TREATIES AND LEGAL ACTIONS AFFECTING WISCONSIN INDIANS

1837 THE PINE TREE TREATY
Allowed exploitation of the pine forests but reserved hunting-gathering rights.

1842 THE COPPER TREATY
Allowed exploitation of copper deposits but reserved hunting-gathering rights.

1850 EXECUTIVE ORDER
US President Zachary Taylor revoked treaty-reserved hunting-gathering rights and local politicians decided to remove Indians to unceded lands in Minnesota. To force the move, treaty payments were changed from La Pointe to Sandy Lake in late fall, resulting in the deaths of nearly 400 Chippewa from cold.

1854 LA POINTE TREATY
Established reservations at Bad River, Red Cliff, Lac Courte Oreilles, and Lac du Flambeau to insure against further removal attempts.

1871 INDIAN APPROPRIATIONS ACT RIDER
Specified that Indian tribes would no longer be recognized as independent nations; therefore the US would no longer make treaties with them.

1887 DAWES ACT
Specified reservations must be divided into individual parcels.

1889 State of Wisconsin began enforcing state fish and game laws against the Chippewa/Ojibwe and restricted their access to ceded territories.

1983 *Lac Courte Oreilles Band of Lake Superior Chippewa Indians v Lester P. Voigt*
Allowed Chippewa access to recreational and subsistence hunting, fishing, and gathering on public lands in their former ceded territories.

---

The 1887 General Indian Allotment Act, better known as the Dawes Act after its sponsor in Congress, had required that reservations be divided into individual parcels: usually 80 acres per tribal member. Earlier treaties, such as the La Pointe treaty of 1854, had given smaller allotments and monies to mixed-race people and tribal members, largely to get them off lands whites wanted for settlement and resource extraction. But those who did not register as part of a tribe during the allotment proceedings after 1887 gave up claim to tribal status and so to sharing in the distribution of reserved land. "Left-over" land, land that was not allotted after all tribal members

*"Symbolic Petition of the Chippewa Chiefs." When the Lake Superior chiefs went to Washington, DC in 1849 to request permanent homes in Wisconsin, they carried with them this pictograph. The clan animals, with their hearts and eyes linked by lines to ceded wild rice lakes, travel eastward along Lake Superior.*

had been assigned parcels, was frequently sold to the public for a pittance, usually timber and mining companies in the Great Lakes region. Graft, corruption, and embezzlement plumbed depths seldom seen since. The Dawes Act, because of its misguided intentions, precipitated a massive land-grab by whites that was unprecedented. Bad River was especially rich in timber and so especially vulnerable and, undoubtedly, John Morrison saw the need to help protect relatives, move closer to town, and receive an allotment as well.

He was an astute and energetic businessman. He had homesteaded 160 acres near Spider Lake after 1875 when homesteads became available to Indians who were not connected to reservations, sold the timber from it for a good price even as he insisted that the lumber company pay the

taxes until they took the timber off, then sold the homestead after he and his sons took up allotments on the reservation at Odanah. The State of Wisconsin and the railroad companies were blanketing the East, Midwest, and Europe with advertising designed to sell their lands in the Cutover, as the lumbered-over region of the northern Midwest was called, and the Morrisons would not have had trouble selling a "proved-up" homestead with buildings and cleared land near a railroad in a place that was being touted as wonderful for farming.[12] The reality was that most of those farms would limp along or fail because of the climate and soil, something the Indians had figured out five hundred years before when they gathered summers at the few places that would support agriculture, one of which was the Old Gardens at Odanah.

John Morrison, like many of his generation on the frontier, had become nimble at doing whatever was necessary to earn a living, using either traditional Indian methods of hunting, fishing, and gathering, or white ones of farming and working for wages for the government, tourists, or lumber companies, depending on what was available and made the most money. Annuity payments to Indians expired in the 1870s, the country suffered periodic depressions or "panics" as they were then called, the land base natives needed to survive in a traditional fashion was gone, and prejudice against Indians and mixed-race peoples was on the rise. He undoubtedly recognized that it was time to move to the reservation.

Mrs. Morrison may write of the horrific times when they nearly ran out of food after they first began homesteading, and she complains in a later letter of being poor, but the reality is that John Morrison was always a hard worker who supported a large family and later, on the reservation at Odanah, ran "Morrison House" which stockpiled food for members of the community in need. He was also instrumental in trying to get the US government to intervene when the Sterns Lumber Company, which held a monopoly on the rights to harvest Chippewa timber and supply reservations with goods, cheated Indians of their just rewards for the timber and charged exorbitant prices for merchandise. Three generations later, tribal members still recall how two of John's sons were run off the reservation at gunpoint by thugs in the employ of the lumber company for their

efforts on behalf of tribal members.[13] The Sterns Company used several tactics to cheat the Indians. It set fires and then told tribal landowners the timber was worthless, even though the fires burned only the undergrowth and left the prime, old-growth white pine and hardwoods undamaged. It offered Indians less than market value for their timber, logged lands it had not contracted for (known as "logging a round forty," or cutting the forty acres purchased but then continuing on to all the forty-acre tracts around it), it threatened, bullied, and intimidated. John Morrison was not fooled.

But despite the work he did for his community, life on the reservation at Bad River would be difficult. By the 1880s, decades of federal Indian policies, which were misguided at best and catastrophic at worst, were wreaking such havoc many Indians lived in a state of chronic disaster. The problems in the western Lake Superior region had begun with the Black Hawk War in 1832, which triggered harsher federal policies designed to protect white settlers and provide them with land. Few of these settlers engaged in the fur trade or understood Indians or métis peoples; many of them were racist. Difficulties increased in earnest in 1850, when President Zachary Taylor tried to coerce the Chippewa to remove west by changing treaty payments from La Pointe to Sandy Lake, Minnesota. Over 400 Indians died from starvation, disease, and late fall travel. To prevent further attempts at removal, the Indians made a treaty at La Pointe in 1854 that allowed whites access to the last of their historic lands to lumber and mine but, significantly, they retained their traditional hunting and gathering rights on the ceded land as they had in earlier treaties. They also requested that land be set aside, or reserved, which whites could never touch, at Lac du Flambeau, Bad River, Red Cliff, and Lac Courte Oreilles. It was to these reservations that the Indians who had not moved before, accompanied by métis family, would go as the Dawes Act of 1887 slowly took effect. The Indians' retained, treaty-sanctioned hunting and gathering rights on lands outside the reservation boundaries were ignored. Mrs. Morrison's nephew, Michael Morrin, was convicted of fishing with gill nets in Lake Superior in 1907, an example of the increasingly tough stance on hunting and fishing the State of Wisconsin would take toward everyone, including Indians and métis attempting to exercise their reserved treaty rights on ceded land, a position that would not be reversed for nearly a hundred years.[14]

The Chippewa/Ojibwe had always had a relatively loose, egalitarian tribal organization that ensured their survival as a semi-nomadic hunting and gathering culture in the harsh climate of the boreal forest, but which left them disorganized and prey to strong-arm tactics by outsiders once on a reservation where it became difficult for leaders to force compliance with unpopular, but necessary, community responsibilities and requirements. In addition, the practice of treating tribes as sovereign nations had ended in 1871, resulting in US policies that were designed to force Indians to change from a food-gathering economy to a money-gathering one. Assimilation into white culture was compelled by various tactics: undermining tribal governments by inserting Indian agents who were seldom honest, breaking up reservations into individual allotments, allowing missionaries great power in reservation affairs and education, and eventually setting up a system of boarding schools that would attempt to strip Indian children of their languages and cultures. The resulting disaster has been extensively chronicled and Bad River was little different from anywhere else. Poverty was endemic and accompanied by all its usual conspirators: tuberculosis, pneumonia, scrofula, venereal disease, and alcoholism. Timber companies not only exploited Bad River's rich stands of valuable timber, they harmed the rivers in the reservation with log drives without regard for the Indians' fishing, ricing, or ancient sacred sites. Merchants came onto the reservation to sell liquor. Indians who could not farm but found jobs in the industries in Ashland were routinely paid two-thirds less than whites for doing the same work.[15]

# FOLLOWING THE MONEY TRAIL

THE PREFERRED ITEMS OF THE INDIAN TRADE, and the most lucrative, were not copper kettles and knives and guns. Indians could and did go without these when they had to. The most coveted goods were beads and cloth, items that contributed to beauty, and alcohol, which made visionary trances less work than self-inflicted starvation. In the tightly competitive arena of the fur trade, traders frequently used liquor to encourage Indians' loyalty or to pay them for furs, even though every government and most companies forbade it. Trappers who had promised furs to one trader might give their furs to another who supplied them with whiskey, thus bankrupting the trader who had extended them credit. The fur companies could do nothing, since theoretically the liquor trade was illegal. In practice, it flourished when competition was intense and the authorities looked away. Whether or not they used whiskey, traders tried to get as many furs as possible for the least amount of goods; the Indians, not surprisingly, attempted the opposite. Traders cheated each other, Indians changed traders in the midst of the season without repaying loans, companies squeezed out independent traders, Indians got credits from more than one trader at once, and companies undercut each other across the US-Canadian border.

The beginning of the treaty era ended this mayhem, since fur companies discovered that not only could they require that treaties include provisions for repayment of Indian debts, they could also preside over the negotiations, effectively forestalling any oversight. Since in some areas fifty percent of the goods given Indians were never paid for with furs in spring, these debts could be considerable. Traders might write off the debts from year to year, especially métis ones who were related to Indian trappers, but the companies kept finer books. The debts of individual trappers eventually devolved upon the tribes and the only way they could pay the debts was by selling land. By the 1840s and 1850s, the US assumed Indian debts worth hundreds of thousands of dollars and paid the sums out to fur trading companies. These debts were often used to compel the Indians to sell land when the whites wanted it. The companies then inflated the debts owed them, using a category called "depredations," which supposedly meant destruction of posts and goods but that functioned like expense-account padding. For example, during the 1854 treaty negotiations at La Pointe, one Francis Gauthier claimed $600 for depredations and $228 for goods actually sold. In essence, much of the money paid to Indians for land cessions went directly into the coffers of the fur companies.

And they weren't paid much. It was cheaper for the fledgling United States to buy Indians' lands than to fight wars for them (the Indian Wars in the West after the Civil War cost about one million dollars per Indian killed), but a moral justification was still needed. For this the Enlightenment concept of cultural evolution worked nicely, suggesting that "savages" could be educated into "civilization" and thus become self-sufficient farmers in the white tradition. Once Indians were Christianized, clothed, and consigned to the field with a hoe, they would need less land, of course, which was the entire idea. Since the US had no reason to pay a fair price if it could avoid it, if a particular tribe didn't negotiate toughly, they would not be well paid. An Indian agent at La Pointe once calculated that the Indians had sold eleven million acres in the 1837 treaty for less than eight cents an acre. The 1842 treaty paid the Chippewa seven cents an acre for twelve million acres. Worse, the government had been able to extinguish title by paying only about 2/3 of what the land was worth to the Chippewa when engaged in their traditional subsistence occupations. The land's value to resource extraction companies was incalculably high. The agent brought this unfairness to the attention of the Michigan Indian superintendent, who had once run the American Fur Company, who fired him.

Once the land was sold and the annuity process began, former traders rushed in to supply Indians with goods whenever an annuity payout was held. Annuities might vary from between ten to twenty thousand dollars per tribe per year and were paid for between twenty to thirty years. Acquiring annuity money was a good deal easier than acquiring furs and many traders simply switched their trading activities to annuity payment grounds, thus effecting what one scholar calls the switch from the fur trade to the "annuity trade." Once again, of course, profit was the key and many annuity goods were overpriced and shoddy.

When Indians moved to reservations after the Dawes Act, money from sales of timber on reservation land did not go directly to the allotment owners. Instead it went into a trust fund, administered by the federal government. In 1912 the Bad River Band at Odanah, composed of 1200 people, had a trust fund of $2,400,000, monies that could be used only with permission of the government for projects the government deemed worthy. Unfortunately, much of this money was never spent and it was so mismanaged that a class-action lawsuit is now working its way through the courts to determine how much money the federal government owes Indian tribes across the US. This time, instead of the fur companies making money, the attorneys will.[16]

The consequence was that by the 1890s when Eliza Morrison writes, Wisconsin's native population, comprised primarily of Chippewa, Menominee, Winnebago, and a mixed group of Chippewa/Odawa/Potawatomie, had dropped to 6095 persons living on reservations and 3835 who did not. Fifty years earlier, shortly after Mrs. Morrison was born, the Chippewa had numbered 30,000 and controlled lands adjacent to the northern two-thirds of Lake Huron, the south shore of Lake Superior, northern Minnesota, parts of North Dakota, eastern Montana, southeastern Saskatchewan, southern Manitoba, and the lake country to James Bay.[17] Wisconsin territorial status and statehood had attracted thousands of Eastern Yankees and European immigrants hungry for property and timber. By the late 1880s these two antagonistic white groups were embroiled in bitter religious wars between the Catholics and the Protestants which led to partisan political brawls that affected the reservations as well. Into this devil's brew of religion and politics came the 1887 Dawes Act that was intended to make the Indians successful small farmers and free up "excess" reservation land. The unforeseen outcome was that the Wisconsin Indians eventually lost much of the already small tracts of reserved land determined by treaties. Once the land was allotted to individual owners, those who couldn't make enough to pay the taxes saw their holdings sold at tax sales; others were bilked out of theirs by unscrupulous buyers; some allotments became so subdivided by inheritances they were useless for farming. Timber companies and whites were the real beneficiaries of the Dawes Act.

Bad River, because it was home to a progressive band, as well as being rich in arable land and timber, fared better than other Wisconsin reservations, but it still faced problems. The depression of 1893-1897 cut prices and job possibilities, a new white generation raised on ethnic hatreds and intolerance fomented discrimination, and Indian cultural continuity—under attack for over a hundred years—became ever more frayed. The crowded and sedentary living conditions on the reservation led in 1915 to a tuberculosis infection rate of 130 cases in a population of 808 residents.[18] The Morrison's oldest son, Johny, died in 1897 after a long illness, which may have been TB. In addition, Odanah was situated in the rich bottom land at the confluence of the Bad and Kakagon Rivers, and while this made it excellent farming land on which reservation farmers could raise bountiful crops, the spring rises frequently flooded the town and farm lands, ruining plantings and spreading sewage and disease. Writing to Mrs. Gray in 1897, Mrs. Morrison says that "Our poor garden drowned out twice so we have nothing. It almost just makes me sick to see other gardens and we used to have so plenty at Spider Lake."

Many of the problems at Bad River and other reservations were the result of the Bureau of Indian Affairs' shock-therapy approach to civilizing the Indians after the fur trade ended. The government's definition of "civilized" meant that an Indian lived on an allotment on a reservation and farmed, wore "citizen clothing," had short hair, could read, attended a Christian church, spoke English, and dwelled in a log or frame house.[19] As *A Little History of My Forest Life* makes clear, many métis and Indians practiced selective acculturation and had done so for years. Mrs. Morrison describes living under birchbark, Indian style, at sugar or fishing camps, while living in frame housing the rest of the year. (And she also notes how much less work it was to keep up a *wigiwam* than a house.) Clothing would be mixed, as were food choices and economic practices. Like all flexible cultures, Indians and métis took what they wanted and could use from whatever the cultures around them offered: when the train finally came through to Ashland, traditional Indians rode it rather than walk. But Mrs. Morrison also notes how surprised she was when she moved to the reservation and heard so many Indians speaking English. "Now three-fourths can speak English.... Still in all, when I see their complexions I feel like using my native language to talk with them." This was evidence that federal policy was working although at terrible cost, since loss of language frequently means losses of culture, not adaptation.

By the end of *A Little History of My Forest Life*, Eliza Morrison has exposed the

reservation and become Indian, or survive as best they could while living as "the people in between, neither white nor enrolled Indian"on the fringes of white settlement on land that was not yet developed.[20] One could, as the Morrisons had earlier, move to the woods, but that option would not work forever. Not only is much of northern Wisconsin unsuitable for farming, the reality of a frontier homestead was that, after a cer-

*John and Eliza Morrison with Eunice Sero and Grandchildren at Odanah 1910.*
*Blanche Sero on left. Ardetta Sero on lap. Daniel Morrison's daughter Clara on right*

fault lines of Indian and mixed-race acculturation and adaptability on the frontier. With the old accommodating world like that of La Pointe gone forever, Indians and métis peoples were left with stark choices: assimilate into white culture, move to a

tain age, it was physically too hard to manage unless there were children to take over. Even if there were, eventually white culture would surround them once again and prejudices hardened as economic times worsened and more immigrants moved in.

As acculturated métis, the Morrisons could choose, and they chose to go where many of those they had grown up with had gone: to Odanah.[21]

And so, the journeys with which Mrs. Morrison began *A Little History of My Forest Life* became slowly more circumscribed. Despite her delight with her trips on the railroad, the first journey she mentions, that of the Chippewa to collect treaty payments at Sandy Lake that killed hundreds, foreshadowed the future. The Morrison's mixed-race heritage, experience, and education protected them to some degree, but the métis world was affected as much as traditional Indian culture. By the end of the nineteenth century, anyone who was not white experienced prejudice.

When Mrs. Morrison picked up her pen to write Mrs. Gray, to please her friend and please herself as well, her task was a complicated one. She had been asked to write about the Indians, about her life in the forest that was not what she would have chosen, and about herself. "Is this to much nonsens" she queries at one point and, apparently assured, she plunges on, following her memory and her pen. She does not attempt to theorize about race or history, but in the accumulation of daily detail, in her casual use of two different languages, one of them Indian, she creates a portrait of what it meant to grow up as a mixed-race person in a truly multi-cultural place and then live on into an era when race and ethnicity, unless one were white and American, became negative markers of status, class, and opportunity—an era when people noticed if a woman accompanying Indians looked white, since Indian women were considered degraded and fair game for sexual play as white women weren't, when she needed to assert her education by noting she could teach her children English as surely many of her newly emigrated white neighbors could not. On a wide-open frontier filled with immigrants from a dozen different countries, language and skin color, rather than knowledge of the wilderness and the ability to survive there, had become what mattered.

Language becomes identity becomes race, or so hoped the "Friends of the Indian," those liberal nineteenth-century whites dedicated to forcing the Indians to mimic white ways, but it didn't quite work out as planned. Persons with light skin can change languages and acculturate themselves in white values and eventually, if they choose, blend in. Persons of color cannot. Once race becomes a marker of negative difference, rather than a cue to language as Mrs. Morrison uses it, assimilation is nearly impossible. The white ethnic wars in the upper Midwest would eventually fade as European immigrants came to think of themselves as American and as their children grew up speaking English as a first language. For many Indians and métis, this would be impossible. Eliza Morrison acknowledges the new social reality, but she was no sycophant. She does not apologize, nor does she ask permission. She wields the autobiographer's power to choose what she thinks is important to write about, and she chooses to describe a lost and lovely accepting world to which she, and those like her, held the only key.

*Moccasin Made by Eliza Morrison for William Gray Purcell*

# Chronology

| | |
|---|---|
| 3 November 1837: | Eliza Morrin born at La Pointe, Madeline Island, Wisconsin, to Robert Morrin, 37, and Frances (Wabegiah) Morrin, 35. |
| 1839: | Eliza Morrin admitted to mixed-blood rolls of the 1837 treaty. The claims of John and Agathe Morrison are rejected. |
| 23 December 1842: | John Meyer Russell Morrison born to John Morrison, 29, and Agathe Cadotte Morrison, 20, at Pokegama. |
| 1850: | Eliza Morrin leaves school to care for mother. |
| 4 April 1855: | Robert Morrin buys three acres, Outlot #36, in La Pointe. |
| 18 August 1865: | Frances (Wabegiah) Morrin dies at La Pointe. |
| 28 September 1865: | Eliza Morrin, 28, marries John M. R. Morrison, 23, at Bayfield, Wisconsin. |
| 28 October 1865: | The Morrisons are enrolled at Red Cliff Reservation. |
| 25 June 1866: | Robert John "Johny" Morrison born at La Pointe. (Dies 1897). |
| May 1867: | The Morrisons move to Leihy's farm upriver from Odanah. |
| 24 October 1867: | Peter William Morrison born at Odanah. (Dies before 1880.) |
| 1 October 1868: | The Morrisons move to a farm at Souix River. |
| 11 November 1868: | Angeline Maggie Charlotte Morrison born at Souix River. (Dies before 1880.) |
| Fall 1869: | The Morrisons move to Bayfield. |
| 4 April 1870: | Deed recorded transferring to Eliza Morin [sic] from Robert Morin [sic] Outlot #36 in the village of La Pointe for $500.00. |
| 29 April 1870: | Robert Morrin dies at La Pointe. The Morrisons begin living at La Pointe. |
| 27 September 1870: | Ervin Charles "Charlie" Morrison born at La Pointe. (Dies 1950.) |
| 12 December 1871: | George Joseph Morrison born at La Pointe. (Dies 1936.) |
| 18 December 1873: | Daniel Russell "Danny" Morrison born at La Pointe. (Dies 1952.) |
| 29 April 1875: | Thomas Samuel Morrison born at La Pointe. (Dies 1948.) |

*James Red Sky's Migration Chart: The Journey of the Ojibwe from the Atlantic to Minnesota*

| | |
|---|---|
| 1875: | Indians not connected with reservations allowed to homestead land. |
| 19 September 1877: | Benjamin Allen Morrison born at La Pointe. (Dies 1939.) |
| Fall 1878: | The Morrisons move to Ashland. |
| 27 May 1879: | Eliza Morrison sells Outlot 36 in the Village of La Pointe for $150.00. |
| 7 August 1879: | Edward Francis Morrison born at Ashland. (Dies 1882.) |
| 15 September 1879: | The Morrisons move to Pike Lake and begin living with the Bouskys. |
| 4 April 1880: | Eunice Maggie Morrison (Sero) born at Spider Lake. (Dies 1922.) |
| Spring 1884: | Eliza Morrison takes the train to Ashland for the first time. |
| 1887: | General Allotment Act (Dawes Act) passed. William Gray and Nettie McCormick buy land at Island Lake. |
| 27 August 1889: | John Morrison homesteads 120 acres south of Spider Lake. |
| 7 March 1891: | Nettie McCormick conveys to Kate Gray an undivided half-interest in the land around Island Lake. |
| 8 June 1891: | John Morrison homesteads an additional 40 acres south of Spider Lake. |
| 28 February 1894: | Kate Gray conveys interest in Island Lake property to Nettie McCormick. |
| August 1895: | John Morrison sells timber off part of the homestead. |
| Fall 1895: | The Morrisons move from Spider Lake to Odanah. |
| 14 October 1895: | John Morrison sells the timber from additional 40 acres of the homestead. |
| 12 June 1899: | John Morrison sells 80 acres of land to Hattie Vanall. |
| 19 September 1899: | John Morrison sells 80 acres of land to Anne Pettingill. |
| 1 October 1901: | William C. Gray dies. |
| 1901: | John Morrison receives allotments in Bad River Reservation. |
| 30 July 1904: | Nettie McCormick begins selling timber off Island Lake properties. |
| 16 August 1913: | John Morrison dies of cancer, age 75. |
| 9 January 1921: | Eliza Morrison dies of pneumonia, age 84. |

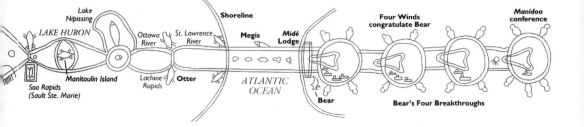

# A LITTLE HISTORY OF MY FOREST LIFE: AN INDIAN-WHITE AUTOBIOGRAPHY

*Eliza Morrison*

OCT
23. 1894

1894
Iron River Oct 27

My Dear Mrs Gray

I send you
all these so that you can pick
out and write the best way
you know that is just the
begining of my story please
excuse poor writing and
spelling I shall do the best
I can for you much.
love to you all yours.. true
friend

Eliza Morrison

October 29 [1894][22]
Iron River, Wisconsin

*Mrs W. C. Gray:*
*My most dearest friend:*

I take in hand to write you up a little history of my life. I will be glad to write it up for you. I am a poor hand for that but I will try my best. It will be a good while before I can get to the Indian stories that I was telling you about when I visited you so long a time. I dont know much about the Indians myself only what my mother used to tell me. She of course knows from her mother. My husband knows more about the Indians for he was among them so much. He was among them six years before we were married, that is the Chippewas. His mother, he tells me, is from the seven brothers. In that line down to the five brothers is his mothers first cousin. The youngest of the five brothers came once to our house to see me and my little boy as he considered my husband his nephew. This was in 1869. Soon after that he died. He has two sons living and two daughters which are older than I am. I will make my letter short. Did you get the plum trees all right. I hope you are well. I will try and get my husband to help me write a little this winter.

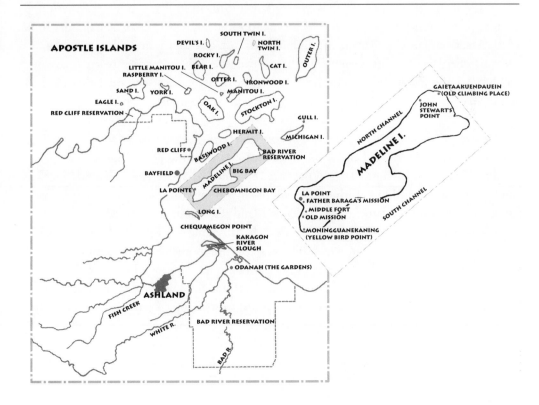

Oct 23 1894[23]

*From Wisconsin*
*Mrs W. C. Gray*

*My Dear Madam:*

In your letter that was written in Sept. 28 wishing me to write a little history of my life, I would like to do any thing pleasing to you but I am not a good writer. But how ever I can do a little.

I was born in Lapointe Island which is now called Madeline Island or one of the Apostle Island. I was born in 1837, Nov. 3rd. I was raised there on the Island. I speak of not where the American Fur Company had the fort, but one half mile south of that, where they called Middle Fort where my father must have bought some land when I was a little girl, where we lived, and there was a Presbyterian mission near by where I went to school, and my sisters and brothers. I did not go to school long, only long enough to learn to read and write. Soon after that my sister got married and I had to stay home and do the work. My mother became sickly. My fathers name is Robert Morrin. My mothers name is Frances Morrin. As near as I can find out her father came from France and my father came from Scotland. When he was a boy, to Canada, to Montreal, where he must have met some of the American Fur Company men and hired out to where they were trading with the Indians, where he must first seen my mother. My mother is been married twice. I have one half brother and two half sisters. In the last marriage of my mother with my father there was three of us, one man older than me and one younger than me.

*[The following paragraphs were written at another time giving additional details.]*
I went to Sunday School and thats where I learned what was good. I loved to go.

I was born on Madeline Island in the year 1837 the 3rd day of November. My mother came from Souix Ste Marie. With my grandmother and my aunt they came in a birchbark canoe, coasting on Lake Superior to Madeline Island. Her name was Frances.

My father was from Quebeck. He was Scotch. His name was Robert Morrin. I have 2 brothers and 2 sisters. I went to school till I was 13. And mother had poor health that I quit. When I was 8 years old I went with my brother in law to Fonderlac where he was preaching. He was a Methodist minister. I was contented for a little while and I got lonesome and they had to bring me home and then I was very happy. I stayed single till I was 27. Mother died when I was 27 years old, the 18th day of August.

When I was 13 years old we took another trip to the same place at Fonderlac. Almost all the people at Madeline Island went, for there was to be a payment made there for the

Indians. We all went there for nothing.[24] When we came back we stopped on an Island and took and cooked some dinner and my dress caught a fire and my brother put it out. He was going to throw me in the lake if he could not put it out. When we got back my sister got married and went away.[25] So then I had to stay at home and do the work for my mother had poor health. Thats the time I quit going to school. My brothers names are Joseph, William, Robert. My sisters names [are] Angeline, Hannah.[26]

I lived with my mother until I was 27 years old and she died. I thought I would stay a while with my father and I was going away to one of my sister, this was in 1865 while I was home where my father lived. I heard of a young man coming to Bay Field, where I stayed when ever I went there. I came to conclusion that I would go to Bay Field after just coming from one of my sisters who lived up to Bad River Falls. I asked my pa if I could go to Bay Field that afternoon. He said "Yes, but be very careful in that big boat." I had only myself to row that big boat. I had my sisters little girl, not big enough to row, [and it was] 3 miles across from my fathers place to Bay Field, what they called the North Channel. In going cross I had to row very hard for fear the wind might rise before I got over. I got over safe. I went to my brothers house as usual, and that afternoon some of my brothers sisters in law was there to his house. I found out through them where Mr John Morrison was. They were camping up the big hill to where the spring is. They are in a tent. Saturday afternoon I went down to the store after some thing. There I seen John Morrison, shook hands of course with him. The next day was Sunday. In the afternoon us girls went up to the camp, stayed a while, and we all went back again to my brothers where I always stay when I am to Bay Field.

In the evening John Morrison came to see me. We of course had a long talk in my brothers house. It was quite hard for me to talk english because I was not very used to it. I told him if he is going to talk much more, use our native language. That is the Chippewa language. I of course spoke in Chippewa language. He began to tell me how he was going to the North Shore of Lake Superior, way out to Misabay mountain to hunt and trap to make money.

"I will be gone about three years" he says "and maybe never come back again."
Here I kept quiet while he was telling me what he was to do.
"Three of us" he says "are going there."
I had no idea he would be my husband in 5 days from that time.
He says "We are 3 in partners. For my part" he says "I rather have one partner."
"Well" says I "what do you mean?"
"I like to find a girl for a partner."
"Not to go trapping."
"Oh no" he says "I mean Id like to find a girl for wife for me."

"Well can you find one."

"Yes. I have found you. Will you have me?" he says.

"I dont know what you mean."

"I mean will you marry me?"

"You mean when you come back from Misabay Mountain" I say "Now or in a week from now? Oh if I know just what you mean, I would answer you."

"I mean just what I say. If you like me well enough to have me we will get married before I go."

"If you mean that, we can get ready and get married, because I like you. But if we get married you will not go to Misabay mountain. You will go home with me to my fathers old place. I got our boat here. You come in the morning and go over with me."

He says "When we get over there you will tell your father why I came with you."

I said "Yes."

The next morning he came quite early. I began to think he meant business. I told my brother I was going now, that John Morrison was going over with me to see pa. I also spoke to my brother in chippewa. Then he said "All right, dont you go over alone." So we started. He rowed across the channel in a short time. I steered. I made a bee line for home. My sisters little girl was with me all the time. When we got to our landing place my father came to meet us. He shook hands with the young man. "Of course I was very glad when I see somebody with you. Come in the house and rest." John Morrison says to me "Now we've got to talk english." Of course he was talking with my father while I was working in the kitchen.

The next morning after breakfast I told my father the intention of the young man. "Well" he says "my girl, if you have found somebody that you like well enough to marry, all right. You are old enough. I know you can get married as soon as you wish. I know the young man is well thought of by the whites." He was out while I was talking with my father. When he came in I told him that I had done my part. "Now you ask my father and it will be all right. He is out to the barn, husking corn."

He went out and commenced to husk corn. And he husked corn 2 days before he dared to ask pa what his intention was. At last he got brave and asked him. For me of course it was all right. The old man told him he could have me. "This is the first time she find a young man that she likes well enough to marry. You and her can get married just as soon as you want to make this your home."

We got ready. We were married by the Justice of the Peace in the town of Bay Field at my brother Williams home.[27]

Iron River
November 10 1894

*Dear Mrs Gray*

I am sending you some more. I am very slow but if it satisfies to you I shall keep right on. Please drop a line and let me know and this winter my husband says he will write about the Indians if you wish it for he knows more about them than I do. Eunice is receiving a very nice sled from Mr Clow.[28] She is so pleased about it. I would like one of her pictures if Willy has finished them. So good by. My love to you all. Next time I write you I will tell you about the house I am living in. I remain as ever your true friend.

*Mrs John Morrison*[29]

After we was married that same afternoon we had a little party and invited a quite number of our friends and had quite a good time. It kept us busy talking to our white friends and our Indian friends. Some of the girls says "Let us have a dance." I says "No, for mother died not long ago." We of course was quite happy to see so many friends. I wrote to my sister and telling her that I was married now [so] I cannot come and stay with you. When she read my letter she knew who he was.

We talked a good deal in our language, the chippewa language. My husband said "I did not think to get a wife so quick. Is this the break up of my going to the North Shore of Lake Superior." One week after we was married he said he had to go back to Saint Croix Falls where he came from. He said he would be gone about twelve days. I said "How far is it by the Indian movement." They say nimidana ashinanogosivin. How many miles is it.

"100 and 90 miles" he says "by the road. Now to go there and back, eighty miles."[30]

"I cant go with you."

"Oh no. It would be to far for you to walk. I will hurry up and make it in ten days."

My husband went off on the 4th of October 1865. He of course left me what money he had with me, to be gone 12 days. Before he went off I asked him if I could visit my white friends while he was gone. He says yes. In ten days he got back all right and well how glad I was. My english language could not explain it. I began to speak in Chippewa to my husband and father come in the house and shook hands with him of course. "You got back all right, I see."

"Yes sir. I did not do so well as I expected, but it will do. I got one hundred dollars" he says. "If I had not went back, I might not got any money at all."

Father says to him "You done some big traveling. Average 35 miles a day for ten days that is counted fast traveling even in my time. You must be some thing like your father. What a great traveler he was."

"There is two days I walked 44 miles each day."

After he got through talking with my father, I commenced to talk with him. He says he dont feel like a young man this evening after traveling 40 miles and crossing the lake besides 4 miles. Here" he says "here is what I went for." He showed me one hundred dollars.

I says to him "As soon as you have a good rest, we must take a trip to my sisters to Bad River Falls." We took our boat from home coasting the Lake Superior [shore] as far as Bad River and left it there for it was hard to pole up the river. We started for up the river. No road but only an Indian trail through the woods. Of course in making this trip it was amongst the Indians. Of course we made ourselfs Indian and wife as much as [we] could. Both had little packs[31] and I had in my hand a little squaw axe to make myself a squaw as much as could be. My husband wore around his waist a red sash. When we walked, my husband walked ahead and me behind. We would not walk side by side but we walked after the Indian style.

We went on our way to the Bad River Falls. About 3 o clock we got to the old Chief Edanigishik, who was the nearest neighbor to my sisters. We of course stopped there for a while. Those Indian family know me well, but[32] they did not know my husband untill I told them who he was. Then the old Chief says "I know his father well. I can tell what he is as soon as I see the red sash. The red and white about the sash. A belt of this kind is an old sign. Represent him what he is, red and white blood. He is a nephew of the five brothers. I know the youngest one well. We are about the same age," he says.

My husband asks him how old he was.

He says "I am now 83 years old" he says.

Then my husband gives him half of what tobacco he had. Tobacco means good friend. Giving half what he had means a respect and my husband went through some motion with his hand and the old man bowed to him and lift one leg and struck the ground or kicked it and shook hands with him. And we went our way to my sisters. Before reaching there my husband says "Wait a while before we get to near the house." He takes the Red sash off from him and puts his suspenders on him. He says "I know Mr Leihy is not an Indian" and I laughed at him.

"You are a curious fellow. You must be pretty near all Indian by the way you act."

"O no" he says "knowing what to do I have not forgot my scotch blood yet. It does not make me an Indian."

"Tell me what was that you meant when you made motion to that old man and [he] bowed to you and lift one leg and kicked the ground?"

"O I cant tell you, wife. That is a secret."

"You must know some secret thing among the Indians."

"Yes" he says "but not any thing to interfere with my religion. I told you I was among the Indians long time before I come here."

We started again, got to the house. My sister seen us coming there. She says "I thought they would come pretty soon. I heard you got married. Is this your husband."

"Yes" I said. "John Morrison is his name. He cant talk english at all. You got to speak to him in Chippewa if you want to talk to him."

She was silent and John went out to look around. In a few minutes Mr Leihy came. He of course know him, shook hands with him. "You come to see us. I heard Eliza was married. We could not see any body here that know you well enough to tell us. All my wife done was to look for you. She know Eliza would come up and see us." Mr Leihy turns to me and says "How quick a girl can get married when she finds the one she wants."

Of course we canot write all what we said. I know we had a nice time while we was there. The next morning we all went to the sugar camp a little way from Mr Leihys house where we made sugar side by side when mother was living. I says to my husband "Let us work and fix up for spring and we will make sugar." Mr Leihy says "Yes you can."

7

but they did not know
my husband. untill I told
them who he was. then the
old chief says I know his
fatther well. I can tell what
he is as soon as I see the
new sash. the red and white
about the sash. a belt of this
kind is an old sign.
Represent him what he is
red and white blood he is
a nephew of the five
brothers I know the youngest
one well. we are about the
the same age he says. my
husband asks him how old
he was. he says I am now
83 years old. he says
then my husband gives him
half of what tobaco he had.
tobaco means good friend
giving half what he had means

8

a respect and my husband
went through some motion
with his hand and the old
mas bowed to him and lift
one leg and struck the ground
or kicked it and shook hands
with him, and we went on
our way to my sisters. before
reaching there my husband
says wait a while before we
get to near the house. he
takes the Red sash off from
him and puts his suspenders
on him. he says I know Mrs
deity is not an Indian
and I laughed at him, you
are a curious fellow you
must be pretty near all Indian
by the way you act, o no he says
knowing what to do I have not
forgot my scotch blood yet,
it does not make me an Indian

After dinner my husband set to work, me to with my squaw ax, he not knowing much about the sugar bush work. I was almost boss over him. We worked 4 days chopping and fixing up for spring. On the fifth day we went home. My sister and the girls come quite a piece with us. We came to the old chief house. We of course have to stop there. Some of them was standing out doors looking at us coming. One of the boys ran to the river. "He is here now" [he] says to his grandpa Edanigishik. Edanigishik means light on both sides. Thats the old chiefs name. The old chief says to my husband "When you get to the garden they want you to stop to *wabanimikis wigiwam*. He heard you was up here. He wants to see you. He heard you was a nephew of the 5 brothers. He says he is some relation to *medueiash*." Thats the youngest of the five brothers.

After he got through talking with my husband, we went on the trail. Wabanimiki means white thunder. As we was walking along, my husband says he did not like to go to *wabanimikis*. When we arrive to the village we went in to Mr Wheelers house. Mrs Wheeler invited us in the house to stay untill the next day. My husband did not go to *wabanimikis* that night. I says to him "Why dont you like to go?"

"Because I heard he was a medicine man."

In the morning one of *wabanimikis* boys came and he gave him some tobacco. First he cut some of it and gave it to him. I said to him "What made you cut some of the tobacco before you gave it to him." He says "The piece of tobacco means a friend. What is cut fine means peace and good will."[33]

Mr Wheeler was a Presbyteran missionary. He could speak Chippewa quite well.

We started for home. It was a very nice morning. This was on Oct 25 1865. From the mission we had to go down the river five miles before we got out to the Lake Superior. When we got to the mouth of the river we could not get out. It had been blowing from the north east. It was big seas. We went a shore and stayed untill noon. The sea went down a good deal in four hours time. My husband was not willing to stay any longer on this beautifull sand beach. I enjoyed it very much on this great sand beach. There was a great deep hollow caused by a great wind. In the hollow we found the most delicious cranberries that I ever eat.

We got out of the mouth of the river in to the lake by hard pulling with oars. I of course helped my husband all I could with my paddle. We had to keep it away from the shore about 1/4 of a mile to be safe from the breakers of the sea. This is the hardest Part of our trip. We had a head wind blowing quite hard, my husband rowing hard against the wind. We would only go at the rate of three miles an hour. We had twelve miles to go like this. After one hour I says to my husband "Let me take the oar for one hour." I went at the rate of two miles an hour. This is the way we had to get home. The last three miles was smooth water no wind. Father was standing on the shore looking at us coming.

He had been setting gill nets. He expected us to be home pretty soon. Oh what nice white fish and trout he had for us. "Pa I shall cook them the old way. I know you liked them cooked that way and John likes them cooked that way."

While we was eating our supper pa says to me "How did you like the trip?"

"Oh I liked it well enough and John liked [it] to, but he did not like the idea of *waba-nimiki* inviting him to his long *wigiwam*."

Pa turns to John "Did you fix it?"

"Oh yes. I sent him some tobacco and had to agree to send more or give if I should come in his way. I heard he was a great medicine man and I sent him the tobacco according to their coustome [custom] by his own son. He heard I was a nephew of the brothers but I made him to understand I was not with them in their old costume."[custom]

"Why pa, you would be surprised to know how much he knows about the Indians. He knows just what to say and what to do and what to wear when he goes among them. He says he use to hunt with them, hunting deer or moose."

Pa says "I hope my daughter has not married a man who will take her in the woods among the Indians."

"Why pa, John has already talked of making a homestead out somewhere 40 miles from here."

Pa says "That would be all right to make a homestead. You had better take a trip over to Red Cliff. The Indian Agent Web is going to Pay off the Indians in Red Cliff reservation on the 29th of Oct 1865. I heard any one that comes there shall get Pay."

My husband says to me "We might just as well go tomorrow morning. We will see what is going on besides a little Pay."

We only stopped over night with my father. We started the next morning for Red Cliff reservation where the Indians were to be paid from the Government. We stopped to Bay Field. We went to my brothers house [to] eat dinner. There was only two of us in that big boat. Brother says "Well now, we will make up a boat. We are going to."

We soon got on the way to Red Cliff and got there, three stout young men rowing the boat. One of the young man is the son of the five brothers, the youngest of the brothers. He happen to meet us in Bay Field. Of course in their language he made my husband his first cousin. They of course done most of the talking on the way to Red Cliff and he was the only full blooded Indian on board with us. The whites called him George, but his Chippewa name is *medueiash*, named after his father. *Medueiash* means Battel by the wind.

When we landed to Red Cliff, the place where the Indians were to be paid by an Agent appointed by the government, we went up to one of my friends house and my husband says to me that he is going to speak to the Indian Agent in Chippewa language through an interpreter. George and him went to the Big Building where the agent was[34] enrolling the Indians. George spoke to the Agent and shook hands with him and told him "This is my cousin. He would like to speak to you. He is from the same country where I come from."

The same time he told him he had no pay for several years. The agent says to him "I am now very busy. I wish you and your cousin would come tomorrow morning. Any thing I can do for you, I will do it. Your cousin is a fine looking fellow. Is he got a wife."

"Yes. Enroll him with us, he and his wife, and give him some thing."[35]

"All right" says the Agent "I give a blanket."

The next morning the Indians were paid and we also got our portion, the amount of four dollars a head. The same day late in the after noon we took our boat and went back home. When we got near to our old landing place, father was standing there waiting for us to come up. The lake was quite rough. It blowed hard that day. Father says to us "You was not gone long this trip. I am very glad you have come back."

I says to pa "We are going to stay home with you. Now see pa what my husband got for you to do. He went to work and bought a lot of gill net twine for you to make nets this fall so he can fish. I told him that I can knit to. We will both get at the business, make them up as quick as we can. He says he likes to fish. I know that will keep him at home. I am glad of that."

My husband set to work fixing up things, ready for fall, fishing right from home. We had three weeks time to fit up our nets before there is any fishing in the south channel.[36] 20th of November is the time the white fish comes in the south channel. He got one of my brothers to come and work with us. That fall, my, he was happy as he could be, getting ready for the business. Got ready by the 20th of Nov and commenced from that time till it froze up. What nice whitefish we use to have there. My husband and brother fished untill Dec 16th. It was very cold. The last time they went to lift their nets, they fished a little over a month, they caught 30 barrels of fish. Most of it was whitefish.

Two barrels was put [to] one side for to be used when we go to make sugar in the spring up to Bad River falls, where we had been fixing up ready to make sugar. Near my sisters where they make sugar every spring and where we used to make sugar every spring when my mother was living. And my brothers use to go to and some times my father would go to and he would take the cows and all the chickens. And then I use to be happy. We all lived quite well in going to the place where we make sugar.

We of course started from Lapointe which is now called Madeline Island. We had to go over the ice 9 miles before we could reach the *ka ka gan* river. The river goes on or through Bad River flats which leads to the gardens which is now called Odanah. [We went] Right to the Indian village in Bad River Reservation where so many chippewas live. We of course would stop over night to Indian village. We always had friends there. We of course starting for the sugar bush was ever hardly alone. Five or six families of us would go together. We always could make it in two days. From home we always had a horse or an ox, some times two oxen and there were few others had ponies. But most of them used dogs, from two to six dogs quite well trained, in going together to go to our sugar bush. Does not mean we stayed together. Every family had a sugar bush of his own, perhaps 2 miles apart all over Bad River flats. These people I am speaking of are not all Indians. There is good many white men of different kind. I am telling about a part of what I use to see the people do, when I was a girl and we use to do the same way ourselfs. When I got married to my husband we both thought it would be well for us to do the same work to live.

In my mothers last marriage their was three of us. My brother William, he was the older, me, and next my brother Robert younger than me. I was the last one to get married after my mothers death. I took good care of her. My father lived four years after my mother died. I took good care of my father when he was sick with the help of my husband.

Is it interesting to you? Please let me know. Or is it to much noncens. My love to all.

*Mrs. John Morrison*[37]

*Dec 4 1894*

My Father died in April 29th 1869 and my mother died 1865 August 18th. Now I have told nearly all I can think of and seen. But have not said any thing about myself and my husband when we used to make sugar the first winter we was married. We stayed with my father at the old home. I of course had hard work to keep my husband at home. There was no work to speak of where we was living. He would fish and trap rabbits. That was not quite satisfactory to him. He wanted to go in a country where he could trap fur. We lived near town but I know if he would go away it would make it unpleasant for me and pa. We past the winter quite comfortable.

In February 28th we moved to our sugar bush where one of my brothers was with his family. I could see my husband was more happy and of course when I see him happy every thing was all right with me as far as getting along to live. We commenced to work, getting ready for the springs work. We had every thing we wanted for the time we were to be there. Every thing was high price. Flour was 16 dollars a barrel, every thing in proportion. There is one thing we always had, that is maple sugar. We had every thing ready by the time the first run of the sap. We went on the old Indian way of tapping maple trees. This was very hard work. The snow was the depth of three feet. We had to use snow shoes the whole time. In three days time we tapped 900 Bark Buckets. The fourth day we began to gather sap, gathered 10 barrels of sap. The fifth day about the same amount and so on for three weeks, hardly any rest night and day. We could not have any time to grain the sugar. The maple trees kept running. When the sap stop running, we had five barrels of syrup had to be attended to, cooked it so to grain to pack into bark buckets for future use.

## MAKING MAPLE SUGAR

THE CHIPPEWAS CONSIDERED MAPLE SUGAR ONE of their most important foods. It was used to season vegetables, fruits, cereals such as wild rice, and fish. It could be dissolved in water to make a summer drink or a syrup with herbal medicine for children. Granulated sugar cakes in the shapes of animals, people, moons, and stars were commonly used as gifts. Strings of small birchbark cones of sugar, like clusters of grapes, were a children's delicacy.

The yearly agricultural round of the Chippewa began in the "sugar bush," or maple grove, about mid-March. It was a

*Indian Sugar Camp*

happy time when groups of two or three families, who may have shared a sugar camp for many seasons, would return to the woods, bringing their kettles, supplies, rolls of birchbark, and any small children or invalids on sleds pulled by dogs. Two structures were generally left in the sugar camp from year to year: a large frame of poles that when recovered with bark or matting would be the lodge, and a smaller bark-covered structure that housed the bark and wood utensils for making sugar.

Sap was collected by using a hand axe to make a three-inch diagonal cut in a tree about three feet above the ground. Below the lower end of this cut, the bark was removed in a four-inch line perpendicular to the ground, then a wooden spile, usually made of slippery elm, was inserted into a cut

in the tree. Birchbark dishes were placed on the snow below the taps to collect the sap that ran during the day when the weather warmed. The size of the sugar bush was measured in these "taps," since each tree could have several. Nine hundred was average.

The collected sap was hauled back to camp in bark containers, pails, or barrels, then poured into kettles and boiled over an open fire in the lodge or outside until enough evaporation had taken place. Thickened syrup was filtered using a basswood mat or clean cloth, then held until "sugaring off," a day when the weather was bad or sap collecting had stopped. At this time, the kettles were cleaned and scoured with stiff rushes, the thickened sap was poured back into them with a small piece of deer tallow to keep the sugar soft, and a maple-wood paddle was used to stir the boiling syrup until it had thickened enough to be "grained." This syrup was poured into wooden trays and worked rapidly with a granulating ladle until it formed sugar crystals. The finished sugar was stored in birchbark containers called makuks, some of which could hold a hundred pounds or more. The finest sugar, usually from the first run of sap, was pressed into molds or wrapped as cakes in birchbark tied with basswood strings. Gum sugar, which everyone loved, was made by taking syrup from the kettle just before it was ready to grain and pouring it on the snow until it thickened, then wrapping it in bark.[38]

*Right:*
*Stacked Dishes and Empty Cones, the Latter to be Filled with Sugar*

*Below:*
*Granulating Trough, Stirring Paddle, Granulating Ladles, and Makuk of Granulated Maple Sugar*

Than came bad weather which gave us time to grain our sugar. Two more days run after this bad weather came. We made that into wax cakes, the amount of two flour barrels of cakes and only two of us to work. We made about one thousands pounds of sugar worth 12 cents a pound right through. But the sugar we use to make we could sell it for 16 cents a pound. Our sugar was much whiter and cleaner than what the Indians made.

We was about two months in all in the sugar bush and started for home back again. This is about the first of may. The lake was all open. Of course in moving from the sugar bush we took a boat big enough to carry all our stuff down the river. We go 20 miles to go down the river before we came out to lake superior and we had 12 miles to go on the lake to get home. I am now telling the distance we had to go to get home, but I must tell some thing about the Indians.

They move of course to go to their sugar bushes all before it is warm enough for the sap to run. They would be on the grounds to build their sugar camps large enough to accommodate more than themselfs. The man who is the head of his family is sure to invite some of his friends to come and eat some of the first sugar their woman make. Woman does not eat the sugar untill they are done. The sugar is put before the man. The wife when she puts it before him she says to him "This is what you wanted for now. Say what is in your mind." The man will call up his friends if they are not to far away. He would say many things as by way of giving thanks to the great spirit for what he got to live on and he would always leave some sugar for his wife and children.

In coming up the River to go home we would stop to the gardens, that is to the Indian village. The Indians would be there nearly the same time. All together they would have a time feasting and dancing. For ten days they were living on good soil, [but] would not take thought to plant any thing untill all is over with. They are great in giving one another things to eat. Some times we would stop a day or so to look at them. How they carry on in their peculiar ways. They would build what they call in their language *ki non da wanan*. That means a long *wigiwam*. This kind of building is framed with small hard wood poles such as the ones they can bend at the top of. It is round as a ball but not high but long. Some times one hundred feet long covered with birch bark half up just so a person can look over. Every body is allowed to look on. But every one that is in the lodge is painted on their faces. In the spring a large amount of all kind of fish goes up the Bad River. The Indians live quite easy and have a good time in their way but we would be moving toward home to the Apostle Island. We had a good boat loaded with maple sugar.

# THE MIDÉWIWIN

THE MIDÉWIWIN OR GRAND MEDICINE RITE began as a curing ceremony designed to purge the Anishinaabeg peoples of the ills, both physical and psychological, associated with European contact. The ceremony, which took place twice a year, in spring and fall when people would be gathered in large groups to harvest food, involved initiation into one of four progressively complicated levels, called degrees, but the basic purpose of each was to promote health by curing sickness and lengthening life. A person seeking treatment was injected with "spirit power"—medicine bundles or, most commonly, the megis shell—shot from the animal skin bags of the priests or shamans. After being shot the candidate fell unconscious; upon awaking the megis emerged from the mouth. Thus cured, a person's power against disease and death was renewed.

Most villagers, including children, were initiated into the first degree, since the fees, originally termed "gifts," were reasonable. But after that the poor were unable afford help without going into debt. Initiation into the upper levels of the Midé took years of study, was extremely expensive to pursue and, by the end of the nineteenth century, was fraught with sorcery. In these late stages, many priests enriched themselves to the point where they no longer had to work.

Like other Nativist religions—the Ghost Dance of the Plains tribes, the Handsome Lake religion of the Iroquois, the cult of the Shawnee Prophet—the Midéwiwin was a new religion that incorporated ancient rituals into a new context. While the rituals may have begun centuries ago, their incarnation as the Midéwiwin began in the mid-1600s, during a time of epidemics and cultural fragmentation. Nativist religions frequently develop as a response to cultural stress when traditional religions, having failed to safeguard the culture and protect the people from inexplicable suffering, seem meaningless. Then a new form of religion, often more dramatic and involving miracles such as raising the dead, sweeps over the culture. Ghost dancers believed their shirts would stop bullets, for example, just as the Midéwiwin convinced adherents it could protect against disease, or Jews believed Moses could part the Red Sea.

Religions such as the Midéwiwin must also fit the economic and social needs of their communities. Historians believe the Midéwiwin flourished because it consolidated the power of individual spirit helpers into a powerful grouping of all the spirits. This encouraged unification of totem groups and encouraged the creation of clans and tribes, which were needed as the land became populated and Indians needed to consolidate their power to negotiate with whites. The Midéwiwin also allowed power and visions to be purchased, thus redistributing the fur trade incomes and making more time for hunting since days-long visions

*Midéwiwin Lodge*

quests were no longer necessary.

Music was an important aspect of the ceremonies and underscored the ancient teachings and beliefs by using many ancient words. The songs were also used to reiterate the conveying of power, so they were performed with a rapid drumbeat suggesting excitement and happiness. Midéwiwin songs were restricted to the ceremonial occasions and to specific members of the rite.

The Midéwewin is still practiced in many communities today and encourages holistic, traditional approaches to healing physical and psychological illnesses by developing the attributes of generosity, love, respect, honor, humility, obedience, and hope. The goal of practitioners is to find the center of the self in harmony with the powers of the Universe and to develop a way of life that embodies respect for all living things. One contemporary form of the medicine lodge practiced in the Great Lakes region is known as the Three Fires Society, which offers ceremonies with English interpretation. Traditional Midé ceremonies are conducted in traditional language.[39]

*1894*
*Iron River   December 15*

*Mrs Gray*

Dear friend. I received your most truly welcome letter and was very glad to hear from you once more. We are quite well at present hoping you are enjoying the same blessing. We are just having the loveliest weather. What a nice thing it is that you went and see your sister. If I only could do that how happy I would be. My sister is a widow now and an invalid. How I would like to go and see her. She lives in Lanse, Mich. Her husband use to be a Methodist minster. Some times I think it is hard to be poor and my mind will just turn and think may be it is the Lords will and than I content myself. I have only Bennie and Eunice with me. They both go to school. All the big boys are gone down to Odanah to work. Johny has build him a house in Odanah. He is going to get a 80 on the reservation. I send you some more of my writing. I shall keep on till I get to the end. They have started a reading room in Iron River. Harry Clow send me some books to donate to the reading room. I was very glad and thanked him very much. I must close so good by. Much love to you all.

I wish you a merry Christmas and a happy new year. I remain as ever your friend,

*Eliza Morrison*

PS

I forgot to inform you there is no body up to the farm. John is stopping with us this winter. He is at his old trade tanning deer hides. Mr Ramsdell is living with his cousin 3 miles north of Iron River. Bennie sees the ponies quite often in town.[40]

We had 12 miles on the lake shore outside of *sha ga wa mi kong* which is now called long Island, where now stands the Government light house. When we came to the end of the long Island we had to cross the south channel the distance of 4 miles. There we will be home. Going this distance along the lake shore it was quite ruff. I was not alarmed at all for I was quite use to being in a boat and knowing my husband has had a good deal experience in that line. How ever we got home all right in the evening. The wind was not favorable for us that day. [When] we were quite near our landing place, pa seen us coming. Oh how glad he was to see us back again at the old home and [with] a boat load of maple sugar. He had been setting nets. What nice fish he did have for us.

John says to pa "We were two days longer than we ought to. We had to stop and look at the Indians dance. You know how they act after they are done making sugar in the spring."

"Pa, John says he is going to turn in to help you to do your planting so if we stay with you next winter we will have plenty potatoes. And he is going to fish between time and make hay and so on. I will be very glad to have you and him to stay with me all the time. I am not going to let him go any where now during the first year."

I became the mother of a little boy. We gave him the name he carries now. That is John who is living now and he is now 28 years old.[41] In the summer of 1866 my husband was fishing. I went out where they were fishing. Of course he did not fish alone. He had a man to help him fish. They salted their fish in half barrels made of pine, hand made barrels. We had no house to live in while we was out there but we had bought some birch bark

*Ojibwe Wigwam at Grand Portage*

made by the Indians that is fishing most all their time. They make some bark in this way to sell it. It is sewed so snug together that it keeps out most any storm. The frame that [is used] to put the sheets of the bark [on] is made like a half of round ball. After the bark is put over these poles, and we put over on top of the bark wide bass wood strings long enough to reach over down to the ground, [we] tie a stone on each end to keep the bark snug on to the frame. In this manner the new married make their *wi gi wam*.

# BIRCH BARK

THE CHIPPEWA CONSIDERED THE BIRCH A sacred tree because of its usefulness. Birchbark was made into canoes, cooking and storage dishes, lodge coverings, carrying bags, fans, torches, figures of dream symbols or totem marks, and patterns associated with craft work. Bark could be stored in rolls or packs of sheets until needed, then warmed before a fire to become pliable again. Large rolls were made by lacing sheets together with basswood fiber. Dishes were made water tight with slippery elm bark. Commodities such as sugar, dried fish, dried berries, and wild rice stored in bark did not spoil; thus the practice of making storage containers, makuks, of bark.

*Cutting Birch Bark Preparatory to Removing*

Because of birchbark's utility, stripping the bark was associated with a formal religious ceremony or at least an offering of tobacco. Bark was gathered in June or early July when it was easiest to remove, sometimes by groups of families who gathered to camp and prepare bark and twine. The largest, straightest, and least-blemished trees were preferred, particularly ones with smooth bark. Once a tree was selected, it was cut down about two feet above the ground by chopping in one direction only. The tree would then fall with one end resting on the stump and the other on the ground. This facilitated stripping off the bark and prevented it from becoming soiled by falling on the dirt. The bark was removed by making a long vertical cut, pulling back the bark with one hand, passing it under the tree, and pulling it free with the other hand. The tree was then used for firewood.

Large trees yielded the heaviest bark of six to nine layers, usually used for canoes and coverings for the dead. The thinnest bark was sheer as tissue paper, but so strong it could be used as wrapping paper. Between these extremes any grade of thickness could be made and either side of the bark used, depending on what was needed. Freshly stripped, or green, bark could be made into a container used for cooking over an open fire. Filled with water, the pot would last long enough to cook meat. Tightly rolled strips of dried bark painted with pitch were used for torches, some of which would burn for hours. Records were kept on birchbark; the sacred scrolls of the Midéwiwin were rolls of birchbark inscribed with pictographs.[42]

But we were not quite custom to that to set on the ground as they do. My husband cut logs 8 inches through, put them on the ground and split small timber, put them on top of the big logs and [put] hay on top of this. Answer for bed and seat. We of course cooked out doors when it dint storm. I of course had no house to keep but I would keep my bark house clean. I was a mother of a little boy that I took Indian style. I tied him on a piece of pine board made very light. A pillow next to the board and other things answer for a bed. When he was 6 months old he would cry to be tied back on his cradle like.

*Cradle Board Carried By Mother*

I was out in this way nearly two months and my husband took me home to the old home where father was farming like. Going home we had nice sailing wind. It took us one hour and half to go 13 miles. Our boat was half loaded with salt fish, the amount of ten half barrels to be delivered to Vaughns dock. My husband was trading with him that time. All this may be considered hard life but we both liked it. We made father quite happy every time we would come home. We are very welcome, he says. He is lonesome for the little boy. "Thats my boy." When he was two months old we were than married over a year. Pa says to me, "Are you going out again. It is getting to cold out on the Island."

"John is going back again after his fishing out fit Monday and then he is going to work diging potatoes and then he is going to fish again till it freezes up."

John went back after his out fit and fished right from home and always could untill the 15th of dec. The last two hauls of fish they dont salt them at all. We take the Indian style in the way of keeping them through the winter so to have that excellent taste. They make a rack about five feet high and make a hole through the fishes tail and tie the two together with bass wood string, hang them up over the poles with heads down and covered over with sheets of birch bark to keep it dark. We always had lot of fish in this way. It was very good and had an excellent taste.

*Fish Drying Over Fire*

Fishing was all over with. My husband then he found a little contract long enough to last about 3 months getting out shingle bolts.[43] Of course I went and done the cooking. This was about six miles from the old home. When we moved we crossed the bay. It was freezing. Making ice. The men had hard work to reach a safe place. We made Mr Pikes landing. It was dark when we got there and then we had to go 2 miles to go to Mr Pikes through pine country. Plenty of water and mud on the road. After dark I could not see some times. I would go in the mud and water above my ankels. I was told to go on a head, thinking I could make one mile before it got very dark. I could not do it. My little boy cried. I had to stop. I know what the men had to do. They carried big packs of bedding. Finally I came near enough to see Mr Pikes light. I was tired and weary holding my little Johny in my arms. I was just a few minutes ahead of the men when I got to Mr Pikes. I came through rough road all alone. Mr Pike was about our best friend in this country then. They done all they could for us that night. My little boy was in their hands all the while. This was in Dec 22 in 1866, the second year of my marriage. This was the hardest time I ever had since I became a mother of a little boy.

We had a nice log house to live in near Mr Pikes. My husband worked there three months making shingle bolts. Than we moved back to the old home again and stayed with pa one week and it was time to go to the sugar bush. My husband engaged a team. There were several familys going that way. We all got ready about the same time to go all together. Our team was loaded down, mostly with fish. We took a good deal more than we want. We might say that was our money among the Indians. We had four pork barrels full lightly salted. Of course we took one barrel of flour and other things. Some of those Indians had ponies and some had single ox, some dogs, some had as many as six dogs. Quite number of white men with the Indians, all making for Bad River flats, to the magnificent flats where the Indian goes every spring to make their sugar.

This was in 1867 March first. We had a very nice day to cross the ice 12 miles of the distance, then up to *ka ka gan* river on the ice and to the gardens where the mission was. We of course stop there and eat dinner to one of our Indian friends house. After dinner we went on our way, 12 miles to go before we got to our sugar bush. My sister was living there. In the evening we reached the place where we were to do our springs work while the maple sap runs. All we know about this kind of work is what we learn from the Indians. The woman makes the dishes out of birch bark. They fold them in such a way as to form a dish. They also make pails out of birch bark sewed with bass wood bark strings, and to make it to hold water or sap they use tamarack pitch or pine pitch so they would not leak. They also make the box out of birch bark[44] to put the sugar in after it is grained. The Birch Bark has a kind of bitter taste but they have a way to take it out. No barrels to be had to pour the sap [in] when gathered, but throughs [troughs] are made out of bass wood.

It is surpprising to know how the Indians work about that time. It seems they will not have the sap to be wasted where ever they are. You cant hire one of them while they are making sugar unless the men fails to get game and they get short of provisions and then they will come and work for some thing to eat. We always have to ask them according to their language. First we give him or her some thing to eat and a piece of tobacco and we ask him or her to come for us one half of ten days. "We will give you some of that we got to eat." If not civilized we got to share what we have got in the line of eatibles and tell him or her to "eat all you can while here." If any hesitation on his part, offer tobacco to smoke while he is working. He is sure to come. If civilized we dont have to talk near so much.

This was the second spring we made sugar after we were married. There were three old women making sugar down the river below us one half mile. One morning one of them came up to our sugar camp, offer to work. The first thing I done was to give her plenty to eat. These three old women, two of them were widows and the youngest was never married. Their names was, the oldest was ma *ka de mi ko kue*. This means black beaver woman. The second is *ki ji i kue zhe zihs*. This means big little girl. The youngest name was *me gin de bad*. This means natural big head. She was only two feet and a half tall. Her body was big in proportion to her height, but her head was biger then any three common heads. I have seen her but my husband never seen her. He had heard of her but never had the opportunity. And another thing he never believed there was such a person among the Indians. My husband gave some fish and potatoes and bread to the one that was there and told her to tell her sister to come and dry a barrel of fish for us and we will give her half what she dries. And she came and cut all the sticks she wants to make the rack to dry the fish on and cut the green maple wood to make sweet smoke. He done this just to see the big headed woman. The next day one of the sisters brought her over to our sugar camp. The last time I heard of the big headed woman she was taken away by some show man. She never came back. She died in some big city. I dont know just where.

After we was through making sugar my husband hired out to run a farm for Mr Leihy for one year. Mr Leihy is one of my half sisters husband. Of course we had a good place to stay and plenty to live on but no white neighbors any nearer than to the gardens and that was 8 miles by the trail and 16 miles by the river. The farm was up the river.[45] What we did not have on the farm, the men had to pole it up by boat in the summer time, but in the winter there was a road part way on the ice and on land. The first of may my husband were to take charge of the farm. That soon came. We moved to the farm house from our sugar camp. Took all our sugar except what I took to my father. My husband hired a man, an old acquaintance, to take me down the river to the gardens where my sister was living. On may third in the morning I went down the river. We had some sugar of course taking it to my father at the old home to Lapointe. It took us four hours to get to the gardens. It was high water in the River. The water Run at the rate of three miles an hour. It was about one o clock when I entered my sisters house. Of course I would not go any further.

My sister says "I am glad you come. About the middle after noon we are going to see the Indians dance." This is after finishing of the ten days dance, what they always do. The last part of it I cant say it in english but I can say it in Chippewa: *wi sa sa ga wi chi ge wag.* "You come with us and see after my dinner." On we went. We had half a mile to go where they were dancing. We soon got there because we was all anxious to see them to perform. When we got to the long lodge, what they call *ke non da wan* where they were to perform, they had not commenced yet. Every white men and woman about the mission was there, ready to look on. The Indians did not seem to care.

The long lodge where they dance is about one hundred feet long and about 12 feet wide. A great post stands in the middle and one at each end. The posts are hewed on four sides and marked up on it [are] the animals they were to show out of their sacks. They first sing and drum very hard and all get up and dance for an hour and the youngest stop dancing and the oldest kept dancing. All at once they stop about half a minute and get up again with their sacks in their hands. These that dance with their sacks is the medicine men. The one they call the mash man was setting down the whole time. He did not dance. The eldest dance with their sacks and each time they came to the post they would oppen their sacks. Animals would come half way out to look at the post. There were seven of them dancing. Seven times one way and turn, dance back the other way seven times. Each time when they came to a post a different animal comes half out of the sack and looks at the post and [goes] back in the sack again. I seen a loon come half out the sack and a mink and a weasel and some thing else looks like a snake. When they got through, that is the eldest ones, they sat down and the youngest got up and dance. Even those that stood out side danced, and when they stopped the eldest commenced to talk about the Great Spirit. They seem to know God, but did not seem to belong there. They say *ni ma ni do mi nan*. This means our Spirit who lives under the mountains and under the water. They seem to know the existence of God. Their Spirit seem more inferior as near as I can understand.

*Medicine Dance in Midé Lodge*

Then it was late in the evening. We all went home to my sisters house. Mr Leihy my sisters husband came from Illinois when he was young man. Took up a farm up to Bad River Falls in 1846. He was a well educated man. We all suppose that he could speak the Indian language perfect. We told him to explain what those Indians was saying at the dance when we was there looking at them and hearing them talk. He could not explain any part of it anymore than I could.

The next morning we started for down the river for five miles before we get to Lake Superior and 12 miles to go on the lake to get to the old home at Lapointe where my father was.  Long before evening we was there. The next morning we [left] again for Bay Field where I was going to do some business for my husband. Bay Field is north west of our old home the distance of four miles crossing the north channel. Why I speak so much of my old home [is that] it is one of the oldest settled place on the Lake Superior, near 50 years older than Bay Field and 50 years older than Ashland. The house we use to live in is still standing today. My brothers live to Bay Field. Of course when I go there I always have a place to stop. Very often I went from the old home to Bay Field to church, crossing the north channel all alone rowing.

*Otter skin Midé Bag*

*Jan. 13, 1895*

I have not been very well for the last 3 weeks. I have a pain in my back I dont know what to make of. Mrs Bousky fell and broke one of her ribs. She is down to Odanah. Much love to you all.

*Eliza Morrison*[46]

I was speaking of my trip to Bay Field. When I got through with my business, we went back where my father was to the old home. Stop there a day and two nights before I return to my husband whom I left to Bad River Falls. The 5[th] day we started for the gardens. On my trip I had plenty to do to take care of my little boy but the weather was very nice indeed. The sun shone bright every day.

We got to the gardens. This is the Reservation where there is about one thousand chippewas in 1867, hardly one fourth of them civilized. What was civilized wear citizen clothes, but the biggest part of them wear their clothes the old Indian ways. Woman of course wear their clothes the old way. Married women and middle aged wore a mettle [medal] about the breast, specially if their husband been to war. The man of course wore no mettel. Only the Chief [wore] what they got from the Government years ago.[47] Any person who is used to the Indians can tell about the men who has been to war. No man wears a feather on his head unless he has been to war. Young man puts one feather on his head for going to war. And if he killed one or two of his enimes [enemies] he takes and puts three feathers on his head. If he is married his wife becomes fited for war dance along with him. And he becomes a speaker of their war. First he is got to go through the motion of his fight before the whole of them. This becomes quite excitible for them. They all come to see him. It is quite a while ago since I seen an Indian war dance. I cannot think of all I have seen but I was Requested by a friend who lives a far distance from here to write a little history of my forest life. And write some things about Indians as I go along.

But I was telling about my trip to Bay Field. Now I am back to the Gardens where my sister lives. I stayed over night with my sister and the next morning we started for Bad River Falls to where my husband was working on a farm. We had to go up stream for 16 miles [with] almost full load of stuff in our boat. It takes about ten hours of hard work to get up to the farm. It is poling up stream all the way. About six o clock in the evening we got up to the old Chiefs place. I got off, took the road one mile to the farm. I was quite tired setting in the boat all day long. It took me but a short time to walk one mile to the farm. I soon got where my husband could see me crossing on the field. We was both quite happy to meet again. Of course we began to speak to one another with our native language.

"Well come wife. Supper is ready. You dont have to cook supper to night. I caught a sturgan [sturgeon] for you this after noon. I know you would come to night. The River is full of sturgen. I heard there was 20 Indians coming up here to make a sturgen rack to morrow morning. One right here and the other down to the old Chiefs."

The next morning the Indians came and set in to work making what they call *mi chi kan*. This means a fish fence or rack across the River. My husband turned in to help to build the rack. We both like fish to eat and this was his first experience of that sort of fishing. It takes men two days to make the rack across the River. Their was not a nail or spike used on the whole thing. The River was about sixty feet wide and about ten feet deep and [had] quite strong current. They use all hard wood poles, about three poles to the foot. Of course some of them was larger. Them went a cross to hold the rest up. About ten men can fish to once on this rack. They fish with hard wood poles about sixteen feet long [with] a hook on the end and another hook about five feet from the end. They dont catch any small fish in this way at all, only big sturgen. Indians catch enough fish to use while they do their planting. Women do the most planting. The men goes off trapping for fur, their last trip for the season. We used a good deal of dried fish ourselfs.

After the last of May 1867 we did not see many white people unless when we went to the Gardens where the missionary was. There was Presbyterian Church and Catholic Church. Quite number of the young Indians joined both of the churches. On a Sundays we would be quite lonesome. The men would go home to the Gardens. My husband and myself and my little boy would be left alone on the farm. We of course would get tired staying all the time to the house. My husband was not in the habbit of hunting on Sundays. There was quite lots of game and plenty of fish in the River. We had a boat. We would only take a little boat ride, go on the other side of the River, look at the Falls and the great Rock Place, and we would go up the Clay Mountain, not far from where we was. From the top of this big hill we can see a good ways off. We can see Lake Superior, the distance of fourteen miles. We of course soon get tired of this and would go down to the boat and take another boat ride. When the water is clear we can see some fish. This made it hard for my husband to keep from fishing on Sunday. He never would take a gun but he would some times take a hook and catch two for us. That would be all. Our men some times would come back Sunday evening. Of course we would get some mail and they would bring little news. These men [who] worked with my husband on the farm were full blooded Chippewas and good workers, but never would stay on Sundays with us. When the busy time was over the men were discharged, so we had to stay all alone most of the time.

October the 15 I got a word from my sister telling me to come down and stay with her. She came after me. After a day or two we went down and I stayed with her untill my trouble was over with. I was than a mother of two boys.[48] After the birth of my boy I wrote to my husband what had happened. He of course was not much surprised. He expected it but was very glad that I got along so nicely. I was gone just one month from the farm, left my husband alone up to the farm. At the birth of my boy many Chippewas woman came to see me. Soon my husband came down the river in a boat to take me and our two little boys. This was in Nov the 16th. The weather was quite cold. Then we had 16 miles to go up stream before we can get home. I was almost afraid we could not make it that day. I spoke to my husband in a kind manner, "Had you better not hire a man to help you up with this boat."

"Oh no wife, I am not one of these fellows that dont know what they say. I have been on the River before. I know what I can do."

"I know husband it always takes two men to get there in one day."

"But [I] just think I can get up to the farm in 8 hours alone when I got you in the boat to take you home."

On we went, scooting up stream. About noon we was to a place where the Indians call *Ma si na bi ka ni ga ning*. This means a man carved out of stone. This is a half way mark. These marks up on those stones can not be told when they were made. The Chippewas suppose they were made by the Souix Indians about 300 years ago. There were two places where those marks were made. One where the Indians call *A ton ga mig*. This means still water. The mark can now be seen but the upper marks that is further up the River can not be seen now since the white man commenced to float logs through there. They wore out the bank. The marks cannot be seen. They sunk in the sand in the river in about the place where those big stones sunk. The Indians will always stop there saying that is the door to the spirit that lives under the water.[49]

I shall keep right on when ever I have spare time.[50]

*Jan 29 1895*[51]

When I am telling about my trip it seem to come in mind what I have seen or heard espec[i]y [especially] where I have been often times. I was telling about one day when my husband took me and our two little boys up the River to the farm where we use to live. It is called Bad River Falls or Leihys farm as near as I can understand it. It is the first farm that ever was oppened in this section of country. This old farm is inside of Ashland County. Now when we lived on Leihys farm [in] 1867 there was only one man in the town of Ashland wich is now quite a city. About eighteen thousands inhabitance in the City of Ashland.

I had not quite finish telling about the day we was going up [the river]. Some people would think it was a hard life. I did not think it was hard life at all. Speaking of my little boys, the oldest one was only one year and a half old and my youngest was two weeks old. I had plenty to do to take care of them and keep my house clean. I always could remember our trip that day going up the stream. Long before sundown we was home.

The nearest neighbor was the old Chiefs place one mile from here. We had to get our mail through them. One or the other would be there to our place most every day. Not one of them could speak a word of english. My husband and me would use the Chippewa language the most of the time. But when we would speak to our children we had to speak english to them in order to learn them.

We was only six months on this farm and [had] six months more to stay [including] the winter which I thought would be the most dreary months for us. And nine miles from any town. I care not much for town but I mean I like to be in town to go to church on sundays. But where I was I could not go to church nor my husband could not go to. My husband and me was not brought up on the same Religion. He was a Catholic. And I was a Methodist. I of course thought if he would not say any thing about my religion of course I would not say any thing about his religion. He was very kind to me of course. I could not find fault about him. If I undertook to say any thing teaching his habits of faith he would say "Now use common sence. Everything will be all right." We hardly ever had any loud words.

The winter seemed very long for us. Of course we was both busy. I had my two little boys to take care of and my husband had stock to take care of and [he would] chop the down[ed] maples in to cord wood to be used in sugar season. And hauled it ready, in fact, everything for sugaring in the spring. The snow was very deep the winter of 1867 and 1868. From our place to the Old Chiefs place it was nothing but a snow shoe trail and it was so clear through to the Gardens, 8 miles. We went quite often to the Old Chiefs, the only place where we can visit that winter. We found the winter quite long. There was one time that winter [when] it snowed for 15 hours. Snow fell about 18 inches deep. This was in February. It did not snow much more after that big snowstorm the last of February. I was determined to make a visit to my sisters to the Gardens and to go to church. My husband was willing I should go and stay a week. Eight miles to travel, part of the way on the ice. Of course I had quite a large hand sleigh and a big dog to haul it. My husband fitted it up for me for the trip for my two little boys to be hauled by the big dog.

The first mild day away I went down the river. I understand driving dogs quite well. My dog went to fast for me [and] I had to walk very fast to keep up with him. I could not trust him away from me. I had a rope tied behind the sleigh which I held. My little boys kept very quiet in the sleigh. But the dog was going so fast it made it quite lively for me. He was not quite strong enough to haul all of us, me and my babies. It took us about 5 hours to get to my sisters house. I was glad indeed when I got there. My sister was quite surprised for me to go that distance with my babies. Of course I had a nice time while I was to my sisters. Soon I had to return home to my husband. Mr Leihy says to me to tell John "In two weeks time there will be a big start here. The Indians is going to turn out with all their ponies and oxen to break a road for sixteen miles up the River. The snow is very deep. You know we will be up there by the 15 of March to be ready for sugar business."

My husband kept busy getting ready for the early spring work. The sugar house is ¼ of a mile from the farm house. Soon came the time to commence to make sugar. My husband was working for Mr Leihy. I was not hired. I made up my mind I would make sugar on our sugar bush. Our sugar bush was ½ a mile from the farm house. I told my husband "I am going to make sugar to our fit out. It is all good yet. I cant stay here and look. All I ask of you husband [is] to come and tap half a day for me and I can do the rest." I got one of the girls to take care of my babies during the time I worked. "I will get ready now and when the snow is off I will begin to boil sap." And my husband hesitated. I would not stop. Finally he helped me and I was glad. It was a very good spring for sugar. Everybody made quite lots of sugar that spring. My sister and her girls with my husbands help made good, over thousands pounds. I made over two hundred [pounds] of nice maple sugar. It was a very pleasant spring, hardly any storm. The spring went off very quick and kept dry.

About the first of May my husbands time was up for Mr Leihy. Mr Leihy wanted to hire him for another year. I did not care about staying it another year there. I wanted to go to the old home to Lapointe where my father was living. We moved back to the old place. My husband was not contended [contented] there at all. He would not stay there. When I see he was not contended of course it did not give me any pleasure at all. I asked him "Cant I go to my sister that lives down to Sault Ste. Marie?" The first steam boat that came down from Duluth I got on and away I went to stay all that summer. I went down on steamer called *Keweenaw*, a passenger boat.[52] It took us two days and a night to get to the Sault Ste. Marie. When I got off to the Sault, my sister was not right there. I found where they lived. My sister had no children. When we got near the place where they were living they seen me. They know who it was with my two children. "Is these your children both of them?"

I says "Yes."

They got hold of both of them. Now they love children. "Will you stay all summer with us and go home this fall or have your husband to come here and live here?"

I was very well contented there. The inhabitance there [were] most Chippewas but quite well civilized and belong to church and farming quite extensively. The name of the place was Iroquois Point, along Lake Superior where they can see the steam boats go up or down.[53] I stayed all summer there with my sister and I liked the place, but I could not get my husband to move there.

In October I returned home again to Lapointe to the old home where my father was. When I got home I found out we were not to live there. My husband had a farm rented where we were to live and where he had a contract to get out shingle bolts that winter with a nice ox team he had. I did not stay long at the old home. We soon moved over where we were to live and farm. This was nine miles from the town of Bay Field and right on the road. We kept a stopping place that winter.[54] We made a comfortable living on the place. This farm is on the flats of Sioux River. This river has been known to be one of the best trout streams in the state. My husband could go out most any time and get what fish we wanted. There were no other kind of fish in the river but speckle trout and good size ones. Good many [people] would come to fish for those nice trout from Bay Field. In that time it was quite good hunting, as I hear my husband say talking with the Indians. My husband was a deer hunter from a boy as much as I can learn from my husband. It is not every man in the tribe is a good hunter. About five men out of ten men is skillful hunters and becomes a good marksman.

There was two families camp close by our rented farm. One was called the best hunter in the tribe. He seem to be very good friend to my husband. He would come very often in the evening and talk about his trips. My husband was trying him all the while to have him to tell him about a silver vein, a mine that was talked of so much out near Spring Lake, south east of Pike Lake. My husband began to talk about this silver vein when we was first married. I of course fought against it. He says "I can never rest unless I go near where I think this silver vein is." I like the woods and wild game to live on. But I was most afraid to go so far in the woods. I prevented him all I could from moving for about fifteen years.

I was speaking about living in Sioux River. My husband he worked all winter. He hired three men to work with him all winter but it was very heavy winter in 1868. Snow was three feet and half deep. My husband had quit working before the winter was out on account the snow so deep. The men who had teames from St. paul had very hard work to get back. The town of Bay Field had to help them to get back. Quite lots of teames use to come through from St. Paul to come and trade for some fish to take back with them. Fish was our money at that time. Very little lumbering done at that time. And some fur, what the Indians catch. In the spring of 68[55] my husband set into work on the farm, clearing land and so forth. The farm we had was next biggest in Bay Field county, large enough to produce 40 tons of hay and other crops. All had to be harvest by hand, together with an ox team. Along in the fall the hay had to be pressed with home made press. This took two men one month. When done [it was] then hauled to market. When everything was done, quite late in the fall, we concluded we would not stay any more on the farm.

My husband had another contract in town to get out oak logs that winter. So we moved in town. My father who lives all alone when we are not there, he got sick. I got my husband to get him over to Bay Field where we lived. I of course done all I could for him when he was sick. He was sick 4 months and he died in our hands at the old home. The old home was left for me.[56] We lived nine years at the old home. What people was there, most of them moved away from the little old town. It was almost vacated during these nine years. I have not much to write. I might say that we were living al most in the pure native quietness of the world. We could see the town of Bay Field four miles across the west channel to Bay Field. I have a sister and two brothers and their children. My relatives would very often come over to see us and we would go over and make them a visit each year we was there. My husband worked on the little farm that we had. Every time he got through

*Mackinaw Boats at Manitowoc, Wisconsin. Note fishing nets drying on reels on shore.*

haying, he would go fishing. Of course I dont mean to go fishing with a hook and line. He had a boat large enough to carry one ton weight or more. Fishing use to be quite a business to the people that followed that line of work. I always hear my husband say, "There two things I like in the line of work. That is hunting and fishing." Its quite hard work about fishing and hunting. Quite good many times my husband telling me he and his man got caught out in a gale of wind when they were out five miles from the shore, where they had to depend on there skill and the firmness of their rig. Thats their boat and sails.

During the time we lived at the old home, there was six years we did not make any sugar. My husband would not make any move toward making any sugar at the old home. Our house stood about ten rods from the shore [on a] nice sandy beach where we can see all the steamboats pass or small boats. Our Indian friends would always stop and see us or some times camp near us as they come to Bay Field to trade. We trade there ourselfs but it was very seldom we got any money, that is cash. Our money was fish or potatoes. We always had plenty vegetables to use and some eggs to sell to the whites, what few there was.

This part of my life was pretty quite [quiet]. I hardly know what to write. We lived at the old home from 1869 to 1878. I did not go anywhere myself any distance, only when I could get my husband to take us somewhere with the boat. This would be in summertime when the berries would be ripe. About that time we had plenty friends come and ask us if we was going out to the island to pick berries. The trips we used to take in this way was very pleasant. There were enough of us always to make it quite pleasant for us all. During the whole time we lived at the old home I could not go where I was mind to because our children was small. I had to stay at home to take care of them.

But if I was to write about my husband I would have to write a good deal about his trips and so forth. I cant write like some people do to exaggerate matters. I dont pretend to know enough for that. I have to tell the truth on any thing I say. Since I was requested by a good friend to write a little history of my forest life, I would not like to have them to think I was telling untruth. Since I am writing little things that I know have occurred in course of my life and thinking of the place what I call my old home where I have lived over half of my life time, it refreshin my mind on a great many things that have occurred at the old home I speak of. [It] is in Lapointe on an island where so many Chippewas used to be paid off from the Government. I used to be very afraid of them. I remember quite well since 1852. I know our folks use to keep us from school while payments were made. It is said it has been as many as seven thousands Indians in Lapointe Island to one time to receive pay from the government Agent. Most all men had 18 dollars a head, children and all. This is one of the bigest payment to my knowledge. There was bigger payments, but beyond my knowledge.

# WISCONSIN DEATH MARCH

*"Tell him I blame him for the children we have lost, for the sickness we have suffered, and for the hunger we have endured. The fault rests on his shoulders."*
Chief Flat Mouth to Minnesota Governor Ramsey, December, 1850

THE POLICY OF REMOVING INDIAN TRIBES FROM their homelands to regions where the US government wanted them to resettle away from whites, an apartheid policy, began with President Thomas Jefferson in 1803 and increased in momentum with the Indian Removal Act of 1830. In order for removal to be successful, three factors were required: disagreement over the terms of an earlier treaty or a failed treaty negotiation, refusal of the parties to compromise, and vested local interests that would profit from removal. These seldom existed in the Great Lakes region, particularly in the Lake Superior country, where centuries of cooperation between Indians and fur traders had established cultural bonds, much of the land was unsuitable for anything except resource extraction which the Indians had already given in the treaties of 1837 and 1842, and whites depended upon Indians for commodities and labor.

The three necessary factors came together, however, in 1842 when Robert Stuart, formerly of the American Fur Company, negotiated the Copper Treaty. He agreed, orally, that the Chippewa would not have to leave the lands they were allowing whites to mine until the "distant future," a term so open to misunderstanding some chiefs refused to sign the treaty. The newly appointed governor of Minnesota territory, Alexander Ramsey, had patronage support to repay, and

moving Wisconsin Indians into Minnesota meant a windfall in annual annuities and management salaries for the surrounding communities. Business interests, particularly the former fur companies now engaged in resource extraction, stood to benefit from complete Indian removal, and most missionaries would follow the government money on which they were dependant.

Ramsey, through his incompetent sub-agent, decided to force removal by compelling the Indians to travel to Sandy Lake, Minnesota, to collect their annuity goods and payments, rather than to La Pointe, as usual. The objective was to trap the Indians at Sandy Lake in winter, 300-400 miles from their homes, forcing them to stay permanently. Three to four thousand Chippewa, mostly men, left the rice harvest incomplete to travel west and wait for annuity payments that never came. When their food ran out, they were forced to buy spoiled commodities unfit for eating at inflated prices. There was no where for them to live and no provisions had been made for them; the area was unfit for hunting and fishing. Dysentery and measles swept the camps; sometimes adults died so fast there was no one to bury the dead. On December 3, with some scanty, overpriced rations finally delivered, the Chippewa left for their homes, on foot, since canoe travel was impossible. Even more died on the march, leading to an eventual death toll of at least 400, primarily the heads of households and young men.

The next year the plan was tried again, although the Chippewa had learned what could happen. They refused to go to Sandy Lake and continued to protest loudly about attempts to remove them. Their resolve hardened, thwarting all further attempts to remove them or to make additional treaties until they were guaranteed reserves that could never be touched. President Fillmore canceled the removal authorization in 1852 and they received their reservations in 1854. They were supported by the general populations of Wisconsin and Michigan, several missionaries such as Leonard Wheeler at Bad River, and Governor Dodge of Wisconsin.[57]

I remember once going to Fondulac when there must [have] been a misunderstanding. The government agent sent a message from below before he came up with there goods and money. By some means or other was changed. It caused the Indians a great trip for nothing from all direction. I remember this quite well. We all started nearly the same time from Lapointe. White man went as well as Indians. Those [that] had any thing to trade on all went by water. They traveled all together with their boats, most of them had birch bark canoes. I remember we had a big birch bark canoe, big enough to carry ten or 15 persons and our things. We traveled at the rate of 40 miles a day. Soon after the Indians got to Fondulac, got another message from the Indian agent that he could not come so soon as he expected and he would make the payment to Lapointe, that he could not come to Fondulac as it would be to late in the fall. This almost enragged [enraged] the Indians. They all came back again and we came back to the old home. It was quite a while before he came to make payment to the Indian. There were so many of them and not much to eat while they were waiting for the agent to come up with the goods and money. I was this time 14 years old. Of course I was not quite old enough to remember much, but I remember the Indian had a great times, dancing war dance and pipe dance and beg dance every day. What people had to eat they had to give to them or they would get mad.

## CHIPPEWA DANCES

WAR DANCE: WAR BETWEEN INDIAN TRIBES was an occupation as well as sometimes being a calamity so there were many rituals, including dances, surrounding the Chippewa art of war. The war dance was danced prior to going on the warpath and the dancers were those men who had consented to be part of the war party. The first dance would be held before setting out, then there would be a dance each night of travel toward the enemy. Before the war party, they also held a dog feast and danced. Then the song of departure

Dances of the North American Indians
(Chippeways)

237 Dog (Sioux) — 243 Snow Shoes. 293 Beggars Dance (Sacs & Foxes)

George Catlin sketched these dances sometime between 1835-1837 and recorded these notes about the center dance: "The snow-shoe dance . . . is exceedingly picturesque, being danced with the snow shoes under the feet, at the falling of the first snow in the beginning of winter, when they sing a song of thanksgiving to the Great Spirit for sending them a return of snow, when they can run on their snow shoes in their valued hunts, and easily take the game for their food.[58]

began and the warriors danced out of the camp and toward the enemy.

PIPE DANCE: The pipe dance was said to be the principal "good time dance" of the early Chippewa. It is very old and, like all other dances, is believed to have come from the manido. In this dance a man carried a pipestem and his body was supposed to represent a pipe. The dancer never rose erect, but took a crouching or squatting posture, trying to assume the form of a pipe as nearly as possible. Many contortions of the body were used, and the antics of the dancers were considered very amusing. Only one man danced at a time. When he had finished dancing he presented the pipestem to another, who was obliged to accept it and dance; he transferred also the rattle which he carried. This procedure was continued

until all the men had danced. Some were awkward, and their frantic efforts to imitate a pipe produced great merriment. It was considered a test of courage for a man to brave the ridicule of the assembly and seat himself where he would be asked to dance the pipe dance.

BEGGING DANCE: A dance to request presents. Those who wished the presents might dance, or it might be danced by a group of young men in their finest attire who were "begging" for others less fortunate. It was accompanied by a high, droning melody and dances that could be frenzied or antic. Sometimes the dancers would yell as loudly as possible, appealing to the Great Spirit to open the hearts of the bystanders to be generous; other times they would make their viewers laugh and so reward the dancers.[59]

The Indian agent came with goods and supplies and money, then everything was all right, enough to furnish them for ten days. While the payment was to be made no liquor to be sold to anyone while the Indians are here. While the Indians were waiting, they use to have great medicine dance. When we would hear of them we would go and see them with my parents. Will and I would go with my mother or sister or friends. I was quite a one to ask questions about what they were doing or saying when they were talking. When I was looking at them, there was one of the Indians sitting down. The most of the time he was dressed different from the others, dressed most all in fur. Of course I would ask what he was. They tell in their language *ki chi me da.* I did not understand this at all. When I got married I asked my husband "What does the word mean, *ki chi me da.*" He being so much with the Indians I thought he might know.

He told me, he is the one who they call the mash man in english.[60] I hardly know what that means myself. He is the one who do not speak, he only gets up and dance once in a while, not much neither. He only goes through motions. *Ki chi mi da* means he who has been through all that can be done in their performances. Once I was looking at them. He got up and danced, went through motions only.

"Husband do you understand some of the motions?"

"Yes of course. I need not tell you what I understand about the motions just now. Perhaps I will have a chance to show you after a while."

*Bear Claw Necklace*

When ever you see an Indian wear Grizzly Bear Claws around his neck and some bones strung up together, he is some thing sure.

This is all about the Indians for the present time.

While I am writing and thinking of my parents, the place where I was raised with my brothers and sisters, it makes me almost sad to think of the storys what my mother used to tell us when we were young girls. She was converted by the Baptists at Sault Ste. Marie and when she came to Lapointe she joined the Presbyterian Church and died in 1865 in Lapointe where she must have first meet my father and lived together for 30 years. Both buried in the same place at the old town of Lapointe. The house stands there yet today. The oldest Catholic Church is in the state of Wisconsin stays there yet as good as ever. It has been rebuilt once to my knowledge [and] stands in sight of my old home. I use to go there quite often with my husband. As near as I can understand inside of the church there are some paintings over two hundred years old. I have seen the pictures myself. The first Presbyterian Church was built in Lapointe Island, stands to day yet.[61] It was been vacated now over 50 years and maybe more. All the lumber that was used in building of these churches was sawed by men with a Rip saw. My father is one of those men that sawed with a rip saw for 18 years.[62] They would only stop for a while for hot weather. For a while lumber manufactured in this way was sold from 30 to 40 dollars per thousand and all the shingles that were used were made by hand out of white pine and ceader.

In 1877 we was still living at the old home at Lapointe. Quite often we would make a visit to Bay Field. Our friends would call us Old Lapointers. "Have you come over here to stay? Is the soil playing out for you over there?" My husband had two failures of crops. This was pretty hard on us. My husband fished all winter under the ice. Fishing was not so good as it used to be. We kept three big dogs while my husband was fishing in the winter to haul his fishing rigg. The three dogs was able to haul the weight of seven hundred pounds.

My husband was quite tired of fishing. By fishing and little farming [we] made our living but both failed. It was time to do some thing else. We

*Fish Skiff and Sled Dogs*

went and made maple sugar at the end of Lapointe Island where it was called by the Indians *ne ia mi kang,* one of the great point for fishing twelve miles from the old home, where my husband had an old friend living. He followed fishing in the summer time the most of his life time. In the winter he did not work at all. This friend of my husband stayed there so long fishing, his name was John Stewart. The place now is named after him, John Stewarts Pointe. His buildings were covered with shingles on the out side. He had all the buildings he wanted for fishing opperation. He farmed some too. Every thing slick and clean around at the place.

My husband went and made preparation, that is to build the place to boil sap and to live in, and done a good deal of hauling to get the stuff there. The snow was about two feet deep on the ice. Horse team could not get around to do any thing. Dogs was used plenty in them times on the ice. My husband done all his hauleing with his three dogs.

After every thing was done to the sugar bush, next is to move to get there. 12 miles of travel to go there and a big hill to climb. One early morning we started. The snow was hard. We could walk on top. Our dog team had a full load to haul, our bedding for all of us, five of our boys. It was only Johny my oldest was able to walk that distance. Me and my husbands sister had to haul a trunk and a sleigh full of stuff. We went the distance of three miles before the sun was up. When the sun was up we could see the point plain that we were making for. This was after the 20[th] of March [and] it was nice bright morning. Evidently we will have a thaw [so] we had to hurry up to travil the distance of 12 miles. After traveling about four hours and a half we were to Stewarts house where he treated us as well as friend could. After our dinner and a good rest, we started again [and] we took the ice in place of the land route to avoid the big hill. It was a good deal further, but [avoided] the high rock on the north east end of the Island. It was wonderful sight to see so high and the deep caves where the water wares the rock away. By three o clock we got to our sugar bush. We worked quite hard but we was all quite happy to be where we was.

Next thing is to carry our things up to the top. Down from the ice to the top it was about 100 feet to the top of the rock and a hill to go up for about 40 rods to the sugar camp. I am told this is the highest place on this Island. We could see a great ways off. We could see the porkapine [Porcupine] mountains. We make out by the map 65 miles off from [where] we was. Some bright mornings we can see the [Mesabi] mountains very plain and north shore is supposed to be the distance of 70 miles across. We can see that quite plain and most all the Apostile Islands.

I was telling about carrying our things from the ice up to the top of the Rock. There was only one place where we could go up for three miles of a distance where the ground fell from the top and lodge on the rock. This caused the brush to grow. By putting a rope from the top to  bottom on each side, by holding onto the rope going up or down was the only safe way. And we could only use this plan while it was froze. The Indian in there language called this place *Ga ie ta a kuen da ue uin.* This means an old climbing place. We found out it was a climbing place by the time we got our things up to the top. First thing was to get our children to the camp. My husband had Dannie and I had Tommy tied in the cradle, a good strap over my head. My husbands sister had a pack on her back. Johny and Charley and George was just able to climb the steps by means of holding to the rope.[63] How ever we got up all right to the sugar camp quite happy and [there was] plenty of hard wood chopped up ready to burn. Our camp was made of most of lumber. For the roof we had sheets of birch bark sewed together. Of course no floor, only a sort of floor made a foot from the ground to answer for seat or bed. In few days we got a little of sap. This was a great novelty for our little boys, to have sugar and syrup to eat on their bread. About the first of April my husband had to go to town for election for to be gone two or three days, the same time to get some more grub. Of course took his dog team. While he was gone we had one good day for sap which made us women hussel [hustle] to gather it all. My husband was gone one day longer than he thought. When he came I had all the kittles hung up to boil the sap. We had kittles enough to boil down ten barrels if we had to. My Johny was just able to haul dry wood with the dogs to mix in with the green wood.

I come to think over the busniss now I think there is quite peculiar charm in this buisness. I dont know weather [whether] to call it a buisness or not, but how ever it use to make it quite lively for us. About that time when ever the sap would slack running we would grain the sugar what we did not want into cakes. We put it in birch bark boxes. Most of them who read papers or books know how the Indian make the sugar and how they get the materials to use them. Their is one thing they cannot get along without it, that is kettles to boil down the sap and axe. These two things they have to have. I see some white men make sugar on the same principle. Those who have learned and can get the materials. And I have seen some who was most unable to get the materials to use [so] they would not have good success. It seems theirs all sorts of ways doing things, but only one right way. To know how is some thing and to do what a person knows is some thing.

From the first of April untill the 15th we worked quite hard. By this time the snow was all gone so it made it better for us. One Saturday evening one of our boys burnt his hand. My husband went after medcine to the big swamp. He told me to come with him and he would show me some deep snow. I went with him and I did see some very deep snow. But it was a place where it has been drifted. We judge it was twenty feet deep. It was that depth for several acers [acres] and allmost all solid ice. The ice on the Lake was about two feet thick. Along about the 15th of April if it's warm weather it will begin to crack and break up to pieces and with the current and a strong south west wind will cause it to drift in to the main body of the Lake. It takes but a short time to do this when the warm weather comes from the hot sun. In the spring time if it should come a heavey north east wind and blow long enough it is sure to bring it back. And cause a great blockade in among the Islands and in the great bay of Deluth. Some people may think this is not worth telling about. But it is one of the greatest sight I ever seen. I have seen this two springs out there when we made sugar to John Stewarts Pointe as it is now called.

In 1878 we was still living at the old home [and] in the spring we went and made sugar once more in the same place. That year there was no winter at all, hardly any snow to speak of nor ice. That kind of winter was hard for the people on Lapointe Island. Nothing to do to make any thing and it was not safe to fish. No one know when it would freeze up. Before we went to the sugar bush my husband and another man was bound to set out their nets out to do some fishing. They went and set all their nets they had. And it come very cold weather, made ice. They could not get to their nets and lost them all. This was the winding up of my husbands fishing on the Lake Superior.

Along about the 15[th] of March we started to go to the sugar bush. We went sailing with our boat. No ice at all on the lake nor any snow to be seen. Sailing in that time of the year never was ever heard of before. There has been such thing as no snow but very cold and very thick ice on the lake. That year was no snow nor ice in this north east corner of Wisconsin. How ever we had quite a nice sail, going in two hours and half we was there 12 miles. We of course set in to work making sugar as the sap run. It was very dull spring for sap that year. My husband bought some more nets from a friend and set them out to get what fish we wanted. What we could not use fresh we would salt. We did not make much sugar to speak of. We were there about five weeks time. We went to the old home. This made my husband quite dull feeling and failure of crops the summer before and losing all his fishing fit out made it quite disagreeable for him. He says "This summer is the last summer for us at the old home. We've got to move away from here. Everything is getting dull for us here."

Once in a while he would mention Pike Lake, what deer country it was and about the silver vein. Along in the fall we moved to Ashland where my husband got a mail contract for six months from Mr Vaughn. In moving to get all our things over at once we had to get Mr G A Stahl scow to move us over to Ashland. We sailed over in a short time where we were to live for a while. I soon got quite a number of friends by going to church. I know I was not going to live long to Ashland because my husband kept talking of Pike Lake most all the time. And when Mr Bousky came in to Ashland he use to come to our house to stop over night just to talk over about the silver vein that is out in that section.[64] He told my husband he thought he could find it if he had any body out with him to look. He would not only talk of the silver vein but the deer and fur and the fish up in that country in those lakes and streams he knows. My Husband likes hunting and fishing and trapping. And my husband would say "I am going out there with my family and farm and look for minerels. Of course I will do some hunting and fishing and trapping."

The first winter we lived in Ashland I had four boys big enough to go to school. We lived right in the centre of the town. That winter my husband done quite well with his mail contrack. I canot tell much about myself, but I can tell about my husband, in what business he was engaged.

Each winter since 1865, when he took the mail he first used his old fishing boat fitted well with sails and oars. From Ashland to Bay Field is 18 miles on the short line by water and by land is 25 miles. Around the bay there is no road and a good deal of swamps and rivers to cross. With his sailboat he would take passengers and freight. He carried his mail this way for a month and cold weather came and made ice in Ashland Bay. He then carried the mail on his back but made nothing more then the mail wages for one week that way. And one part of the bay froze which made the distance of five miles shorter each day and he began to use two dogs to haul the mail and express with a dog team. About two weeks this was and then [he] took his ponies and commence to run stage accross the bay part way [on ice] and part way by land. The first of January the ice was strong enough to hold a team clear to Bay Field and [he] took a beeline from Ashland to Bay Field. Starts on Mondays from Ashland and back the alternative days. Three trips a week and had all the freight he wanted when he had no passengers to take. He of course kept doing this all winter untill spring. When the ice got weak for horses he took dogs again for a while.

*Dog Team, Bayfield, Wisconsin, about 1900. Probably the Booth Fishing Company with barrels of fish in the background.*

Ashland Bay generally opens early in the spring. Along the shore for two miles he took a small boat to travel the piece that was open to reach the other shore. He had nine hours time to get the mail to Bay Field or to Ashland. About the last of April his time was up. The bay was open so the tugs run to Bay Field. Soon big steamers came to Ashland from below. In the spring of 1879 my husband fitted up his boat for pleasure seekers, one for sailing and a little boat to fish with in streams for brook trout. He was engaged at this business most all the time while we lived in Ashland. I had quite a good many of my Indian friends come to see me, that is the most brighten ones. They use to come to trade in Ashland. The Indian Reservation is eleven miles east of Ashland.

From the time I married my husband to 1880 he had the silver vein in his mind. He was bound to take us some where where he thought it was. Him saying so much about it I finally consented to go any where he thought we could live. He soon got ready with the two oldest boys and his team he had and he load up his wagon with provisions and some hay also. Everyone of our friends was surprised when they [heard] of us moving in the woods. Every one would say "Where are you going." I would say "All I know about it is to Pike Lake. My husband is going to make home stead out to Pike Lake."

I did not tell anyone what was the intentions of moving out in the woods. It bothered me a little to know how we was going to make a living out in the woods. I know we did not have much money, hardly enough to buy supplys for all winter. We had a good team and a cow and chickens and steel traps and nets and hooks, in fact everything to catch fish with and guns to kill deer with and other things. And school books for the boys. My husband tells me I have to teach the boys so they can read and write and "I will teach them some myself when I am home. I will be out most all the time trapping or hunting and fishing and exploring for the silver vein and I know if I dont find it I know we can live out there. There is going to be a Rail Road out there next summer so we can come in, riding in to Ashland to trade and get what we want and have a home out there where I can have a good time to hunt and fish and trap fur winters. I am able to do any thing that can be done in a country home. I shall not make a home stead this fall. We will move out there, eather right to Pike Lake or to where Bousky is living on the old St Paul road so we can have them for Neighbor." He first took his team and the two boys with him to make hay out to Pike Lake. And no hay to make to Pike Lake [so he] went to Spider Lake and there found some hay. In three weeks time they came back home to Ashland. The boys had great lot to tell me about lakes and fish and praries. They seen deer and other game.

In 1879 in September the 15th we moved. Our team was so loaded the little ones could only ride and a very bad road untill we got away ten miles from Ashland. I had to walk behind the wagon but we went very slow, only went seven miles the first day and the second day 13 miles. On the third day about three o clock we see the north end of Pike Lake. I went down to the Lake with my three oldest boys. We found a boat, got into it, we went scooting for about two miles to wards the south west to the other end of the Lake to the old Bear trap trail. Mr Morrison went on with the team to wait for us at a certain place. My feet was quite sore from walking. I did not mind this [as] I was quite happy with my three little boys that was walking with me. They was just as happy as they could be. Soon we got to the place where my husband was waiting for us with the team.

"Well wife how do you like the lakes and the country? One and half mile to old Bousky's place. I told him what day we shall be there and to have plenty duck on hand for us to eat when we come. I brought quite lot of tobacco for him."

When we got in sight we could see her cooking outdoors, a great pot full of wild ducks and other things such as there was in the country and [she] had a little garden.[65] The shanty he lived in, Bousky told us to live together that winter. My husband made an addition to the shanty, builded our part of the shanty four feet under the ground so to be warm in the winter. Before he got done it came a big snow storm. This was about the 15th of October. This one storm spoiled the hunting. My husband began to think that it was going to be hard for us that winter. So much snow fell at once made it hard for them to hunt deer. We was sure we did not have grub enough for the winter but it came warm weather [and] the snow went off, most all of it. We had time to make a trip to Ashland after a load of supplies. When he got back he commenced to hunt [and] killed 5 deer. That's all that fall and a big bear, weight four hundred pounds.

That winter was hard winter. The snow was very deep and [it was] very cold, almost to cold to do any thing. My husband told me he feared that we would have to go without bread before spring. He was afraid he might not get through to Ashland if it comes any more snow. The snow was two feet and a half deep that winter. In January first Bousky and his wife went off to Ashland. They had no grub for the winter. They had to go on snow shoes. When they seen we was going to be short they went away with the intention of coming back in three weeks time, but they did not come back. My husband and oldest boy got ready and started for Ashland.

My husband says to me "Do not be surprised if we be gone for two weeks away from here. You keep courage wife untill such time we will come back. I will try to come in ten days if Providence will permit. It looks to me [like] I have betrayed myself when I made up my mind to come here. Here I have a big family away out here 35 miles from here to Ashland the nearest pointe to go and trade, and no road, only what we make ourselves. The snow is deep [and] our ponies is not able to go through to haul any thing here [and] almost out of hay. I am sure wife you got grub enough to last two weeks. I will be back about that time. I mean with the help of God. The way our situation looks to me wife there is no one man can do all that I see to be done to bring our family safe through this winter, and there the ponies and the cow and ourselfs to live. You can just think wife, it's my fault. I know you was unwilling to come here. I see my mistake now, bringing you here and the children. We have one boy able to be with me."

I just did not know what to say to my husband when he was talking about his trip to Ashland to get provisions to save us from starvation and to save the horses and cow. I had made up my mind if they wasnt back about the time our provisions was consumed I would commence on the chickens to keep my children from getting hungry.

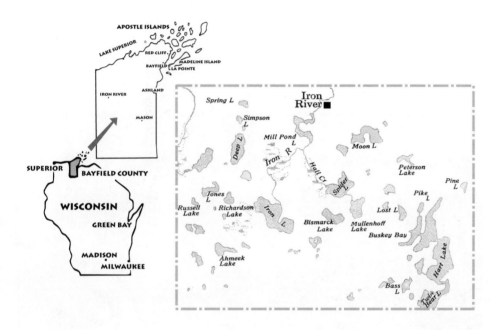

So one morning on they went to make Spring Lake that day. No one left to Spider Lake but me and my six little boys. Of course I had enough to do to take care of my little ones every day. I done some reading for my little boys evenings. After they are all to bed it was quiet. I would stay up untill ever so late at night. I could not sleep much thinking of my husband and my boy, the great task they had to do. I not only thought about them, I prayed many times.

I even thought of the old stories my mother used to tell us about hard winters and the scarcity of food in their time when she was under the care of my grand mother. Of course they had their belief in regard to their spirits in same manner as their parents did. My mothers father was a french man. My grand mother was a pure Chippewa woman. Mother use to tell us her father died long before middle age, left my grand mother to support her two girls and a boy. My mother was the youngest of my grand mother's children. [Grand-mother] had some brothers that would help her if she could only but follow them around where ever they moved.

The Indians had places to hunt and places to make sugar, many of them together according to the size of the maple grove, and places to gather rice in seasons and for fishing and some particular pointe where they come together in certain seasons, generally some good place to catch fish and where the young men can raise a good play ball ground. This ball game is one of the greatest sport for young men. In this kind of game they soon find out who is the best man and got the most indurance. I being a woman I feel so that I ought not to say much about mens games. The Chippewas woman has a game a good deal like men only they have no catchers on the end of their sticks like that of men. The women wore in the old time very light deer skins or some such like and made into short skirt to hang just below their knees and leggings of course and moccasins and over their bodies they have Broad Cloth when they can get it.

## LACROSSE

*Ball Play of the Dahcota Indians near Fort Snelling, between 1841 and 1848.*
*Notice the broken stick in the foreground.*

BAAGA'ADOWE, WHICH MEANS "PLAYS lacrosse," is often called the "little brother" of war, since its fierceness mimics combat and many rituals were the same for both. The color red decorated the players and their equipment; the thunder spirits were associated with war and with the game, which was once akin to a religious ceremony with religious leaders serving where coaches would today.

The game was played on a large flat space, which might be nearly a half-mile in length, with goals at the eastern and western ends. In winter it would be played on a frozen lake or river. The size of the playing field was determined by the number of

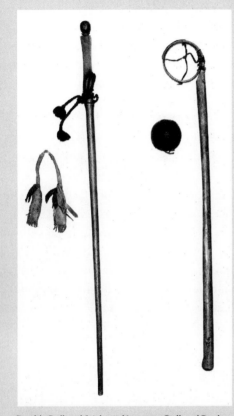

*Double Ball and Stick, and Lacrosse Ball and Racket*

players, sometimes numbering in the dozens, who used a ball of wood or stuffed skin slightly bigger than a tennis ball and a stick with a net pocket four or five inches in diameter on the end. Both balls and sticks were decorated. The only invariable rules were that the ball could not be touched with the hands and that each team had to be of equal strength. Everything else was allowed, including violent fighting, in the attempt to strike one's own goal with the stick with the ball in its pocket, hit the goal with the ball, or run past the goal with the ball. Two out of three points won the game, but some games could last for days. Although the games were played with teams, as in war, spectacular individual performances were highly praised. Betting on the outcome, sometimes lavishly, was the norm for both men and women.

Women played a variant of lacrosse called "double ball," so called because it was played with two balls or two short, heavy pieces of wood joined by a short thong that were thrown by a curved stick. Double ball was played in a field, often about 300 feet in length, with a goal at each end, and the object was to grab the balls after the toss up and carry them through the opposing team's players to the goal. Lacrosse is seldom, if ever, played by Indians in the Great Lakes region at present. It has, however, become an elite sport at universities and private academies.[66]

I was going on and write about my grand mothers stories, what I learned from my mother when I was a young girl. I use to ask my mother to tell us some of my grand mothers stories as far back as I can remember. My mother seems to remember well the hard times they use to have and the way her mother use to tell her. And I remember some of the [stories] my mother use to tell us in my grand mothers time and young days.

She was brought up in this country near here. They lived the most of the time up the head waters of St Croix River up to the Lake St Croix not far from here. They never hardly went down the River for because the sioux was near by. The Chippewas were in war with them. The Chippewas got more enraged against the sioux and drove them more south west away from St Croix River. St Croix River was known by the Indians to be well supplied for game and fish and rice and ducks and such like. Of course they fight for it. After the Chippewas drove the sioux more west they lived better and safer.

Some white men use to come up Mississippi River and up St Croix a ways to trade with the Indians. My grand mother was by this time full grown woman and married one of the men. He did not live with her very long. He died. My grandmother did not stay long to St Croix because the sioux was hard against the Chippewas. They came from [the] west, so many of them the Chippewas had to keep back, and my grand mother was afraid. She did not want her children to be killed, her two girls and boy.

She took a canoe and started up St Croix River and made the long Portage from St Croix to the head waters of Brule and down the River Brule of course not well supplied with food. Her only hope was to see some other Indians to get some thing to eat. She worked hard to get some where so she can see somebody. Three days now and nothing to eat. On the fourth day in the morning she seen a canoe [and] come to find out it was one of the meanest Indians in the tribe. He would not give her any thing to eat when they had plenty meat and rice. All he said to her [was] "Keep on to the mouth of the river. You will see one of your uncles there." Near night she came to camp near the mouth of the river. It was one of her uncles. They had plenty to eat but they would not let her have any thing but drink a little broth for four days, and her children only let her eat just a little at a time.

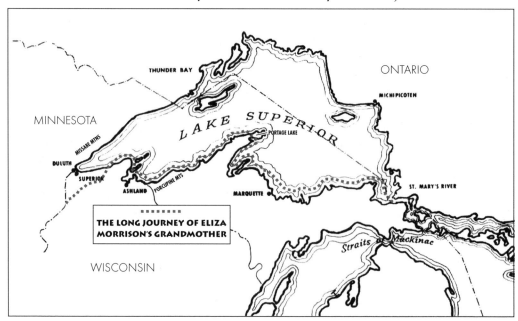

# THE CHIPPEWA-DAKOTA WAR

THE COUNTRY AT THE HEADWATERS OF THE Mississippi did not always belong to the Chippewa. The Gros Ventures, who now live far to the west, occupied it first, perhaps for many hundreds of years. They were driven out by the Santee Sioux branch of the Dakota, who occupied parts of Michigan's Upper Peninsula and the northern parts of Wisconsin and Minnesota. The Dakota lived by hunting small game, berrying, fishing, and harvesting rice, which is much different from their later history as buffalo-hunting Plains tribes. They were pushed onto the Plains and into a completely different way of life by the twin forces of the Chippewa/ Ojibwe and the fur trade. As the Chippewa were forced from their homelands by the Iroquois Wars and white settlement, they moved west into Dakota territory and the Dakota pushed the Gros Ventures west in turn. When the French traded guns for Ojibwe furs, the Ojibwe turned those guns on the Dakota, people they came to call the Sioux, which derives from the Ojibwe word for "stranger" or "snake." Once the latter obtained arms as well, open war broke out in the area that is now eastern Minnesota and western Wisconsin in 1736. By the mid-1740s, the Chippewa had driven the Dakota out of much of Wisconsin, and by the 1780s, the Dakota had been pushed west of the Mississippi. Chippewa then occupied their lands, which gave them more resources, but which also fragmented the close-knit culture that had once existed at La Pointe and Chequamegon.

Although white histories of the United States and Canada barely mention the Chippewa-Dakota War, Indian commentators dwell on it at length because it lasted so long and caused such mayhem to their peoples. Indians may have fought in the whites' Revolutionary War, War of 1812, and Civil War, but they often fought as hired mercenaries or as businessmen protecting trading partners and those actions, except for Tecumseh's organization during the War of 1812, seldom merited much comment by Indian historians. The war on the upper Mississippi is quite different. William Warren devotes a large portion of *History of the Ojibway People* to the war and to particular skirmishes and battles; Andrew Blackbird's *History of the Ottawa and Chippewa Indians* does the same. Like white wars, the Chippewa-Dakota War was fought over territory and economics: who would control the rich fur-bearing lands of the upper Great Lakes country. Although there were few pitched battles, and Indian methods were seldom as destructive as white military campaigns, the attrition of decades of skirmish and attack and threat took its toll. Warfare was as important as hunting, since only in war could young men attain glory and reputation and respect.

The French, British, and Americans spent more than a hundred years attempting to end the conflict, which was not resolved until the La Pointe Treaty of 1854 caused the removal and confinement of most Indians on reservations. Before then, the threat of the Chippewa kept the Dakota confined to the Plains, leading to the development of one of the most colorful and beautiful American Indian cultures: the Great Plains horse and buffalo tribes of the Dakota.

She remained fourteen days with her uncle and aunt. Then she told him she was on the way to Souix [Sault] Ste Marie, that is the lower end of Lake Superior. She told him "I do not want my children to be killed by the sioux." He told her "You are going there you got to start pretty soon. It is getting late in the summer. You see the leaves is getting yellow. We have plenty of rice to give you to take with you. I will hunt and kill meat for you to dry so you can take it with you." To start from the mouth of Brule River to go to the lower end of Lake Superior always takes twelve days where men are running the canoe, but a woman all alone. The oldest of the girls could help a little.

When ready she starts with her cannoe to coast the great body of water. She made up her mind to make the journey in a month time. She was bound to go where there was no sioux to save her children. She struck good weather and made the trip in twenty one days to the *ki ji sa si ji wa nong*. That is the name of great falls of water or great current going at a great speed. She got there all safe with her three children. The youngest of the girls was my mother. My Grand mother she found friends where she was. She lived round at the Souix St Marie a very long time untill her children was all grown up. My Mother and her sister and brother was half French. Their mother use to tell them never to marry a full blooded Indian because they were too white, both of the girls. Both of the girls stayed with their mother till they were full grown and stayed among the Chippewas. Of course had plenty chances to get married among the Indians but they both promised to their mother they would not. Of course being among the Indians they learned all there was to be, that is in their work and habbits and ways, but no education neither one of them. They could not talk any english or french but chippewa language was there language.

Their brother went *ki ji ni sa ji wan*. He would not stay among the Indians. He went way below about the time of the treaty was made by the Government with the chippewas. Their brother came up with the Indian agent. A large number of men came up to *ba wi tig*. This means the lower end of Lake Superior. Those men came up at that time, good many of them, and stayed and lived their to Souix St Marie. Went to work [and] made log houses to live in. My mother and [her] sister both got married to white men and lived to Souix St Marie.

After a while my mother [said] her man wanted to go back to Canada, but she would not go with him to leave her mother. She told him go and come back again. He went back. She waited three years for him. He never came back to her. Her brother was married and he went up north to Lapointe, quite good many went at that time. He left his wife with his mother. Lapointe Island was called *mo ning gua ne ka ning* by the Indians. This means Yellow Bird Pointe. Three days after the people left to go to Lapointe my grand mother got a big canoe and her daughter and daughter in law and 4 children, started to coast the great lake the distance of two hundred and eighty miles. 3 strong women paddling, making the canoe go at a good speed. Five days time they got to Portage Lake. There they caught [up] with the people that was going to mo nig gua ne ka ning. That's to Lapointe which is now called the Appostile Island.

They were now traveling with a crowd. Their eight big batuos [bateaux] or boats, seven men to each boat. Each one of their boat had in them the weight of six tons. It is immence work to unload even one of these boats. They had to go in the River at night or some good harbor. As near as I can learn this was about the first goods landed on Lapointe Island of any amount. They all got to Lapointe all right with their goods [and] commence to work. My mother was living there several years before she met my father.

Now I will write about things [that] transpired in my time. I am living in the town of Iron River in Bay Field County, state of Wisconsin near the North East corner of the state. In 1881 I was to Spider Lake, left all alone, just with my children, in about the middle of a very severe winter.[67] The snow was very deep and very cold. My husband could not get around to do any hunting. The snow was so soft it was impossible to go in [to the woods] any distance. They were two persons with us the first part of the winter. They left us on account of not having enough grub for the winter. My husband is a middling strong and quite resolute man and proper age to be good. But when he explain to me our situation at that present time, and he feeling most unable to endure what he had to do to keep us from getting hungry, it made me quiver. Thirty five miles from here to civilization. Three days after my husband and my oldest boy went away to be gone several days. Me left with my children. Three days after they had gone I began to think [of] the hard times my mother use to tell us girls when she was with her mother. Should my husband and boy fail to get through where would I be with my six little boys away out here.

Fifth day in the evening I seen some body coming across the lake on the ice. "Two men" says the boys "it is Uncle Bousky and shang wash, a young Indian." It got quite hard for Bousky in Ashland. He came to get some deer skins he had left. They stayed over night with us. They said they met my husband and boy ten miles this side of Ashland. "We camped together one night. John was quite happy that night because I told him, you will strik[e] a good road little ways from where we camp. They were to make Ashland before noon and it will take them two days in town before he starts to come back."

Oh how glad I was to hear from my husband and boy. And my six little boys [who] stayed with me seemed to be very happy. I of course would teach a little during the day. They would get out and chop wood. On the tenth I began to look for them enough to blind me almost, untill it was dark so I could not see. All my children went to sleep. I went to bed but I could not sleep. The eleventh day in the morning I commenced to look again. Only had grub enough for two more meals, not all we want at that. I kept a good watch. I did not lose any time. About four o clock in the evening I thought I could see some body coming down the hill. It looked very small across the lake. But it was some body coming with a pack. The little boys ran to meet him. It was Johny coming with a pack alone.

He says "Pa went back about 4 miles to get his other pack. He will be here tonight with a pack." Johnys pack was about 40 pounds, little flour, sugar, and fresh pork and tea and coffee. Oh, how nice it was. "Mama" he says "we have got quite a load of grub down to the road."

Quite late in the evening my husband came with a sack of flour on his back. We were all glad enough indeed. My husband got a team to come with a load as far as they could. They came ten miles, that was all they could come with a team. Next was to get the grub to Spider Lake where we wanted it. They took one of the ponies and tryed him on the snow shoe track. It was very hard for him. They went a mile and come back. My husband thought the pony could get through by driving him very slow. He set to work, made a flat sled for the pony as quick as he could to get the stuff that he left 25 miles from here. So one Monday morning they started, to be gone six days. He thought they could make the trip in six days time. I [was] being left alone again with my six little boys but I was quite satisfied that our grub would last us untill they came with some more before we would get out. Of course my husband succeeded to get the pony through to where they left the stuff and was back in six days with about five hundred pounds feed and grub for us. He made three trips with the pony to get the load.

Since I want to or required to write a little about the Indians. In the fall after we came to Spider Lake, a month after, there was twenty Indians past here. They was going to Odanah to interduce a new dance which is about [the] half and half. That is, they made an exchange to other tribes. They came from the mouth of Yellow River. My husband is been there [and] he knows the most of them. There are three of them from the five brothers. They claims a relation to my husband. They called him cousin. They told him "You had better come where we are to raise ponies for your boys, plenty of hay." I heard them talking with him down there. They started one fore noon, eat dinner before they went off. One of them came in the house, kind of hiding from the others, began to tell John about the big bear track they seen not far from here. He says "Just keep quite [quiet], dont say any thing to the others. I had a notion to tell you that through our motion." So John made a few signs and began to cut tobacco fine and gave it to him. The head man of them was one of the five brothers boys. He was the one who would state matters in their line. He is chairman like in every thing and general. After they eat they started.

## JOHN MORRISON EXPLAINS SIGN LANGUAGE

THAT IS NEARLY FORGOTTEN. ONE A FEW KNOW anything about it, and they are old men. The sign language was what deaf and dumb people have, only it was simpler, and all the tribes understood it. For example, if you came a stranger to a wigwam or a village, a stamp of the foot on the ground meant that you were welcome, two or three stamps that you were very welcome. Hunting signals were made with the hands. Four fingers and the thumb down meant a bear, with the thumb up, a deer, if a lynx or other climber, climbing signs; if the animal were running, the hand with fingers down made bounding motions; if a man, the forefinger was held up; if the man were hiding, the finger was closed down to the hand. Picture writing was done on bark. It was a map with various signs and animals here and there upon it. A circle meant a yell—by which the reader was meant to call when he reached a certain point.[68]

*Drum (or Dream) Dance Drum*

# THE DRUM DANCE

THE DANCE ELIZA MORRISON REFERS TO AS "half and half" or "four days dance" was the Drum Dance, or Dream Dance, which probably arose among the Santee Souix branch of the Dakota sometime after the 1870s when a girl fled from US soldiers taking over her tribe's camp. Tailfeather Woman hid in a lake under the pond lilies, forced to remain there without food until she saw a cloud settle over the water. In it was the Great Spirit, who had come to rescue her. For four days he taught her the ceremony of the Dance and instructed her to take it back to her people. The purpose of the Dance was to recreate Tailfeather Woman's vision to bring peace rather than war, friendship instead of hatred, and to ask for the blessings of the Great Spirit. The Dakota gave the dance to the Chippewa, who taught it to the other tribes farther east. As with other songs and dances of the American Indians, it was considered a sacred ceremony and a form of prayer.

The dance took place in a circular enclosure, outside or in a building, four times a year. The center of the ceremony was the sacred Drum, which was supported by four legs that kept it from touching the ground. This was a larger drum than most Indians had used before, and the drumhead was painted half red (symbolizing south) and half blue (symbolizing north), with a yellow stripe, signifying the path of the sun, dividing the colors. Dancers believed the Great Spirit imbued the drum with sacred power and that it symbolized the world, thus it was addressed as *gimishoomisinaan* (grandfather), treated with the greatest respect, and aligned so that the yellow stripe would exactly mimic the path of the sun. The beating of the drum, combined with smoke from ceremonial pipes, carried prayers to the Great Spirit.

During the dance, the drummers knelt in a circle around the drum and each beat the drumhead with a slender stick. As they drummed they sang, assisted by women who sat behind them and hummed in a nasalized fashion, while the dancers moved clockwise around the circle in time to the rhythm of the songs. Dancing was interspersed with speeches, prayers, stories, and the recitation of the creed of the drum; there was also a feast. The ceremony took place during the day and usually lasted four days, although some meetings could be longer.

The Drum Dance was of Woodland origin and should not be confused with the Ghost Dance of the Great Plains which figured in the massacre at Wounded Knee. Ghost dancers believed they could cure the sick and raise the dead, that through their dancing the world the Indians knew before white colonization would be recreated. Although Drum dancers believed they were communicating with the Great Spirit, they did not expect to create a future world free of whites; they did not encourage trances and they did not expect to heal the sick. Healing was the purpose of the Midé or Medicine Rite, a much older ceremony that was held twice a year. The Drum Dance may have developed from the Plains Grass Dance, and it may have been a ceremony that attempted to bring peace to the perennially warring Chippewa and Dakota, thus its instruction to pass on the Drum after a few years to establish tribal peace and brotherhood.[69]

There was only one woman with them. I could not understand that so I asked my husband "How is that?" "Well" he says "that was *ki che me de*,[70] This is the mash man's wife and he is dead not long ago. She shows it, Did you notice what she had in her hand. A piece of birch bark doubled and sewed one end and one side, one end open flat like. In it she has pieces of other barks and marks of all he has done since she married him. On one piece of the bark for certain there is thirteen moons mark up on it which represents one year. Each moon she passes, she rubs off one each time. When she rubs the 13 moons out, then she is clear from her husband that died. Before the year is up cant no man approach her without strong blemish. The brothers or cousins of her husband's will abuse her or kill her if she dont behave. But if she is young woman perhaps they will bring her a man in place of the one that is dead. If so she is married again. She cant refuse but they always pick out a man of the proper age for her to show the rememberance of her former husband. She must go to the grave with some stuff cooked and call others to come and eat with her, and its got to be some thing she makes herself. Rice or maple sugar.

And another thing I seen the Indians do just before they started, one of them had a great big red pipe. And a stem quite fancy, When he filled the pipe with tobacco and *ki ni ki nic,* lit the pipe, handed it to each one of them, some drawed smoke and some did not.

"How is that?"

My husband says "A person takes notice can tell how that's done. Any of them that takes the pipe in his mouth [that] is the first move to join their habbits. The stem has a mouth piece like any other pipe and beyond this there's a little hole. They put their lips over the hole and draw the smoke. Those that do not know how can not draw out any smoke out of the pipe. Anyone [who] draws the smoke out of the pipe is considered a true member of the tribe. The most of them does not know how to draw or do not put the pipe [in] far enough to draw any smoke."

For the first three years we lived at Spider Lake, Indians past there twice a year. Of course they stopped every time. Some times camped near the Lake. When they are on the way they drum before going to bed, after this smoke and tell stories to one another.

I will now go back and tell some thing of ourselfs. The winter of 1879 and 80 was the hardest I ever experienced, that is I thought so when I saw my husband half discouraged. I began to think we was in a hard place. We never was any time out of grub but [we had] a close call. And my husband did not like to see such a close call. But there was one good thing. After they broke the trail from here to Spring Lake they could catch plenty brook trout out of the lake which was as good as money. My husband had a friend in Ashland who would take the fish, all he had any time, and he would send them to Chicago to certain parties.

The spring of 80 I became a mother of a little girl April the 4th.[71] When this was over with my husband was entirely a new man. Mrs Bousky was to be with us, but she went away before the time came. So this held my husband right to home with me. He could not go to Ashland to get another load of grub. This was quite hard for him, yet he was very happy to see me up again. I was up the first week doing some of my work. In ten days time I was doing my work same as ever. By the time I got perfect, well it was impossible to get through to Ashland to get provisions.[72] So one morning we made a move to go to the sugar bush where Bousky was making sugar. That's to Bass Wood Lake. The lake was all open. Great place for fish and ducks. Bousky had only 100 pounds of flour. This is not enough to last very long for all of us. My husband and my oldest boy and Bousky started for Ashland to get some flour and some other stuff. They were gone three days. Took no horse, pack the flour from Ashland. They did not seem to mind the packing. When they came, they brought ammunition and nets to [get] more fish if necessary. We did not have much of a fit out. We could not get all our things, nor half of them, out from Ashland. But if any people was glad and happy because it was spring time, we was some of them that [was] glad and happy.

The snow was all gone by the 20th of April. Lakes all open, birds and ducks and loons to be heard in all directions. The strong sun shone, seemed to dry the ground quick after the snow was all gone, so it seem comfortable to us to see the change of the season. After a severe winter is past, we of course did not have any extrys in the eatibles [so] we was quite satisfied to get what the country natural[ly] produce and [to know] all our children in good health and ourselfs.

Well but some people would be surprised to know twelve days after the birth of my little girl I took her in my arms and carried her for 8 miles over ruff trail. The last two miles it was hard, thawing made it hard walking. After being in the sugar bush one week, my husband went back to Spider Lake, what we call home. We left the ponies and cow and chickens. When he got there he could not find the ponies. They were gone. He found one of them but one he could not find untill the next day. When he found him he was dead. He got to a creek and fell in and could not get out and there he drowned and we had only one left. This was hard on us. We could not replace or buy one to mate the one that was living to make a team. We had to do with the one we had to get our provisions. After we had done making sugar we all went back to Spider Lake. My husband was quite discourage after he lost the horse. When we was back to Spider Lake we had plenty fish and meat and sugar, but not much flour. We tried to live with out flour for a while. We could not do it. My husband and Bousky went out to make Bear traps without any bread. They could not stand it. No place to get flour shorter than Bay Field. That's 40 miles from here. My husband started one morning on horse back to get some flour. Our children did not seem to have any life in them without bread. My husband was back in 4 days, brought one hundred and 50 pounds of flour. On the horse back it took him two days from Bay Field [to] here.

"Husband we cant live here. You can see that now. Here you have lost one of the horses. If you lose the other what will you do. You say you cant buy another. How can we get along with just one horse way out here."

"Dear wife dont be afraid. Let me alone this summer and if I cant make money enough by fall so to live here we will go back, but I dont like to. I will not try to get our things here this summer. I am sure there is going to be a Rail Road here next summer. If it is not right here it will be close by and if there is no Rail Road near here we shall not live here. I shall not mind [plan on] clearing any land this spring to raise any thing. I am going to work for [a] St Louis party that is coming here to stay all summer to Pike Lake."

The fishing parties [was] numerous that summer. My husband had plenty to do and good wages [for him] and my oldest boy. We had plenty grub all summer and quite a lot put up for the winter. When the party went home my husband set to work and made a house for us to live in. In a months time he made a pretty good log house, quite comfortable to live in. "I will not hunt the silver vein this fall. I am going to hunt deer. I am going to try to kill enough to do all winter so if it comes another severe winter we will have plenty meat and plenty to do to tan deer skins all winter."

It is now one year since we left Ashland. During that year we lived with Bousky and his wife in a quite small shanty. He and his wife lived in that country for 19 years before we came to live with them. No children. She told us she never gets lone some when her man goes to town to trade. He would some times be gone for 15 days. She was all alone during the time he is gone. Many times [she] would stay down to Pike Lake on a small island. She of course had a canoe to get round with to catch what fish she need to eat. She had a little dog with her when she stayed on the main land. She always carried a big knife and a little hatchet around her waist. There was quite a number of pine hunters at that time in these woods.[73] She was more afraid of white men than wild animals. Most of them would want to see people but [she] kept away. She did not want to see any body. She understood some english but she never let on she understood any. In acting this way she found out what kind of men they are, if any was around there where she is. She some times was taken by surprise.

1895
March 4
Iron River

*My dear Mrs Gray*

Yours of the 25th was received stating you sent me a box of provisions. I have not received it yet. How long does it take to come. I hope it will not be lost. You are so good.  I just got a telegram that Mrs Bousky was dying. Our love to you all.

*Mrs John Morrison*
*in haste* [74]

Somebody would come all of a sudden when she would be in the shanty. When she would be caught in this way she thought there were some danger for her. The first time she thought there were danger is one time late in the evening four men came to the house and ask her if they could stop over night in the house. The men showed her some bread and some money. She did not like that at all but she made up her mind what to do. The men seem to stay up late talking to one another, except one seems to have his eye on her all the while but did not seem to say any thing bad as far as she could understand. But they did not seem to want to sleep. There were only two rooms in the shanty. When she found out they did not sleep she went out doors. When she got out she ran as hard as she could with out making noise. After some ways she stopped. She heard the door slam, evidently looking for her. She ran down to Iron Lake, got into her canoe. Away she went to a certain pointe that run out in to the Lake. There she stayed untill day light and then she went through the woods to go to Pike Lake. Just as she was getting to the road she spied the men. She ran back and hid again untill she thought they had passed and she took another start and she got safe to the landing and got in a canoe and to the Island. There she know she was safe. She was not afraid of men with good character but she could not tell. All she depend on when she was left alone is to show her character as much as she could.

Her man use to go to Ashland to trade. He would get to drinking whiskey. He was in no hurry to get back home where he leaves his wife alone. And often times when she is left alone she would go to Pike Lake on an island and there she would stay till he comes back, maybe a week or so at a time. She tells us she has past several winters without seeing any body. Just two of them all the time and she would be alone most of the time when her man would be out trapping or hunting. She was a great worker. She would not keep idle unless she was sick. She would tan deer skins and make them up into moccasins or mittens and sell them and other things. She was brought up among the Indians down on St Croix River or thereabouts. She was a full grown woman before she married Bousky. She was then babtized when she was quite old. I see she has some of the old Indian ways about her. She shows them but she will never say any thing unless she is asked. Still she likes religion quite well.

Bousky him self has some of the Indians superstitious ways. He was brought up a Catholic. He has lived so long among the Indians he almost got in with them in their habbits. He lived to Spider Lake since 1861 and he died in 1887 at 67 years of age. Bousky was a very strong and powerful man and a great traveler. He has carried the United State mail for two years during his life time put it all together before he came to Spider Lake. He use to live at Lapointe [during] the time of the American Fur Company. He was one of their right hand man in many things. The Company's headquarters was at Lapointe but they would send men and goods with them a great ways off north and west.[75] They had to have the best men in the country to indure what they had to do. As for their food they had to depend on the Indians to get some from them, that is while they have meat and wild rice what the woman gathers. If there is a failure of crops of rice chances are they will be hungry before spring, specially if there is a severe winter and deep snow.[76] A severe winter and spring is what causes the Indians to get hungry. The deer and other animals seem to gather in some thick timber country where the Indians is not custom to go on account of the great distance to travil and [because it is] to hard for them on to soft snow so it is to hard travling for them. A severe winter is very hard for the Indians and it causes fish to go in the deep water where they cant be caught or be reached any way and where the water is warm for them. Those men who was out for the American Fur Company had large experience of this kind.  My father and my husbands father both worked for the American Fur Company for a long time. Those men that worked for the Fur Company were married with chippewa woman. Some of these woman had great endurance, all most like men. They would go with their husbands. They would pack all most as much as their husbands would. Mrs Bousky is one of them who use to go out with her husband. She would take a pack all most as heavy as her husband and travel with him right along.

## Mrs. Bousky's Winter Walk

Grandfather turns to Mr. Bousquet, who is making one of his rare visits to our camp. "Mrs. Morrison says the year of the great blizzard your wife came out this way on snowshoes to bring you some grub. She says you found her near that first little lake just a mile east of here."

"Yes, Dr. Gray, that was a time I was on the way up to Bayfield, you know. It began to snow one Friday about dusk. We were there by Big Ox lake five or eight mile to north of Gordon's at forks of Eau Claire. Looked bad and I thought, better make camp in the big woods while I had a chance. It snowed hard all night.

"Next day that northwest wind was on the warpath. I hitched up the dogs all right an' we tried to make a go of it. But *Kabibonaka* he came along to tear at us with his bitter cold from the Big Lake off north. You know there where Ox Creek crosses road is good shelter in the hemlocks—you have fished there, Dr. Gray—well, me an' the dogs camped again—all we could do.

"Next day we just had to make trail somehow—dog feed getting low. But five or six mile was all we could make. I never seen such snow. I had to pack most of mail; dogs just pawed along. Trouble was I had to go ahead and break trail. The old toboggan was bucking and slewing. Snow piling over from that-a-way—no one to steady it behind. Late that day—must have been Tuesday by then—I was just passing your Island Lake here—*Minnesagaegun*. In that day no one was living around here. Over east of where your barn is now I smelled smoke. It was just about dark. 'Whose smoke?' I say.

"We go along through those popples and jack pines to first little pond hole couple of rods off south of trail. Then I smell smoke strong. By that time it was good and dark. Dogs they picked up the scent and started to yip. Pretty soon we see a little light ketched on a snowdrift, and someone standing there. The dogs, they know her all right.

"My wife, she had come eleven mile from our cabin to meet me and bring grub for us and dogs. She got that far and couldn't go no farther. Guess I couldn't neither. When she quit, she scraped out a little place alongside big Norway windfall where she could lay against the trunk and get some good of fire. Fire was for sign if I came 'long.

We give them dogs the last of the fish—one all round—then keep that little fire going and make some sleep. . . ."

"Name o' sense," says Grandfather Gray, "what did you have left to eat by that time?"

"I had nothing. She brought along some jerked venison, bread, dried blueberries. We made tea in her little lard pail. It was good. The snow was not so deep after we hit the jack pines this side Eight Mile lake. But it took us all next day to go only those few mile to Spider Lake. She carried half the pack. I couldn't have made it if she hadn't come along."[77]

The time Bousky use to go west to trade with the chippewas he went so far west that they use to go on the sioux hunting grounds. When he would come back he would tell his wife. She would be afraid because she was a full blood chippewa. If the sioux would find out she was there they would kill her. She went with him two winters way out there. After that she would never go again. She use to tell me when ever they would be ready to come back to Lake Superior she use to be very happy to think she would be safe away from the sioux. When she gets home to Lapointe back again she thought she is in the other world. When we came to Spider Lake to live where she lives so long, we might say all alone, she would say this is nothing. When she would think [of] the fear full experiences she had when she was of[f] west, here is like living in paradise. Here had no sioux to fear, but white men.

She says "Since you are here, I fear nothing. I can only tell one time when I was most scared by a white man. It was a St Louis fellow. He came in the house one after noon. Commenced to talk to me. I understood some of what he said and I bowed my head to him. Just so, I understood all what he said. I was cooking my dinner. I of course offered him to eat. He shook his head. I eat my dinner. After this was done he commenced to talk to me again. Finally he asked me if he could sleep here to night. That made me very mad. I pointe to the door, made motion for him to get out quick. I took the butcher knife and said [I would] kill him. He got out very quick and when he got out doors he ran like every thing. This is the nearest I ever came to fighting what they call a white man. I did not think there was much white man about him. I after wards found out who he was. They say he is one of the best lawyers in St Louis, that is my husband found out who he was. He knows law well but he is apt to violate the law like the rest of the people."[78]

How Bousky and his wife came to live at Spider Lake [was] by taking the mail to carry it in the winter's times. Bousky had one arm off half way up to his elbow. He done it himself long before middle age. He was out in the woods. He fell over a log and his gun went off and shot his hand. He had to walk four days to get to a place where there was a doctor to have his hand cut off. He could pack well with one arm off. He has been known to carry one hundred pounds of flour and go 30 miles in one day. When he was carrying mail he would take the weight of 30 pounds. It was nothing for him. Quite often his wife would make a trip with the weight of 30 pounds, go 18 miles and back the same day with the mail bag on her back. She is a great woman to work. She would tan deer skins and make

*Chippewa Leggings*

them up to moccasins and mittens. She says she likes to live to Spider Lake because it is quiet, nothing wicked going on there. Our men are happy hunting deer every fall.

Since her husband died she has made her home with us the most of the time. Her mother died five years ago. She was 89 years old when she died. Mrs Bousky has a sister living and a brother to Odanah in the Reservation. Neither one of them belong to any church. Her mother was babtized. She died a Catholic. Quite a number of her friends joined the Presbyterian church there in Odanah.

Mrs Bousky when she made her home with us, she told me all about the Indians and their habbits and of their marriage and so on. Her mother when she was old enough to get married, the man who would come to see her would come right in the lodge where she was

and set down long side of her to talk with her untill bedtime and he would go home. If the old folks see their girl make some thing for him it is a sure sign she is going to marry him. The next time he comes, he stays a little longer and he gives the girl some thing for herself to make up. Then he goes home about middle [of the] night with the intention of not coming again for ten days. About the third time he comes he brings her a bundle of some thing, beeds for her to make some thing to wear around his legs, fancy things. The fourth time he goes to her he takes some of his things and puts it near where she sleeps. This means he will come to stay the next time. The fifth time he came to her he takes all he has got with him, a gun and traps and ax and a bow and arrow, all he has. The girl says to her mother "I must get a new mat for him to sit on for he is coming tonight." The girl can tell what kind of a mat she wants to get for him from the kinds of paints he uses on his face. All the paints he uses she must use them herself along with him.

# MAKING MATS

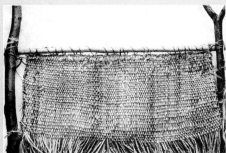

*Unfinished Reed Mat on Frame*

FLOOR MATS WERE MADE OF DRIED BULRUSHES, a swamp plant similar to cattails. The rushes were gathered in bundles, then hung to dry. Once dried, they were boiled, and portions were dyed different colors. When the rushes were ready to weave, they were tied one at a time to a basswood cord the length of the finished mat. This cord was fastened to a pole, and the pole was placed in a frame that would support the weaving. The mat was created by weaving basswood cord over and under the rushes to create a patterned mat.

Aside from the creativity required for color and pattern placement, weaving could only be done with rushes that were slightly damp. Dry rushes became brittle and broke, necessitating a difficult mending job. Women who wove on portable frames kept these covered and in the shade. Others had small lodges facing north in which to store their materials and weave on a larger, more permanent frame. [79]

WILLIAM GRAY PURCELL TOOK THIS PHOTOGRAPH in 1894. His notes on the back read: "I cut the rushes holding a scythe behind the scow while grandfather rowed. We had seen her, wading fully clothed, skirts wet up to knees, cutting handfuls with a hunting knife—that was too slow—How she cheered from shore as the reeds fell in a wide swathe.... All summer she got up at 5 a.m. to work on mats while reeds were pliable ('to wet them turns them dark'). I went 17 miles to Iron River to get dyes, lost them out of my pockets on the way back, but some one following found [them] on road and brought them in. Mats were gold or brass color with lines of green violet yellow—about 30" wide—6' to 8' long. Sort of a continuous braid—interwoven with concealed string reinforcement. String made of basswood fibre in early days. These mats used on floors—and as under mats and side mats of wigwams—but were not water proof. Just protection against wind and drifting rain—or for extra warmth—sort of insulators."[80]

*Mrs. Bousky Curing Rushes for Mats*

First day after their marriage he brightens up his gun and other things he has. On the third day he takes a trip with his wife some where on a hunting trip. Like if it on the lake or on a river, if he catches fish or kill animals of some kind, the same day they go back to the old folks to give what they got that day. But if he fails to get any thing the first day they stay and camp out untill the third day. If he fails to get any game on the third day he takes his wife to his father and mother's *wig gi wam* or teepe to stay there untill he can get a deer or some other animals to give it to the parents of his wife. When he fails on the fourth day than he speaks to his father by taking the old mans pipe. Filling up his pipe means some thing more than common. He lights it for him and gives it to him, to his mouth, saying "Some men would say, pa take this for me." The old man would smoke. After this is done he tells his other son "You get up early in the morning and help him to make his return thanks to his father in law." They all go make a strong effort to help the brother to make up a return thanks for the girl who is his wife. One or the other will kill a deer for him or he will himself. If it be too long in getting the game to give to the father in law it becomes double on him. When he kills the deer he takes it right to the fathers in law's door, lets it down close to the door without saying a word to any of them. Then he goes home [and] tells his wife what he has done. The father in law and mother in law is looking for this. And the second animal he kills he takes it the same way and his wife goes with him to her fathers to stay with them again. In doing this way if the wife should die any time thereafter, shall not be any blemish on the husband if she should die. He should stay with them just the same for one year or more. If he mourns much after his wife and the old folks see he is sorrow and lonesome, if they have another daughter old enough they place her with him as the nearest relation for his wife. This seems to be the habbits or law among them.

In these marriages or ceremonies that is one way. And they have a different way where a young man wants to get a wife to take her to his home. The girl goes out to chop wood for the night to pack it into her folks lodge. The young man goes out to meet her where she is chopping wood. There they have a conversation. When comes dark they make a little fire and sit on each side untill the time is up. [This is] what they call *nin go do pua gan*, that is measuring the time with pipe, certain amount of time specified according to the custom. That is for good character. If the young man does not smoke she makes fire twice, that is little fire, and he goes home and she does the same. The next [time] he goes hunting right from his home and if he kills a deer half goes to the parents of the girl who he wishes to marry. He gets his mother to take [it] to the folks and sends his little sister along with the mother with a piece of deer meat and a small kettle. He sends that to the girl who he intends to marry to have her cook it for him and send it to him after she cooks it. Doing this way shows they are going to be married soon. He giving them meat and other things shows kindness to them. The third time is the last time. The deer must be whole or some other animals. If it should be a bear it is some thing of great importance to them. They will bring [it] in whole to the place where they live without stopping to see what the bear skin is worth. They will go right to work and burn all the hair off and cut it up in such a way [that] the father in law and mother in law would have the best pieces, and his parents and his nearest relation next. Then after eating only the men would talk loud. The young man who is to be married to the girl, he cuts up tobacco fine to be smoked by them right there and than. He cutting up tobacco fine and giving it to them means goodwill and peace.

The girl who is to be married she goes with her parents to stay for good with her husband. All she takes with her she carries it on her back, mat and blankets and seamless sack made of woolen yarn of her

*Indian Women Procuring Fuel*

own make and her clothes of course. About the first thing she makes for her husband is a new sash, a belt to use around his waist to show her skillful hand in their line of work.

*End and Fringe of Netted Belt*

*Yarn Bag*

The Indian seem to have no record for any thing but could remember quite well what they know for themselfs what they use to do long ago. But now they have no regulary way same as they had in the old times specially since liquor is sold among them. They seem they dont know what injure it does to them to drink whiskey. Men will give it to their women. They all drink now, that is those who are not civilized and those who do not belong to any church. They seem to be ruin. This what I write about the Indians is true the most of it. My husband knows a good deal about the Indians, and Mrs Bousky tells me some things about the Indians and I know she is one of them, what people may call [a] true character. She is full blooded chippewa woman and she was brought up right among the Indians on the St Croix valley and I know her mother to be a very good woman. She died not great while ago. She lived to be 89 years old but Mrs Bousky is still living this present day. She lived to Spider Lake a long time with her husband. Bousky came to Spider Lake with intention of carrying mail and to hunt and trap.

I came to Spider Lake in 1881 with my husband and my family of boys.[81] My husband had a strong idea that he could find the silver vein that was found very long ago by the Indians. It is some where here in this part of the country. My husband was bound to spend ten years time in hunting silver vein. At the expectation [expiration of] five years he thought he had better quit. He did not hunt the silver vein the whole time during the five years time. He traped a good deal and made enough so we could live. In the fall of the year, the time when the deer is very good, he would hunt steady and our oldest boy with him the most of the time. He got to be as good hunter as his father was. The next younger boys they drove the pony to gather up the deer what was killed to bring to the house. My husband often killed four deer in one day. We did not only sell what we did not want to use, we give a good deal away. There was always somebody around here that was glad to take

*George and Ben or Tom Morrison with Deer*

what we had to give away. When the snow is to deep to hunt he would quit, turn in to tanning all the deer skins ready to be sold at any time.

Of course we took quite little time to learn our boys how to read. We both had some education in english of course. We felt like learning our children what we know. We had some friends who would send us some books. Some times most of the people would think the woods is a bad place to live but since I see my husband was satisfied, I was. He says "There is some virtue in living in the woods. We make honest living and we do not here swearing or see drunking men, but only few came to steal our meat when they come across the place where it was left. But they come from town."

I would say it is quite hard for me to make up a good history of my forest life in english because my husband and me when we are talking to one another, we speak the chippewa language. But to our children we would speak to them in english as much as we could.

I said before now that my husband was brought up among the Indians but he was not always with the Indians. He had some chance to go to school to learn to read and write.

He can write english and chippewa if necessary and he can also talk french when it comes to that. He was brought up catholic. He was taught the catechism, all about the commandments of God and the commandments of the church and rules and regulations of the church. I of course was brought up in Presbyterian doctrine. We neither one of us forgot where we belong. Not that I want to say we are good christians but only to show that people can live in the woods and remember what they know.

Two years after we left Ashland, we [were] living in the woods. During that time we had a sad experience. Our youngest boy got scalded with boiling water.[82] I was out doors washing one after noon. He was running where I was and had just let the kettle down on the ground to get my tub. He ran aggainst the kettle and up set it the whole of it right onto his little body. He lived a week and died. Mrs Bousky and her husband was not at home. Only one of her sisters was with us and one of her boys. Our boy Johny, the oldest, went to Bay Field to get a load of grub. He came back the same day his little brother died. The horse was very tired. My husband and our boy Johny and Mrs Bousky's nephew started with the horse to take the little dead body of our little Eddy to be buried in the burring [burying] ground to Bay Field.

They started in the evening, in the cool of the evening, to travil all night and part of the next day. In the evening he was buried by the Priest and by St Joseph society because my husband belong to it at that time. My husband prayed to God before they started that evening with full of sorrow in his heart I know. He traveled all night with his dead boy. The next day about 2 o clock he was to the church to Bay Field where the Priest buried the little corpse in the church yard. After this was done he came right back. He know I was alone only with our little boys.

This was in 1882 about the middle of August. I could not go with them because we had only one horse. I was left at home with my little girl who was 2 years old then. This was a sad experience for us. The woman who stayed with me and the children she kept talking to me about their peculiar ways. She did not belong to any church but [knew] hardly any thing leading to virtue in the manner I was taught. Oh how lonesome I would have been if I had no little girl to look at. I could not sleep in the night. Day time was not quite so bad for me.

On the third day my husband came back with a load of provisions and other necessary things. My husband would not leave me long after that time. He worked on the place clearing land with his boys. The only time he would go any where is when he goes hunting to kill meat for us to use later on that summer and fall. My husband would kill quite a number of deer so as to [keep] us busy drying the meat for the winter and he would tann deer skins and part of the time to have them ready to turn into money to give us a living. The first five years we were here to Spider Lake my husband had a great notion to dry plenty of deer meat from Sept first untill the time it freezes to keep [it] fresh.

Two months after my little boy was dead I was very sorrowful. I could hardly rest in the nights. Day time it was not so bad for me when they were all at home with me. When I refresh my mind of my sad experience, my english language cannot explain my feeling when I think of the pain my little boy must had from the hot water spilled on his little body. Of course I thought it would not do for me to show only sorrow to my husband and to my children. Many times I prayed to my God for comfort to be relieved of my sorrow. For a long time my smallest boys would play close to me. [They] seem to know I was troubled in my mind. They was all good boys, mind me well.

Later on in the same season some of our Indian friends came here to hunt. They camped near here which made it more pleasant for us because we could talk with them and we would trade with them. The women would tann deer skins for us and the men would come to our house in the evenings to talk to my husband about hunting that day. They knowing we lost a little boy made them come often to us. They ask my husband if he was using the same trails since his boy died. "Oh, that's why he is so sorrow." That was all that was said that evening. The next day or so one of the women came to ask me if my husband did not want to change his hunting trails. "One of our men would change the trails for him. Will you ask your husband to have new hunting routs. You will see he will be relieved of his sorrow so much and you too. Will you ask him to night when he comes home and if he will come to the conclusion to make new trails tell him to come to our camp to night."

"Well I will tell my husband when he comes but dont be a bit surprised if he dont come" I said to her. "He is *we mi ti go shi a na mi a.*" This means he belongs to the Catholic religion.

Late in the evening he came. After supper I told him what the Indian woman said about changing his hunting trails. "Oh I understand what she means. She was sent here for that. What did you tell her?"

"I told her *we mi ti go shi a na mi a* all right."

"The Indian is very superstitious about many things. They make remarks according to their dictates of their own conscience. Of course it is good to be friendly with everybody but it may not be good to take the course as they do to gain morality, but how ever I shall go there now and show as return thanks for their offer. You know wife our little boy who died here had a good burial by the St Joseph Society in Bay Field. This is a great sattisfaction to me you know. I even do not take their medecine when they offer it to me. That is what they call hunting medecine." These Indians always stay here to hunt untill the snow is quite deep. That would be the middle of December and [then they] would be left [would leave] for all winter. They would all go back to Odanah where they belong.

The winters of 1882 and [1883] was quite severe winters. My husband ordered a load of provisions from Bay Field. Along about the middle of February we began to think our supplies would not last all winter with us. We had some tanning done by those Indian woman and my husband tanned quite number himself. We worked, made moccasins and mittens to sell when my husband goes to Ashland. That winter Mrs Bousky stayed with us untill my husband got ready to go to Ashland to trade. About the 20th of February they started. The snow was very deep, hard traveling with snow shoes. Without them, they could not travel. They were 7 of them and the horse. They were quite able men, that of my husband and two nephews of Mrs Bousky. The horse walked behind all of them with quite a load.

That winter there was not a track to be seen, only what our people made when they went away. I was left once more alone only with my little children. We was the only ones that was to Spider Lake. My husband told me that they might be back in 7 days with our load of provisions. "You got enough of everything but sugar in that time I know." I know very well they would have hard work to get to Ashland. I did not look for them before the time he said he would be back.  After they were gone the dog we had to the house kept barking off towards North. He would run on the ice out [on] the middle of the Lake. There he would sit and bark untill dark. This was quite strange thing for me. The dog never acted like that since I lived there. I let the dog in the house for a while that evening untill after supper and I let it out again to see how it would act again and watched it. He looked that way but did not bark any more. But two days after, the dog barked again in the afternoon. Then I mistrust. There must be some one around here. About three o clock I see two men coming across on the ice coming towards the house. When they were nearby I could see they were white men. The biggest boy stayed out doors to speak to them. First thing they said was "Is your father in?"

This was George that stayed out doors to speak to those men. He says "Father was to come this evening. We are looking for him."

One of the men asked Georgie if his mother could talk english. By this time I was out to speak to these men. "Wont you come in and set down."

One of the men said "I know Mr Morrison. We came to see if we could get some meat. Are you Mrs Morrison?"

"Yes sir" says I. "I expect my husband will come this evening. This is the seventh day."

They spoke to one another. "We had better go back and come tomorrow to see him. We are out of provisions and we have got plenty of money. You tell your husband we will give big price for any thing we get here. We got out of grub. If we buy any we got to hire his horse to get a load for us. We are hunting pine lands. This makes a month since we left Ashland. When your husband comes back we are going to make this our trading place for the ballance of the winter."

"My husband is gone after a load of grub. Most likely he will spare you some because he can go after some more since there is a trail through to Ashland. If they dont be here soon I am quite sure they will be here tomorrow."

At three o clock they went off to their camp, four miles from here they say. My husband came that evening. Oh how glad we was. He brought all the horse could haul, the weight of five hundred pounds of provisions. "I am going to get another load" he says "before long, so we can have plenty for the next three or four months."

The pine hunters came again to buy some grub from us. I have not much to tell about myself. Of course my husband went with those pine hunters quite a while that spring. Soon after the pine hunters had gone, some more men came from the line, the survey line for the north P R R running to Ashland from west.[83] The survey party started from Ashland to locate the Rail Road line. The party of course had Indians for packers to supply them with grub. When they be come quite a ways it became very hard for the packers. It was very deep snow that winter. They did not have quite men enough to supply them or the packers was gone a little longer than usual. The party got short of grub [and] came to our place to see if we can get some grub of any kind. They had no flour no meat [but] they had plenty of dried fruit. This is what the head man told me. My husband came with a load of grub and stayed home a few days and went back again after another load so to be sure to have enough during spring.

The same morning he went off the survey men came to see us about getting some grub. They wanted flour and meat and potatoes. They came six miles from here. My husband was gone. I could not tell what to do but they must have flour and meat. Of course I let them have flour and one whole deer. The white man took the flour the weight of 50 pounds and the Indian took the whole deer weighing one hundred and fifty pounds and froze at that and [they had to] go on snow shoes and six miles to pack it over hilly country. The white man told me he was the strongest Indian he had in the crew. I of course made up my mind he was strong when I see him packing a frozen deer weighing one hundred pounds.

My husband came back with his load of grub. That spring we did not make any sugar. My husband went to work and made an ice house and filled it with ice. This was the first house made on the shores of Spider Lake during that spring. Mr Bousky and his wife made sugar down to Bass Wood Lake. I took a trip down there to stay a week with them. I took one of the boys to pack our blankets. I of course had my little girl to pack. She was then 3 years old. She was quite heavy for me to pack. She made pack enough for me I found, walking in the woods and through brush and going over down falls and over hills and some snow to contend with and packing my little girl weighing 45 pounds and carrying a bundle besides and my Charley about 14 years old packing our blankets. I know some people would think this was hard life. We do not think it is hard at all. We think it is just charming. Of course we do not see any thing wicked nor learn any bad language. The boy who was with me to go to Bouskys sugar bush he was very happy indeed with his bow and arrow, shooting birds and other little things.

The distance was eight miles to go to the sugar bush. It took us about 5 hours to go that distance about half way [with] no trail. When we got out of the timbered land, got to the opening, there was no snow. This seems to increase our courage [and] we walked faster. My boy says "Ma we will be there in good time for dinner. If Uncle Bousky has not got any fish all ready for you ma, I will take the dug out and go out and catch fish for your dinner. I know ma, you like fish. All I am going to eat for my dinner is syrup and bread."

"While we are there, you fish. I am going to dry some to take home with us when we go. Pa likes dried fish."

When we got in sight to the sugar lodge Mrs Bousky was looking at us coming fast. She says "You are just in time for a good dinner" she say. She came to meet us a little ways and got the little girl off my back and kissed her of course. She had the dinner ready. She cooked duck and pork and dumplings. This is supposed to be a good dish for Indians. Soon Mr Bousky came in with more ducks and other game what he trapped. Mr Bousky's father and my mother were brother and sister. This makes us first cousins. He said he would give us packs enough when we were ready to go home.

We stayed there three days with them and came home. When we came home we had both heavy packs. I must had the weight of twenty pounds besides my little girl which is now three years old. My boy he had all he could carry. We went half way and left our load. My boy climb up a little hard wood tree, bent it down with my help and tied our stuff to the tree to spring up off the ground so it will be safe from wild animals. After we got through hanging our stuff up we went on our path. No trail but [a] little brush broke to guide us through and to keep our right course.

Every little brush was so old once in a while I could see my husband's mark. Wherever he would stop, he would make a mark. This mark was given him when he was a small boy by one of his mothers cousin. It was his mark when he lived. It is a long life mark as it is called by the Indians. I remember my husband told how he made it on a tree with an ax. As near as I can learn every man of the Indians has to have a mark from which they can tell from the mark who has been there and when, almost to the hour, wether sick or not, or had any sad experience. I will tell more about that after a while but I will tell about my husbands long life mark that is which was given him when he was a small boy. I will tell in a way to pronounce it in the Chippewa language. *Ki chi a ka ka de bosh. O shi bi I gan. O do de man.* The meaning of this is an Alligator or life supporter in long duration, an emblem or contain. My husband makes a mark on the tree with an ax like an alligator just to know that he has been there before but not because he believes any part of the Indian superstition. He also understand the marks what the Chippewas has and signs. Of course I dont know very much about the Indians out in the Interior. Of course I know about those who lived where I was brought up. Their habbits and ways are not exactly like I found since I been married with my husband. He tells me quite many things of their habbits, the

Interior Chippewas where he was brought up.[84] I was brought up on one of the Apostle Island where the Indians were half civilized. They were not so strick as those that lived where there were no religion taught. There old habbits are more strick. Since I came to Spider Lake to live where we made our home there were not many Indians that would stay all the time but quite many would come in the fall of the year to hunt deer.

# John Morrison's Long-Life Mark

THE ALLIGATOR ELIZA MORRISON REFERS TO as her husband's long-life mark is a symbol of John Morrison's clan totem (*dodaem*). A totem was a clan mark, like a family crest or genealogical sign used as a signature, that identified group members and sometimes implied certain community duties, such as policing duties at campsites (bear) or leadership (crane). Persons could not marry others from the same totem. Members sharing the same totem, even if they lived miles apart and had never met, considered themselves relatives.

Historians believe the concept of totem began as a way for people in a village band to identify themselves to outsiders; each band, which could be composed of between 30-100 members, used an animal symbol to describe itself. This symbol, or totem, was carved into a post put up in the camp and also inscribed on birch trees as the band moved to let others know who had passed. Bands were patrilocal; that is, the totem of the men was the totem of the band, although wives belonged to different totems. Gradually, over the course of the 18th century, bands united to form a single large group, the Chippewa/Ojibwe, that was composed of many totems, each of which came to identify a certain clan. Clans regulated marriage and integrated neighboring bands.

Normally a man would have used his father's totem. Children of white fathers or men who lacked totems were given the totem of their mother's clan or of the eagle. According to William Warren in *History of the Ojibway People*, at the time John Morrison grew up the Chippewa had twenty-one totemic clans.

There was no alligator, but since *kichi-akakadebosh* translates as "great short-legged reptile," there are three possibilities. John Morrison's parents were married near Detroit and his mother may have been part of a family from farther south. Alternatively, Mrs. Morrison may have been referring to Micipijiu (Missipeshu), the great horned underwater lynx who is the creation of the Ojibwe/Chippewa and was used as a totemic figure by bands near the St. Croix River. Micipijiu is one of the most powerful creatures in the Ojibwa universe and would have been associated with leaders. If so, this suggests Mrs. Morrison did not believe her readers would understand the concept of an underwater lynx and so substituted another creature. The third, and most tenuous explanation, is that the totem refers to a species of creature now extinct in the area. The explorer Radisson described an alligator-like animal in the 1600s, but scholars consider the report bogus.

A totem is not a spirit-helper, however. To receive the aid of a spirit helper, John would have undergone a lengthy fast at puberty when he would have received a vision of the creature in a dream. He would have had to earn this creature's help through fasting; it could not have been given to him by his uncles when they adopted him. A spirit helper was personal and private, a creature to be called upon in times of need. It would be highly unlikely for someone to use it as an identifying mark on a tree since it would mean little to anyone else. It might be the same as one's totem, but it could also be completely different.

A totem is not a personal name. Many Indians considered their "real" name to be sacred and private, and it was rude to inquire what it was. People might have as many as four or five names during a lifetime. John Morrison's father's Indian name was "Metance." "Ma Danse" was John Morrison's name, which perhaps translates as "belonging to this place," a name that may have been given him when he was adopted by his mother's family after his father died.[85]

I came away from Ashland in 1881 and in the fall of 83 I took a notion that I would go and see my old acquaintance in Ashland. When we came to Spider Lake I said when I go to Ashland I will ride on the cars to Ashland but it was most to long to wait. I told my husband I would like to go. He says "You better wait untill next fall. Then you can ride on the cars." I [had] never rode on the train yet.[86]

About the 20th of September we started for Ashland a foot. There were ten of us counting my little girl. Of course she could not walk. I had to pack her on my back through to Ashland. We took the old Indian trail to fish creek near Ashland. It took us 2 days to get to Ashland. I stayed one week with my friends in town and I return home with the crowd. There were nine of us coming home to Spider Lake. We did not come the same way we went. We was told the rail road was graded for ten miles, that we would find good walking and not quite so far. We did find it so but I did not like to see so many men to look at us that works on the road. Some would say "There is a white woman among those Indians." Some would speak to me. They would ask what my name was. Of course I would tell them, "I am Mrs Morrison."

"Where do you live."

"To Spider Lake sir."

The next day we came within six miles of home. There was one hundred and 50 men was working there. We stopped. Bousky went and asked the head to see if we could eat dinner there by paying him so to save us from cooking. He says "Yes you can eat dinner with us." The head man waited on us him self. He found out I could talk english. He says "I heard your husband is a great deer hunter. I wish you would tell him to come here and hunt for me. I have 150 men working here. I will buy all the meat and potatoes you have. I will give you a good price for it."

"We have some potatoes to sell. How much will you give a bushel for potatoes sir, so I can tell my husband when I get home. It is about seven miles from here sir. We can get home this after noon easy."

"Tell your husband to come here. I want to see him."

Soon after we eat we started, got home quite early that afternoon. My husband he had been out hunting, killed a nice deer for us to eat when we come. I enjoyed my trip quite well and I was glad when I got home to my husband.

He went down the next day to see the head man to trade with him. Going to Bay Field for grub was ended for good for us. [He says] "I can now get all the grub we want for the winter awfull easy." My husband kept hunting deer. He got plenty of provisions for the winter and sold one hundred bushels of potatoes.

In the spring of 84 we came to conclusion we would make sugar once more together with Mrs Bousky. They had part of a fit out and we had [part and] by working together we could make quite a sugar camp down to Bass Wood Lake. We had to use our dog to haul our things to the sugar bush. My husband when he was hunting in the fall killed a big Buck near to where we was to make sugar that spring. He hung it up after the old hunting style so it would keep good all winter. After moving down there and camped in good shape he thought he would go and see his big fat deer. He found it but there was not much of it left. The fisher had found it and eaten most all of it.[87] My husband set a trap for Mr Fisher. He caught five from that very thing. Each morning he went he had one in his trap caught. He called that fair reward for the damage they done for eating up the deer from us. Fishers skins was worth at that time nine dollars apiece. Five times nine is quite a little sum to get out of the woods. Their is quite plenty of game to get in these woods that we can get money for but nothing like getting five fishers in side of a week out of a wooden trap.

That spring we made quite a lot of maple sugar. We were all in good health to work. We had no barrels to put our sap [in], but troughs to hold from two to three barrels. My husband made 7 that spring. Of course in making sugar out here where we was 30 miles away from civilization we had to use a good deal of the old Indian style. Frame stuck in the ground and wooden hooks to hang our kittles on and the old way of stirring it to grain it off to put away for future use. After we got through, there was the moving our sugar to get it home to Spider Lake. No road to use a horse. All had to be packed to the lower end of Pike Lake than two miles to Spider Lake west ward. There we used the horse to haul our things home. It took us three days to get our stuff home. Next for me was to clean my house. That took quite a while.

My husband says to me "Now wife we've got through with the old Indian style working. Now we will try the white man style for a while, that is clearing land and planting potatoes and so forth."

*Cabin at Spider Lake built in 1878 or 1879 and abandoned in 1894. Thomas standing in the door,*
*George is standing to the left of the door, Daniel is seated in the chair at right. The dog is Sanko.*

On one of his early trips to northern Wisconsin, William Cunningham Gray wrote the following letter to his wife, Catherine, at home in Oak Park:

Morrisons, in the Woods
Monday June 23 '87

My Dear Wife

We came through to Ashland all right and had time to make our purchases of [?] things this morning at Iron River. We were dumped in the woods, and found George and young Mr. Morrison waiting for us with an excellent team and wagon. Of course it was raining, and it rained all day. It was quite cold at Ashland, an immense contrast with the temperature at Oak Park. I slept last night under heavy blanketry. I came in the rain nine miles through the woods, and we did not think but to go on in toward the lake. I was glad to get in my flannel-lined hunting regimentals.

Here we have a primitive life. Mrs. Morrison is a motherly lady of about fifty, a good cook and her cabin floor of puncheon is white as a table. There are no boards about the house, excepting hewn or riven ones—no ceiling, but the low roof of clap-boards, and yet there is an air of neatness and comfort here that is genuine. There are no neighbors within six miles excepting one old couple of Indians—very old, near here. Mrs. Morrison has five boys and one girl—the youngest girl about Millie's age. I undertake to say that you would take solid comfort in this humble cabin for a few days. It is the essence of comfortable primitive life....

Affectionately WCG

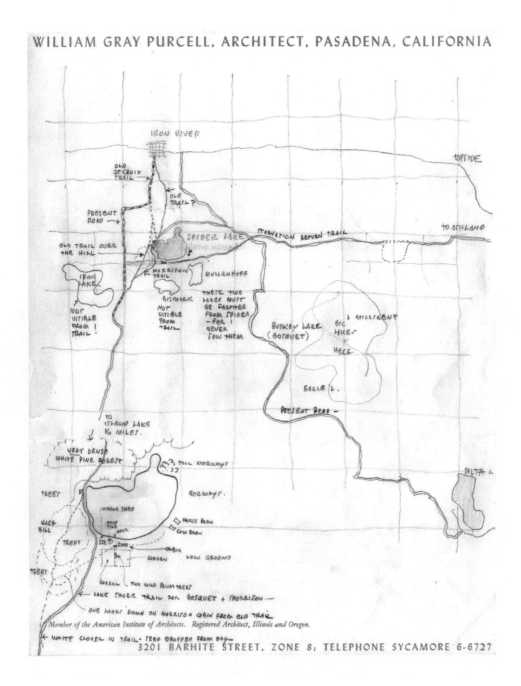

*Purcell's Map of Spider Lake*

They put in twenty bushel of seed in the ground among stumps and roots and stones. The land is quite good to produce a crop if it is a good season. One contractor on the Rail Road kept sending word to my husband to hunt and to kill meat and fish. He want it for his men. After planting they set in fishing and hunting some, but not much. They went quite hard on fishing in Pike Lake to sell to the Rail Road contractor and sold some maple sugar also.

That spring before our planting was done I took a notion I would make another visit to Ashland. The NPRR was not completed yet. Bousky and his wife was going down to, not to be gone long. There was some things we had to have before we could complete gardening. So one morning we all started. Bousky and his wife and me and one of my boys and my little girl on my back of course. But my oldest boy could pack his little sister quite well and walk faster than I could and dont get tired out at all.

When we started we made for Masion [Mason]. That is on the Odanah road. Thats twenty miles from here to Masion. We was trying to get in time to get the train. Five o clock is her time at Masion. Bousky was bound to get in time for the train so to get in Ashland that evening. Twenty miles is the biggest walking I ever done, part way no road and oft time packing my little girl. I dont believe I could have done this much walking if I had not thought of riding on the train the ballance of the way. I never rode on the train untill that evening going from Mason to Ashland the distance of twenty miles. My boy came home the next day to bring some seeds to finish the gardening and I stayed for a week. Going to Ashland in one day and back the next day was some thing new for us.

While I was in Ashland I had five days to myself visiting old friends and acquaintances. I did not stay at any one place long, only over night and a day to one [each] friend. In a week time my boy came for me. He started from home four o clock. When he got to the rail road it was only 10 o clock soon after he got there, to the place where they called 31. It was a station ten miles this side of Ashland. He got a chance to ride on the freight train that was going to Ashland. He was to Ashland at 11 o clock. This was the quickest time made going from Spider Lake to Ashland in our time. This was some thing new for us. The best of our men all ways takes one day.

The next morning we started for home to Spider Lake. It was ten when we started from Ashland and we rode for ten miles and walked the rest of the way, 24 miles over ruff road and muddy. I had a pack of course weighing 40 pounds. My boy [was] packing his little sister all the way home. About dark we got home to Spider Lake. When I got home that night I was not tired, only my feet was sore. My husband told me I better not go again untill I could ride the cars all the way through to Ashland. "I will go once more if I have to walk. That is in October before you [go] hunting. I will take some tanned deer skins. I shall have money for them. Quite a number of our Indian friends asked me if I had any deer skins to sell. Next time I come I will bring some to sell."

We past the summer same as usual but doing a little better to wards living than before. My husband got over his silver mine. As soon as he got over that he done more hunting and cleared more land and [had] a little better [to] show to live. In the fall of 1884 the NPRR was not completed. I told my husband I would go again to Ashland. "There is things I want. I will go myself once more this fall. Bousky and his wife is going Monday morning. I will go with them but I shall leave the little girl at home this time. But Johny will go with me so we can carry lots of stuff home. They are going towards Mason. Not quite so far to walk. We got to start very early in the morning so as to make the train in time."

When Monday morning came we started about 4 o clock. We had twenty miles to walk from home to the Rail Road to get a chance to ride the cars. We got in time to get the train that goes to Ashland. We walked twenty miles and we rode on the cars twenty more. The walking was ruff. The road was cut up by the wagons and made it muddy.

Bousky and his wife did not stay long. They only went to trade and we went on the same business. In three days we was on the way home. Rode to Mason. We got off at 11 o clock. We of course made tea for our dinner. Before one o clock we was on the way but I almost bought to much stuff for us to carry. Our packs was almost to heavy to carry. Johny had about one hundred pounds. I had about 80 pounds. Mrs Bousky had some where about 100 pounds. Of course we all had [all] we could walk under. We went 8 miles that after noon. I have been used to pack but not such a long distance.

The next day at noon we arrived to Pike Lake. There we had a boat for four miles. This was a great help to us. The boat was big enough for us all and all our stuff. I enjoyed the boat ride very much indeed. After packing 16 miles in two half days this day we was bound to make the hunters camp. Thats where the Indians called *sa gi ga mag*. In english would be thoroughfare. About one o clock we was to the hunters camp where we was to eat our dinner. When we was there I asked them if they had any deer meat. They said no but we have plenty of nice fish. They say "dont undo your pack. We will give your dinner. You always give us dinner when we go to your house."

One of them says "It is to bad you have to pack like this."

"Well I enjoyed the trip quite well untill today. I begin to think it was to much for me."

"One of us is going to your house this afternoon to get some potatoes. Who ever goes will take your pack for you."

"If you take my pack over for me I will give you half bushel of potatoes because my neck is sore and my boy is near tired out packing. Only two miles more and we will be at home. I am glad of it. I dont think I will take a trip like this any more very soon. My husband wanted to send the two oldest boys with Mr Bousky but I insisted on going myself."

In an hour or more we reached home. When I got near I seen my little girl standing near a fire where my husband was drying deer meat. He had killed two deer the day before.

This was in the fall when the deer is fat. Of course we talked a good deal about our tripp and my heavy pack. The man who carried my pack from Pike Lake says to my husband "Mr Morrison if I had a woman like her I would never make her pack from Mason here [even] if I went without goods."

"Sir I told her it would be hard for her but nothing to do. She must go herself just because she wanted to ride on the train from Mason to Ashland and back and I told her not to buy to much stuff to try to pack it out here. Her pack is enough for me almost."

The man says he must go back.

"Oh dont be in a hurry sir. We will have supper in an hour. Sit down and stay and have some supper with us. I am cooking in Indian style."

The Indian when they have deer meat and pork and potatoes and dumplings they think that's the best dish in the world. Tea or coffee and sugar of course when they can get it. The man says "This is not only good dish for an Indian it is good for any body."

Bousky had to cross the lake yet to get home. We told him to stop and eat with us so we all eat well that evening. Our children was very happy that evening playing with the mouth organ. My husband had made a rack to dry meat on. This made some work for the boys, cutting hardwood to make smoke. The man that came with us from Pike Lake went back after supper happy as he could be, seen that we were happy. My husband talked so much with him about hunting, seem to give him life. He said he wished he was an Indian to be able to follow this kind of life.

My packing from Mason home is about the last packing I done this fall of 1884. My husband had quite nice time hunting. There were not many chippewas around here that fall. He hunted right from home the most of the time. He killed 30 deer and 5 bear and sold the meat to the Rail Road contractor. This gave us enough money to get quite a good supply of provisions that winter. About the first of December the train was running through from Duluth to Ashland. My husband went to Superior to buy our supplys for the winter. This was a new thing for us to get grub here so easy in that landing the stuff to Iron River. No one living there than. From the rail road to our place made three miles of a haul for the horse. We did not have a reagular road that winter to the rail road.

In the spring of 85 my husband ordered some chairs for our house. We had been using benches. Us women went down to pack up the chairs. They had not made the road yet for the wagon to go through. During the summer we made the road from our place to the rail road which is now known [as] morrison's road. It is now a publick road. Now there is a town to Iron River and quite a large town. It is over 1000 inhabitance, two big school houses where now the two youngest children is going to school. After the rail road was completed we did not see many Indians come through. The most of them went by rail.

Since I am requested by a friend to rite a little history of my life and some things about the Chippewa Indians. I do not claim to know any thing about other tribes of Indians but the Chippewas. A good deal of their habbits may be the same as other tribes. The Chippewas has motions and signs with their hands and marks so others can tell almost the very hour [when they have passed] and there songs marked out on a piece of bark. The signs with hand seem to be known only by certain ones and only men, not woman. My husband who claims to know some of the signs, he tells me the signs is from old ancient time. It seems they was doing some great work and all at once they scat[t]ered for some thing they knew not. What seem the sign was given them to use so they may know one another and understand one another and go together. The Indians now claims it is so long ago since the signs were given them, they cant say the date and explain what they were doing when they were scatered. So the Indian leaves marks up on trees where others can tell by marking the quarters of the moon or half quarters. They also have a mark for their sick. [A person] leaves a mark for others to know a mark for the sick. If a man lay down and one of his elbows on the ground and his hand is on his head, this means sick. And if very sick, lays down and his head [is] covered up. But mark for the dead [is] laying flat on his back and his two hands up. For any sad experience, using coal to mark with.

## PICTOGRAPHIC LANGUAGE

ON SATURDAY, AUGUST 5, 1837, JOSEPH NICOLLET was traveling near the St. Croix River, heading for Lake Superior and La Pointe. "A few miles before Snake River we found a fine lodge and a bark canoe, both abandoned. A piece of bark hanging on the door informs us that the family has moved to Lac Court Oreilles, that the family is composed of the father and mother, two boys and three girls. The father is of the bear, the mother of the eelpout totem."

These "elementary characters," as Nicollet called them, were not sacred like much rock art (petroglyphs), but simply a shorthand way of communicating

without a written language. Pictographs were used for many of the same purposes writing is used: records, reminders, histories, magic, ritual ordering, communication. The pictographs John Morrison speaks of are prosaic, such as the one below found by Nicollet. Others could be carved on trees to mark battle sites, or used in a Midé scroll to

*Nicollet's Drawing of Pictograph*

show the stages in the Ojibwe migration from salt water to the Great Lakes.[88]

The Indian has not a bible nor history. No record of what was given them but all in memory and signs. They believe in the existence of the Great Spirit. They believe a person is got a soul that goes away when he is dead or her's. When they bury their dead, if a man, the man digs the grave, gets every thing ready, puts in all his things what he had with him or her's, what he did not give away before he died. When they are ready to burry him or her, one of the men gets up and holds up one of his hands, begins to speak [the] same as he would say "My relations and friends, the one [who] died just before this one, I spoke on his be half. I will now speak for this one who is about to leave us for ever. This is the last we will see of her. The path is now very plain but very great distance but many is gone ahead of her. We must all tell her to be very care full in crossing the narrow bridge when she comes to the dangerous river where so many makes mis step and fall in the river where they can never get out and [will] be lost forever.[89] The bird they use to use to cross [to] our ancestors is not in existence no more for us." If there is any man that is a warrior, they sing war songs and drum a few minnits. The man stops at once and says to the rest "This is enough." For a woman "she does not need so much as one of us. This is to please the Great Spirit to take care of her on the way untill she gets across the dangerous river." If they can cross safe they will [go] to the next country.

From what we can understand [from] the Indian, there is been a great size bird in this world to carrie them in those dangerous place. Now it seems more danger without that great bird. They have an idea the height of the bird was as high as three common man. The Indian also claims it is by this great bird that [they] came in to this continent from other part of the world. The Indian have a great story about the great bird and they have them in their songs. When any member of the family dies they band [bury] it there usual way of course. But about once in every moon the first year they cook and call their friends to come and eat with them near the grave. If they fail to do this every moon they make up. They leave enough stuff to the grave to be taken. They have no choice who may take it. The first one they see they tell him to take it. Some times a good blanket is found there or some other article of some valuable or a big sack of rice of their own make or some sugar or deer skins.

When I was a girl my Uncle told me a story about finding things in this way near the grave. Once he was going to Fondulac which is now called Crowkey. As he was going past the mouth of Brule River he seen some thing hanging he thought. He was in a boat. He turned his boat and went a shore where the Indian had a graveyard. When he got near it he seen a moose skin hanging all tanned and one moccak [makuk] of maple sugar set up on two logs covered up well with other barks. He look around, seen some marks. Evenditly [evidently] they had been there six days before he was. He took the skin and the sugar and left a piece of tobacco about three inches square. With the Indian a piece of tobacco means good friends. He would like to leave more but he did not have it. Tobacco than was only four dollars a pound at that time. It is no wonder an Indian would be friendly to the man who gives him tobacco. In my Uncles time there to the mouth of Brule River was a quite village [of] Indians camping there, in number about 100 and 50 some times more, where theres none now. My Uncle was one of them that was round in this country since he was young man. He use to tell us about his trips when we was young girls. And about the chippewa Indians. He was 75 years old when he died in 1869. He was most of the time lived on Lapointe Island. He came here when he was a young man and was round 50 years or more. That old man Bousky was my Uncle, my mothers brother, [the father of] young Bousky who used to live to Spider Lake. He died in 1886. My Uncle lived near us ever since I could remember, there to Lapointe where he died and where mother died and my father died and where I first met my husband and where we made our home so long and where six of my boys was born and what I use to call my old home.[90] The old house stands there yet. My Uncle use to work a good many years for the [American Fur]Company there to Lapointe and made quite number of trips to St Louis with Birch Bark canoe from here.[91] Some of the members of the Company lives to St Louis and use to be taken through by canoes from Lapointe up to Brule and portage to reach the St Croix River and down the Missippi untill they reached St Louis.

When I am speaking of the old home there to Lapointe where we was surrounded with my mothers friends and relations it puts me in mind of many things what transpired in my girlhood. When ever I go to Lapointe I would spend a good deal of time in looking around what I call the old home and to the old graveyard. I think it does me good yet my anxiety is mixed with sorrow. But somehow other I like to go over the ground where I was raised. There is now only two houses standing there. The old mission and the old house where I use to live. It was built by my father. What I call the old mission it was built by the Presbyterian mission. I could just remember. I am now 57 years of age. To my knowledge use to be 37 houses on the flats, all made of round logs roofed with ceader bark.

My Uncle I speak of he build alongside of ours where he lived so long and died. He being with us of course I became finmiller [familiar] with his stories about the Indians and even other experiences. He says in a period of 30 years he was with the chippewa Indians half of the time off west and north of here. What made him to be with the Indians so much [was] because he use to trade with them. He use to get goods from the Company. In the summer they take canoes to go out to where to eshtablesh [establish] their post which would be their head quarters during the winter. There they use dogs when they have them. The dogs were very large ones. I use to see some of them brought in. They were yellow and had long hair, stood about two feet and a half high when full grown and quite long and look like a wolf. My Uncle tell us it was hard to buy dogs from an Indian. They would not sell them but would only hire them [to] those who is out trading with the Indians. They would come in the spring quite late in June. They would be gone eight months from home each year.

When I was a young girl my Uncle use to get me to do a little writing for him. He use to want me to write a book about the Indians, that he would help me all he could while he lived. I never undertook the mater. I all ways thought it would be to hard for me or I did not know enough or some fear of that kind, untill I found a good friend or friends to request me to write. I then thought I would write some of the matters of [the Indians] and a little history of my forest life. And my experiance is quite long now and the experiance of my husband is quite [a] little about the Indians. As for myself I have consummate,[92] although I know about the Indian. But when I come to talk to my husband about the Indians, their habbits and ways and ceremonies and custom, that is those that remains uncivilized, is a good deal like that of my Uncle whom I speak of [who] was so long in this country before he died. When I am writing a little about him it refreshins my mind on some of the legands he use to tell us. It was about four girls. Indian girls of course. This was not long before he came here him self.

There were than an Indian village at the mouth of Iron River. Those four girls use to live there with their parents. They were very pretty girls but the youngest was the most beautist. A young man who lived on the north shore of Lake Superior and away out to some of the interior lakes heard of those four girls. All at once he got ready to come over to get one of these girls and told his parents "I am going to the south shore of Lake Superior to get a woman for me. Dont be surprised if I dont come this summer. I am going to stay untill I get the one I want."

He of course had a good canoe and other things in porportion in their style. When he came out of the river to the Lake Superior he camped. It was too ruff for him. Here he had to go by water for six days to get to the mouth of Iron River where he thought there were girls to suit him. He never seen any of them, only heard of them and never come on the south shore of the Lake before. The tenth day in the afternoon he arrived to the place. Those who was camping there when they saw a canoe they spoke to one another. "A stranger" they say. "Higst [hoist] the flag."

He came a shore and got out. Went through motions to the one he thought was the head man, asked him "Am I welcome on this land or ground?"

The man made a sign, lift one foot, down with it and bowed his head saying "Yes sir you are welcome on this land."

They see he was a nice young man. The head man cause his woman to cook and told him eat with them. One of the four girls came. The oldest one came to eat with them. The young man seen her, thought that one is good enough for him. After he was there four days he began to court her in their old way. He soon got acquainted with all of them but he had an eye on the youngest girl the most of the time because she was the best looking of the four. All to once he stop courting the oldest girl and took a change in his mind that he'd rather have the youngest girl for his wife. It was a good while before he could court her. Finily [finally] he got her affection and court her according to their old style and married. This enraged the oldest sister, but [she] could not help it. He stayed there the length of one moon and told his wife to get ready. They would go back to his own country. She said she would not go. He would have to stay right there. "You see my father is got no boys to help him to kill game. We must stay here."

"Well if you cant go with me, I've got to go back to my country for a while before it is too late in the fall. I will go back the same way I came. I cant promise you to come this fall but I will come next spring to stay with you and your parents."

The oldest girl never spoke to him while he was there. She was mad enough to kill him if she could.

He went off with his canoe all alone back to his country where he came from. Spring came. He did not come yet. The year was most up. He did not come. His wife gave birth to a child. She died from that and the child died all so. Than the girls was ever so mad. The oldest one says "If he comes I will kill him sure. He will never go back to his country no more." She told her father "If he comes you take me and place me on his side and if I am not accepted by him I am going to kill him for sure. But if you will take me and set me by his side and [he] take me instead of my sister for his wife he may live with us and I will never go to his country with him to live there with him. He is got to promise to stay with us and if all this is refused by him he's got to die here on our grounds near where my sister is buried. I just think he is the cause of my sisters dying so soon, and when he first came he spoke to me about marriage and married my youngest sister. Where is she now. And he is not here him self. Will he come or not. Here it is most a year since he left us. If he comes he will come the same way of course. I will go and put a mark so he can tell when he gets to the landing, but if we see him coming we will let him know." How they can let him know [there has been a death is] by histing the flag low for a woman. That is in day time. But in the night to know they take coals off of the fire, put it on a stump or stone and spit on it and strike it with some heavy stick. It will make noise like a gun. [They make] two strikes for a woman and three strikes for a man.

The oldest girl was very anxious for him to come back. She was mad enough to kill him right there if it was not to see him, how he would act. One day he came. Got to the landing place he seen marks and the flag hang low. Evedently the woman died a little while ago. They told him it was his wife and he fell in sorrow. He took off his best garments and took some coals and mashed them with grease and blackened his face down to the collar bone, showing deep sorrow for his young wife and child. He went to the grave. There he began to dig the sand with his hand. After he dug quite deep there he sat for four days waving his hand in the air and [making] signs of sorrow, fasting not eating nor drinking. Every midnight the oldest girl would bring him meat but he would refuse. The third night she quit. She would not take any thing to him. Then the father of the dead wife came to him asking him if he is yet alive. "If so, you come." Then he turns to him, made a sign [that meant] "I will come before noon."

The morning of the fourth day one of the head man went and seen him, told him to come. Then he made sign to him to bring the drum and men to sing and war dance. They came for him. He claims half of his life was gone. He got up and walked to wards those lodges. He went in to his father in law's lodge and set down [on] the side where his wife use to stay. His mother in law gave him some thing to eat. He eat a little and went to sleep and slept for two days. After two days he got up and looked over his things that he brought over for his wife. At that time the Indians made their blankets with fur, quite valuable, and carrieboo [caribou] skins. He gave it all to his father in law and told him he did not want any thing himself. The old man and the woman liked him but the oldest girl had a trap for him if he did not marry her.

After ten days or so the old man took his oldest daughter and place her to his side. He did not speak to her for a long time. He showed signs he did not want her. She told her sister that "he did not care for me. Now we will soon fix him." The youngest told her sister not to kill him, but the elder sister insist on her sister to help her to kill him. Then the youngest consented to help her sister. "You are going to kill him. I will help you to do that." The oldest girl kept insisting upon her sister to help to kill the young man. Now next is to make up a plan what way they must do it to get away with him. The youngest of these girls name was *wa se gi she go kue.* The interpretation of her name is very bright day light woman. The oldest of the sister, her name is *nin go io.* She was very long at her sister to get her consent to destroy the young mans life. It was great hesitation in her part. She said "Let him live with us. May be he will take a notion to take one of us after a while."

The oldest girl said "If I thought we could bring him to time by let[ting] him live with us I would soon wait and see if he would, but you say sister he make take one of us. But I want you to know I want him to take me. If he does not take me he shall not live." The youngest says to her sister "It is about time for us to take a trip to gather rushes for to make mats and other things. Say nothing to him about it and when we are ready to go I will try [ask] him to go with us and if he goes with us I want you to promise not to kill him because he is the second brave and not been to fight. But you know if our second brave knew we killed him they may not like it. You know sister, he has all the appearance of a good warrior and when I hear other young men speak about him they all speak well of him there to our village."

The oldest says "I want him to be my husband or else he cant live."

After quite a number of days *wa se gi she go kue,* the youngest of the girls, began to think it was impossible to prevent her sister from killing the young warrior. She told her she would help her to get away with him. "I know you can never do it alone. He is ours anyway untill the mourning year is up. We shall not tell even our pa nor ma because they may prevent us. We always showed good will to ward him, and done all we could for him and you treated him like your husband and he will not except [accept] of you. I say kill him."

(From what I can learn from the story from the Indians, they seem to think they are justified to kill one an other for such cause. Those two girls seem to think if he did not come their youngest sister would not have died. When any one of the Indians is old enough to have a daughter or daughters to be married, of course the oldest [is] first. Very seldom the youngest will be the first to be married. When the young man first came they gave him a name. *O mash ke go.* When the old man took one of the girls and gave it to *O mash ke go* he seem to have a right to refuse because the mourning season is not over with him, so their is not any blemish on his part from the old folks. But according to custom, he not excepting the oldest girl for his wife when she came to him seem to be very offensive to the girl. Seem the whole nation would look up on her as such scornful way and shame. She could not bear it without revenge because he would not marry her.)

Soon after she got her sister to get him out a little ways from the camp. He of course never mistrust what they were after. He went with her a ways. The oldest followed them. The two girls made up a plan about what to do with him. The oldest says "I am strong enough to hold him and you strike him on his head untill he falls to the ground. He is the cause of the death of our youngest sister. It is right for us to kill him. Besides he dont want neither one of us. So you see he is no use to us."

The youngest hesitate, but [it was] no use. They must kill him. When they got him a little [to] one side of the camp they told him to sit down on this log with her. [At] the same time [she] was ready to clench him. She was very strong for a woman. Soon she held on to him to get her death hold of him. He would not get away from her. The youngest [was] striking him with a club. They soon got away with him. They left him dead on the ground to get up no more.

"Now we will rest in our minds like our youngest sister that is dead and buried. He will soon be with her now. He is not far behind her. Our sister shall be glad to see him come. We shall bring him near her and put some of those nice things he brought for her. And we shall put this nice robe for him that is made of nice fur and we will wash his face nice and clean. The medicen man shall paint his face in our style and the men shall bury him. We shall have them to sing war songs for him and they shall hyights [hoist] the death flag up to the top. And we ourselfs sister shall both mourn for him [so] there may be no blemish on us. We must show sorrow for him before our men and when our medicine man is ready to bury him, he shall require me to sing for him so he may be remembered by our tribe. If I cant sing for him what may be the conciquance for me I dont know. I shall live single all my life time unless his brother comes over after me and I cannot refuse him if he comes and wants me for his wife. I got to go with him when ever his mind is made up to take me. What the concequence will be for me I do not know."

She insisted upon her sister to help her to make a song for him. When she be required to do so, they had but a short time to make up a song for him before they bury him so that he may be remembered by the tribe. When they were ready to bury him they called up the two girls to sing for him. The oldest sang for the dead young man who they killed for their sister so she might not get lonesome in going to the far world. The Indian do believe when any of them dies, goes into the far world, believing also it is a better world than this world is.

The name of the oldest girl is *nin go iou*. In Indian language is called *Nin go ious* song, which shall be remembered as long as the chippewa nations lives.

*Nin go iou o na ga mon ue ni ban i dog. Ke ni wa wa sa bua ie suad. I ma ua gi di big ki ji ga ming.*
*Gu ie tchi ua si de nig in a ji man. Ima ua gi di big ki chi ga ming.*
*Gaie gebigosh kan iw nouaia. Ima ua gi di big ki tchi ga ming.*
*A shi gwa gi ki shi ta ni ma jad. A ni ke ka mi gong. E shad mi na ua ui ka ji wa ba ma si uind a nsa a king mi e ta negadang o shi bi i gan oma a king.*

I will now give the interpretation of *ningoius* song, what she made up for the man who she killed.

We do not see his shining paddle upon the surface of the sea. Neither do we see the shining of his canoe upon the surface of the sea. And do not break the air upon the surface of the sea but ready to go in the far world never to be seen again upon the surface of the sea neither to break the air upon the face of the earth, but to leave a mark upon the face of the earth in where we live.

(The Indians who lived on the borders of Lake Superior on the south side did not [get] communication from the northern Indian. They did not live near the lake shore because away from the lake they had nice large lakes. From three to five days from Lake Superior right direct north there are Chippewas. They speak our langauge. The Chippewas on the south side of the lake, they call them Swamp Indians. We understand years ago quite lot of them went from here to go and live with them over there and they did not like it because it was swampy and wet and they came back and would not stay with them and call them Swamp Indians ever since. The word *o maski go* is Swamp Indian. The Swamp Indians talks little different from what we do in some things.)

Now about *nin go iou*. She lived with her parents 2 years. A young man came after to marry her. She could not refuse because he was a brother to one she killed. He came right to her father's lodge and she was there of course. He showed dangers weapons. She did not know what the consiquence would be for her. He told the father "I am going to the east end of Lake Superior where my mother's two brothers are. I am to stay one year with them. I want *Nin go iou* for my wife. My brother has refuse her but I can take her. If I had been here my brother would have handed her to me of course. Now that I am here I will take her."

The father took her and gave her to him. "She is yours if you wish." She then took her mourning knot off her hair and paint her face good with the sign of joy.

"And sing to me the same as you did to my brother when he was buried, that I might be good to you."

After she was fixed, he came in [and] blackened his face but light, showing not very deep sorrow yet. This gave *nin go iou* joy. When he would mourn deep for his brother, he would show angry. "I am only going to stay three days and I am going where I said I was. *Nin go iou* can get ready." But he did not take any thing from her. She did not understand this. She was afraid of him when he refused everything from her. She know she had not long to live with him.

The third day in the morning they got in the canoe for the south east end of Lake Superior, way down to his Uncles. When they had traveled a day and half they came to a place called Crow Rock, *gagagiuabikong*. That's a rock that stands out of the water. The height is six fathoms, stands some ways from the main shore. The bank there is all rock for 2 miles and that is six miles south of where Bay Field is now. The rock stands there today. When *ningoiou* and her husband got to this rock he said to her "Here we will stop." *Ningoiou* says why to her husband.

"I want you to go up and fix a place for me up there. I got to fast four days."

He got a cord out of his sack, all of 12 fathoms long, and got a bow and arrow purpose to shoot the rope over on a tree purpose to higst her to the top of the rock. They were a few little trees on top of this rock. How ever the husband got her up here. After he got her up there he says to her "Do you remember the song you made up for my brother after you killed him. You shall now have a chance to sing it all you a mind to." He pulled the rope down and shoved the canoe away and he went a little ways off and talked with her about his brother.

"You killed my [brother]. You being a woman of course it would not look right for me to kill you. According to my dream, if you can get down without getting hurt you might live and go home by land." It was very high and very deep and was ruff, so he told her good by. "Tell my brother its me that sends you there." Off he went down the lower end of Lake Superior. This was the last *Ningoiou* was ever heard of. He came and got her just to punish her. He had it in his mind she killed [his] brother unjustly.

*Profile Rock, Apostle Islands*

*Ningoiou* was the second girl that was left on this high rock. A few years before my Uncle came up to Lapointe one girl was left on this high rock. She was left there through jealousy by a young man who was about to marry her. While he was courting her some how or other he got jealous of her. He insisted on her to go with him to this place to get some eagles eggs and to try the new canoe. She finally consented to go with him. When they got to the place, he told her "Do you know what I am going to have you do for me."

She told him "No. What is it."

He says to her "I brought my bow and arrows. You go up this rock and after you get up you make noise. The eagle will come and I want to shoot them. I like the male eagle for its feathers. I want to kill him if I can."

She went up for him with the aid of the rope they had. He would throw it over the trees to enable her to go up to the top. After she got to the top he pulled all the rope down. He told her not to make any noise for a while. At the same time he was shoving his canoe away from the rock. He went some ways off and he told her "If you can come down and swim a cross the lake and get home that way you might live. But you cant get home through me. I am going to leave you right where you are to die. I am going to the north shore of Lake Superior to get me a wife and I am going to live there. You shall die."

Away he went out of sight to wards the North with his new canoe. The girl who was left there on the rock, her name was *ne ga ua ji kue.* That means Sand Mountain Woman. When she seen he went out of her sight she began to think he meant what he said. He went North ward. She was sure he was not going home. She could not rest. She began to cry very loud but no one heard her but the eagle that flew over the top of the trees. When evening came no one was in site to save her. When dark she was almost exhausted. She went to sleep. Morning came. No one in site but the eagles. She began to cry very hard, but no one to hear her but the eagles. When she stoped crying she thought over her dream about the time she entered woman hood from girl.[93] She dreamed her second man came to her. She said to herself "It can not be these eagles I dream. It was a man I am sure. I hope he will come. My first man is gone, left me to die up on a rock. No one knows but the eagles."

The evening came on the second day. "I see no one but the eagles." Dark came. She slept, resting up on what she dreamt, but how she was thinking no one knows. But she slept. Morning came of the third day. She sat up hardly alive. She was so thirsty she thought if her second man does not come soon she'l die. She rest on thinking he might come before she dies, from her dream. She thought if he would come to day she would get saved her.

On the third day in the morning her second man got lonesome. He seen he was left. He took his new canoe to take a trip a cross to the main land which was about six miles cross from the island where their camping ground was. On the way he thought he would go around to see the eagles. He made a bee line for that place. There was no sea to bother him. It was very calm. He made head way fast toward Crow Rock. He had no idea what he was going to find there.

Poor *ne ga ua ji kua*. She looked. She thought she could see a loon. In a very little while, she could tell that was a canoe coming to wards the rock where she was. Oh, how glad she was. Soon she seen one person in the canoe. It was a man sure. He comes here to fast. He was close when she got up [and] he seen her. He spoke. "Who are you. What are you doing up there. That's no place for a woman up on this rock where men comes to fast."

She motion she could not speak loud at all. He understood her to say she is most dead but he had no rope to help her down to the canoe. He told her he could after he goes to the main shore to get some bass wood bark to help her down. He had to go a mile and half after the bass wood bark to use as a rope to throw it up to her to let herself down to the canoe. The young man of course did not lose any time for fear she might die before he got back to the place. He wanted to save her. He soon got back and first he shot up a small string of bass wood bark to reach her and tied a big string strong enough to hold her. She came down into the canoe all safe and drink some water with some sugar in it and eat little crushed rice and dried meat mixed. She soon revived. She began to talking with him. She told him how she came to be left there. She says "He will never come back here again. He is gone for good. He expect I shall die there but you came and saved me. I am yours now if you wish. I did refuse you when you asked me to marry you on account of him. He is now gone. I am now yours if you want me."

"Well" he says "we are all most home now. I will give you three days to make up a song for me. You know this is quite remarkable thing for both of us. You make up a song for me and you will sing it before all that it may be known and remembered by our nation."

On the third [day] he told his parents to cook a lot. That this afternoon *ne ga ua ji kua* was going to give a song for me after they all eat. *Ne ga ua ji kue* began to sing to the young man of course. She had three days to do it in, that is to make up the song.

*Mang go dog nin di nen dam ima ua gi di big ba na go sid go uen gish uin mi iaw ge sa gi ag. Api be ka ka ba mag go uen sa gish uin mi aw ge sa gi ag ba na gui sid ua gi di big ima anwating. Kauingoningi inendasi awgebi i shad im wagidibing anwating meeta nendauenimag ge bi na gue sid inaa uagidibing anwating a shi gwa be sho baiasas ni ni si da ui na wa a ua ge sa gi ag ima uagitibi.*

I will now give the interpretation [of] words used in *negauajikue's* song. First *mang go dog nindinenclam.* When I first seen a floating spot on the smooth of the sea I thought it was a loon in site. But no it was he who I shall love. When near enough so I could tell it is he who I shall [love] that came over the smooth sea. Did I think he would come. Why no [I] never thought. But it was him that come over the smooth sea to save me. First I thought in my weak mind who could that be. When near enough it was he who I shall love that come over the smooth sea.

As near as I can find out this song was kept on a piece of bark [and passed] from hand to hand even to my days. When I was a girl I use to hear part of this song. The Indian girls use to try to sing it but I never know how it was originated untill I was asked from a friend to write a little about the Indians and a little history of my life of course. Not long ago since I seen my friend who caused me to write a little in this line. I not being thoroughly educated it was quite hard for me even to do what I did. What I mean is, if I had good education I would been more able to write up matters in better shape. And the english language not being my native language. There is one blessing for me. I could spell quite good. That is what my teacher said when I was to school in my young days. That is one thing why I undertook to do some of this writing about the Indian, there lives and habbits and their peculiars ways. Of course I got along quite well with the aid of my husband.

Many more things about Indians a person can write, that is wars and so on, what I have heard and what my husband knows, even [about] the sioux Indians what his father told him about the big battle in Hudson between chippewas and sioux there. About one hundred and fifty chippewas was killed. This was in 1837 right after the timber sale in St Peter. I cannot say much about this. My husband say he is getting quite well. He is going to write a little history about the Indians himself.

I of course will say some thing about the oldest person I know. That was an Indian woman. She died at Lapointe to my knowledge. I dont hardly remember of even seeing her but my sister who is living seen her very often. She use to go from home to go and see her. Quite many years before she died her children kept her in a box to keep her from danger. She would set up and lay down and sleep is all she done for five years before she died, eat but very little. She was baptized long before she died. As near as I can find out, she died in 1842 and she was one hundred and eighty three years old when she died. It was to Lapointe where she died and was buried.

Lapointe is what I call my old home. I am now living [in] what [is called] the Indians garden. I of course have told before now where I have been living before I came here. It is up to Spider Lake or near the headwaters of Iron River where there is quite a town now. The latter part of June my friend who I speak of came up from chicago, up to Island Lake where they take an immense pleasure. That is such as fishing and boating. Of course every time they came from chicago here they would [ask if] some of us would go up and see them when we lived at Spider Lake.

The fall of 1895 we moved from Spider Lake to Odanah, that is to the Indian village where I am living now. A person would naturley think it would be very pleasant to live with my people, but when I first came here I kept thinking of my old homestead to Spider Lake, the wild game we used to have. Still in all when I see my husband quite happy and my boys, I am quite satisfied to be where I am with some of my old acquaintances. Twenty years ago, in speaking of the Indians in Bad River reservation where I am living now, thirty years ago there was about two out of every ten could speak english but now three fourths of them can speak english. That makes [it] quite pleasant for us. Still in all when I see there complection I feel like using my native language to talk with them.

I have nothing more to write. I might say I have almost consummate the history of my life, that is what I know to be true in speaking of the Indians in this locality. I say they are pretty well civilized. There is some here yet who follow the old style of dancing and pow wow and their medicine dance and other old habbits. The Indians in this vicinity is selling their timber off their allotments. This enables them to build quite good homes. Not one family lives in a wigiwam like they use to. There is a big saw mill here where they can buy lumber. Some of them has quite large fields, raise quite a large amount of vegetables which they sell to the whites. And their hunting and fishing and wild fruits in the summer and wild rice, what they call *ka ka gan* rice beds and it is a great place for hunting ducks in the spring and in the fall. Well, I believe this is the end of my story.

The end.

# ADDITIONAL LETTERS

*Odanah*
*Aug. 23, 1897*

*My dear Mrs. Gray*

As I was alone this afternoon I thought I would drop a few words to you. We are all quite well at present, hoping you are enjoying the same blessing. I feel lonesome for Island Lake when I read the Camp-fire Musings. If we hadn't had death in the house I should have come again, and besides Mrs Bousky was very sick at the time. She is a little better. If Mr Wilson hadn't take her just at that time she would have been incurable, but she is much better now. Oh Mrs Gray it is hard to lose a grown-up child. All my boys are here except Georgie. He is up to Brule. Oh Mrs Gray I wish you could come down this way when you go back. How we would like to see you. I suppose Gordon has a nice garden. Our poor garden drowned out twice so we have nothing. It almost just makes me sick to see other gardens and we used to have so plenty at Spider Lake. My sister from Michigan are living here at Odanah. We have nice side walks here so it makes it nice. So good-bye hoping to hear from you I remain as ever your friend.

*Our love to all*
*Mrs. John Morrison*

*Odanah, July 2 1907*

*My Dear Mrs. Gray*

I received your most kind and truly welcome letter and wich we was very glad to hear from you. I have often thought to write but did not know where to write to because Gordon told me last fall that he did not know where you was. He heard that you had left your place, but did not know when you went. Gordon told me that Cyrus and Harold was to Island Lake last fall and he invited me and my husband after they had gone, but we dint go. We was to Iron River a little while, but John could not hunt. He had rheumitism in his leg. But he could go out a little while and kill some rabbits. John is quite well. He is able to do a little gardening for ourselfs. It is quite nice here in Odanah, only in the spring it overflows and makes it very unpleasant. It over flowed twice this spring. I just wished myself back to Spider Lake where it don't over flow. Year ago I and Eunice was over there looking over the old place. And now somebody burnt the old house. I have not been since the house is burnt.

Well now about my children. They are all here in Odanah by me except Tommy. He is in Virginia, Minnesota. He is there at his trade barbering. Ben is at home. Ben and Charley keeps a clothing store and George keeps a confectionary store. Dan, he is farming. Dan has 3 children. Charley has 2, and George has 4. First Dan and Ben had a hotel and they got tired of it and Dan bought out Ben and now Dan rents it out. Yes Mrs. Bousky is living yet and that is all. She is helpless. She had a stroke this winter and she never got over it. For a while she could not speak, but the last time I went to see her she could talk quite plain. She is down to her brothers. I never could have taken care of her. I am troubled with my feet a great deal if I stand on them much. Oh Mrs Gray I wish you could come and see us. We would do every thing to please you.

I forgot [to tell you] Eunice has a nice house. She has a little girl 2 years old. Eunice is very kind to me. We are going to have a camp meeting here in Odanah this summer. It will commence the 3 day of August, just about one mile from Odanah going towards Ashland.

Our best regards to you from your loving friend

*Eliza Morrison*

PS I hope I will hear from you again.

*"Democracy": Evening Gathering, Island Lake, 1898*

*Front row: Dorothy Gray, Ralph Purcell*
*Second row: William Gray Purcell, William Cunningham Gray, Margarette Bousky, Catherine Gray, C. A. Purcell*
*Third row: Jonathon Gray, unidentified, Annie Zeigler, Eliza Morrison*
*Top row: Albert Muther, Willie Gray, Gordon Young*

# INTERPRETATION
## ELIZA MORRISON'S JOURNEYS

*Those who hold the power tell the stories.*
*Plato*

WHEN A VOYAGEUR IN THE FUR TRADE became a brigade leader, the head man of a flotilla of canots du maitre, the thirty-six-foot birch bark canoes paddled by eight men that could carry more than seven tons of cargo between Montreal or Quebec and the *pays d'en haut* or "upper country" of the western Great Lakes, he was given a raven's feather to wear in his hat. Indians wore eagle feathers to celebrate achievement, but the French or mixed-race voyageurs, despite their daring journeys over lakes and rivers, could aspire to no such accolade. For them it was the raven with his unmusical croak and his canny way of insinuating himself into human culture, as if he were half bird and half human in his mischievous, observant ways. Like red and white sashes, multilingual *patois*, and mixed-race families, using ravens' feathers as a mark of leadership was the creation of a unique culture that was not Indian or white but new: a North American métis one that could range freely over thousands of miles of country and engage with all the other, more traditional cultures found there. The raven's feather signified not just competence and bravery, but the respect that adaptability is accorded. It was not sacred, as eagle feathers could be to Indians, but instead it marked a pragmatic ability to figure out what was

wise and logical even when, in a new place with a new culture, there were few traditions and there was little guidance.

Ravens still come to the old Protestant cemetery at La Pointe, living in the pines high above the floor of the forest the burying ground has become, and their feathers float down on the cracked and broken tombstones that remain. They drift on the marker of Frances Wabegiah Morrin, and in the cold rain of a late October afternoon, the ravens' cries are a distorted echo of the voyageur songs Frances would have heard nearly all her life. To a mixed-race child of the fur trade, like her daughter after her, a raven's feather would have been an instantly recognizable emblem. Wabegiah's daughter, Eliza Morrison, never makes clear whether she thinks of herself as Indian or white, or if she felt the need to choose. Asked for a racial definition, she would have described herself as both, and it was a mixed-race community down the path from the cemetery into which she had been born and where she had grown up. People she knew were Indian or white or both and there were angels and devils in all three races. Skin color was pragmatic, useful for predicting which language one needed to speak to someone, but not for defining one's moral stature or intelligence. Race, ethnicity, and culture, as Mrs. Morrison demonstrates, are not eternal characteristics, but historically determined social constructions—a network of influences and choices—and as history changes, so do they.[94]

Eliza Morrison had been enrolled as a "mixed-blood" as a child under the provisions of the 1837 treaty that acknowledged the métis reality of Old Northwest and guaranteed payments to mixed-race peoples as well as to Indians as a gesture of devotion and respect for the new world the fur trade had created. As *A Little History of My Forest Life* shows, the Morrisons spoke Chippewa and English fluently, they had white and Indian friends, lived in white and Indian communities, and spent their lives crossing back and forth across the shifting borders of race and culture in a place and a time where many others did the same thing. In part this was a result of having grown up in the village of La Pointe on Madeline Island which, like Mackinac Island, another fur company headquarters further east, was for many decades in the eighteenth century and the beginning of the nineteenth a financially comfortable town where the important differences were between Catholic and Protestant, not Indian and white, since nearly everyone was mixed ancestry. The major cultural concerns, which Mrs. Morrison dwells upon as well, were how moral one's behavior was, whether or not one was a Christian who lived in town or a traditional who lived in the woods, and if converted to which church one belonged. It was the legacy of

this old, accommodating, métis world of the Great Lakes that allowed people to be Indian or white or métis at the same time in the same place, depending on which was necessary to qualify for treaty payments, or homestead land, or take up an allotment on a reservation. They could, like Mrs. Morrison, note their mastery of white customs and in nearly the same breath praise their foremothers as being "pure Chippewa" who could achieve feats of strength and endurance European or North American white women would never contemplate, much less accomplish.

Can it really have been as easy as she makes it seem? Was negotiating between racial and cultural identities as simple a matter as her husband taking off the red and white sash identifying him as mixed-race that he wore when with the Indians and putting on suspenders to meet his in-laws to demonstrate he was acculturated enough in progressive white ways to wear "citizen clothes"? Did the Morrisons' ability to move easily in both Indian and white cultures complicate their lives, or did it give them more opportunities than they otherwise would have had? Or both? What did it mean to have two, or multiple, racial and cultural identities, and what happened to those identities as the nineteenth century came to a close and Indian and métis peoples were coerced or forced to choose between taking up allotments on a reservation or remaining in white society? When a métis woman living in frontier America picked up her pen to write her autobiography, historically a white European form of narration that frequently concentrates on self-analysis and interiority, how would she recreate the form she had inherited? Would she write a métis autobiography and, if so, what might that be like?

THERE ARE CLUES IN ANY NARRATIVE that suggest how it might be interpreted, beginning with how much time a writer spends on particular subjects and with what emphasis. *A Little History of My Forest Life* devotes a surprising amount of attention to journeys and so recalls the annual hunting and gathering round of the Chippewa to the sugarbush and fishing grounds on Bad River in spring, to the berrying places on the Apostle Islands or near present-day Iron River in summer, to the wild ricing beds on the Kakagan River in fall, and to La Pointe to fish or to the interior woods to hunt in winter.

The cyclic journeys of traditional Indian seasonal movement to gather food are reflected in the circular pattern Mrs. Morrison develops as she writes, her stories progressing like traditional, oral, Indian narratives that can pause mid-event to loop back on themselves to add more detail or to tell another story to make a slightly different point, then resume to add another layer of meaning. She is leisurely and discursive, writing as if simply putting events down as they occurred to her without any real plan of organization save that which mimics the yearly round practiced by native peoples for centuries. She writes about the Indians,

then pauses to add to her narrative of the Morrisons' personal lives, then picks up, like a waiting thread strung with beads, more stories about Indians. She is gossipy and talkative, replicating conversations directly, inserting little jokes on the people she describes and, when she is baffled by a custom of either whites or Indians, giving the verbal equivalent of a shrug. She begins her autobiography with the story of her marriage and, making another circle, ends it with a traditional tale about the rescue and marriage of young girl who was as isolated on a rock as the young Eliza may have felt at La Pointe before she married John. She calls up her memories of the stories of the lengthy journeys fur traders made between fur trade posts and Indian camps, between La Pointe and St. Louis, between the native world that produced furs and the white world that consumed them, recalling into the present moment the vanished fur-trading world of her childhood. She writes of her own journeys back and forth to her various homes by foot, fishing boat, canoe, dog team, steamboat, horse-drawn wagon, and finally, to her great delight, by train.

But to write of journeys is also to acknowledge they will end. *A Little History of My Forest Life*, by concentrating on journeys, hints at the larger, and less positive, circle the Chippewa made beginning in the 1600s, from La Pointe to the Sault and back again in an ever-narrowing hoop until they were confined at last on a few small reservations by 1900. Early in her narrative Mrs. Morrison writes of the Indians' doomed journey to Fond du Lac in 1850 that spelled the demise of traditional life-ways, since it led to the 1854 treaty which created reservations. At the end, as if closing the circle, it is on a reservation where she finishes her story.

Later, in one of her last letters to Kitty Gray she notes that there are sidewalks in Odanah "so it makes it nice." But is the cold confinement of a sidewalk, however easy and safe, a positive change from her grandmother's freedom to make unlimited canoe journeys of hundreds of miles from the St. Croix River country to the Sault and back again to La Pointe, even if the journey began in a war zone? Especially since Mrs. Morrison makes clear her life in La Pointe was hardly as exciting as her grandmother's had been decades earlier. When she writes of the family's years there in the 1870s, she seems at a loss for a subject: "This part of my life was pretty quiet. I hardly know what to write. We lived at the old home from 1869 to 1878. I did not go anywhere myself any distance, only when I could get my husband to take us somewhere with the boat. This would be in summertime when the berries would be ripe." In other words, if she hasn't been anywhere on a journey, there's no story, although by this time she's borne six children, buried two, and moved repeatedly. But if she wasn't traveling, it wasn't interesting, so she described other people's journeys instead, and in so doing gave them voices they would not otherwise have had. She became not only a ghost writer for the living, like her husband and Mrs. Bousky, but also a writer of ghosts, weaving them into her story along with the stories they had once told her.

To braid together voices and literary traditions from two cultures as Mrs. Morrison does, combining Indian stories, American experience, métis culture, and European-American autobiography to make her chronicle, creates a new kind of literature known as *métissage*. Put simply, this is a cultural creation, such as a narrative, that is a mixture of artistic traditions, much as a métis person is a mixture of races. For Mrs. Morrison to write in English of her mixed-race life while using the metaphor of a traditional Indian yearly round to give order to her narrative is métissage. Métissage texts can be complicated because they are written by people of mixed race; if the dominant culture is not, or if the writer is angry because of acts of colonialism, slavery, or uncompensated appropriation of land or resources but is afraid to express that anger openly, the métissage narrative may contain coded attacks or rebellious subtexts that must be decoded by the reader. If the writer creates in a language not used at home, the prose can seem ragged or incorrect. Rituals and life-ways might be misunderstood by readers unfamiliar with the writer's world. The form may be seen as "broken" or "flawed" by readers who don't understand how texts that braid together the writer's different worlds conform to no traditional patterns and, in fact, frequently create new ones. Often, the writing can be marginalized, then ignored and forgotten.[95]

Although métis writers from certain areas of the world, such as the Caribbean, have struggled to make themselves heard on their own terms, particularly during the past century, the context from which Mrs. Morrison wrote was quite different. In the 1890s the United States had not yet entered the Progressive Era with its focus on racial purity, so the decades of intense racialism between World War I and the 1960s were still to come. More significantly, for many generations in the eighteenth and early nineteenth centuries, métis people had been the dominant culture in the Great Lakes region. They were no longer, and Mrs. Morrison acknowledges race as a category that affects her in any number of ways, but she is not confrontational and, more revealingly, she writes with a confidence born of generations of people who had controlled their own destinies.[96]

Before the eighteenth century, Great Lakes Indian peoples and Europeans had forged a unique "middle ground" of negotiation and compromise because neither culture was strong enough to impose its will on the other. Race or social status gave little advantage; in order to survive, prosper, and do business, everyone had to accept everyone else's cultural premises. This middle ground of acceptance and respect, and the mixed-race families that came from it, endured until the Americans took control after 1815. But even into the 1830s and 1840s, whites were still a minority in the western Lake Superior region, English was useful but not always necessary, and the only enthnicity that mattered was to which tribe of Indians one was related or aligned because, as several of the stories

Mrs. Morrison weaves into her narrative make clear, being a Chippewa in Dakota territory was dangerous, if not deadly. That the self-confidence born of a proud métis history had not been destroyed by racism at the time she wrote is everywhere evident in her narrative, a project that was her idea, and that she refused to turn into a detailed ethnography to please her audience.

More than simply autobiography, *A Little History of My Forest Life* is a type of métissage described as autoethnography. Autobiography has been defined as auto *(self)*—bio *(life)*—graphy *(writing)*. Auto-ethno-graphy substitutes ethno *(culture)* for an individual life. Traditional autobiography begins with the writer's childhood and proceeds through introspective self-examination toward a climax of belief, often of faith, and a changed self. Clearly, this is not how Mrs. Morrison organized *A Little History of My Forest Life*. Autoethnography not only tells one writer's life, but employs a type of memory that is archaic as well as modern, a cultural memory that interweaves the events of an individual life with the recollections of a culture.[97] This adds another layer of complexity onto the already complex form of autobiography, since mixed-race writers like Mrs. Morrison who are creating métis autobiography or autoethnography are not only writing about themselves, but about three cultures and the interface between those cultures. Since it becomes impossible for them to be inclusive, and they may not be objective about personal memories, the crucial question becomes what events and recollections does the writer relate, and what do those choices tell us about the writer and the time in which she wrote?

Like many oral Indian narratives told to white ethnographers, some of the important details are frequently the details Mrs. Morrison does not give. Readers are not told about the deaths of two children, and she avoids entirely mentioning the birth of one, a daughter who is stillborn or dies in childhood. She does not speak of the La Pointe Treaty of 1854 creating reservations that changed Indian lives forever when she was seventeen, even though it took place nearly on her doorstep and would eventually change her life as well. She never clearly explains Midéwiwin ceremonies, Indian hunting charms, or anything else of traditional spirituality or ceremony except some accounts of marriage and mourning rituals, by then largely unobserved, and these come from Mrs. Bousky. Mrs. Morrison professes to know nothing about any of these things which, even though she is an acculturated métis, is difficult to believe because she grew up surrounded by Indian culture with many Indian relatives. She evades sensitive issues by saying her husband will help her, or will write himself, but while John may be wemitigoshianamin, or Catholic, he respected native religious practices enough to refuse to be co-opted by curious Protestants from the city. Ethnographers describe this sort of reaction as "resistance," that is the quiet refusal of ethnic informants to share important information with an outsider even while appearing to cooperate by providing less important knowledge.

Therefore, although Mrs. Morrison's narrative appears to spend a good deal of time writing about Indians and Indian lifeways, and in its form incorporates the traditional seasonal round even as she relates a linear history, she tells us little beyond what an astute observer living in the region could have seen. She alludes early on to the catastrophic events at Sandy Lake, but she does not dwell on them, either because she is distancing herself from traditional Indian culture, or from public life as a white woman writer might, or because she is employing a traditional Indian method of narration where one word or image stands for an entire chain of associations that only others with knowledge of Indian culture will understand. Readers cannot know and the effect is to make her seem simultaneously apolitical and political, retiring and assertive, while making a coded reference she knew her readers might not comprehend but which she felt, because of its significance, must be included in any history that touched on those years.

Her intentions are additionally complicated because she was writing to her summer employers, urban intellectuals who had, apparently, requested information about native peoples. The Grays may have been engaged in a mild bit of what is described today as "salvage ethnology," that is preserving the art and customs of a traditional people who were, at the end of the nineteenth century, popularly considered to be "doomed to extinction." Most of the great collections of traditional American

Indian myths and tales now available were collected by scholars doing just such work with people they assumed would soon either be dead or assimilated into white culture. When the Grays hired Eliza Morrison and Margarette Bousky as summer help and then discovered the rich trove of tales and experiences they brought with them, the Grays would have felt it their duty to try to preserve what they could, whether or not they ever intended to make any use of it. That Eliza could write well, as evidenced by her letters to Catherine Gray, simply made it easier.

Mrs. Morrison was not a paid informant, as were many Indians who talked with ethnologists, but the links between herself, the Grays, and *A Little History of My Forest Life* are tangled nonetheless. According to the Gray's grandson, William Gray Purcell, she wrote as repayment for the barrels of clothing and food the Grays sent to the Morrisons in winter. Purcell describes them as poor, as does Eliza in a letter to Mrs. Gray. This is not surprising, since they had eight children and, during the mid-1890s, the United States was suffering through a profound depression. For those who were not as privileged as the Grays and their friends, the years when Eliza wrote were a time of privation.

Despite this, why would Mrs. Morrison reciprocate the Gray's kindnesses with a narrative? Especially since, according to Purcell, she was an accomplished craftsman. "She made baskets of birch bark for picking berries; she also used birch bark to make large and small shallow bowls called

muckuks and tall pails with a small round top opening and broad square bottom called kaso; these could not easily tip over when being filled. And of course there were toy birch bark canoes for us children, in addition to gloves for Grandmother Gray who liked going fishing. Many of the objects Mrs. Morrison made were decorated with beads or dyed porcupine quills, and were painted with colors she extracted from roots and berries. She knew all the lore of the woods, what every plant was good for, and how to tan all kinds of hides—with hair on for furs, without hair for shirts and shoes."[98] Indeed, Purcell related that every spring the Grays bought a bushel of moccasins from the Morrisons for the summer and paid them "top dollar," handwork he so loved he kept one moccasin his entire life. Why then wouldn't the Morrisons have repaid the Gray's gifts with handwork?

*Moccasin made for William Gary Purcell by Eliza Morrison*

Because nearly everything the Morrisons might have given the Grays could have been also turned into cash, except her story. And cash money, as she says at one point, was something they seldom had. She knew the Grays were interested in information about the Indians since they had been listening to her stories around the campfire for years; she felt obligated to repay them for the gifts they had sent, and writing about the Indians was the only way she could reciprocate without foregoing income. Her predicament is an example of how a gift can introduce an elaborate web of social relations, a symbolic order of class and duty, because there is frequently an expectation of a return.[99] When the gift comes from someone of a different race and class, patronization is difficult to avoid. In this situation, a return gift is imperative to reestablish relations of equality. Historically, this expectation of reciprocal exchange was what enabled the fur trade to function: gifts cemented relationships between trappers and traders while business agreements floundered without them. Thus Eliza Morrison was both free and not-free when she sat down to compose, and that is evident in her text. As her own story keeps enrupting into the information about the Indians, she repeatedly pulls herself back from it to the subject she knew the Grays were interested in and that she felt compelled to relate in repayment for those barrels dropped off the train at Iron River.

Nevertheless, she refuses to silence her own history, and with that decision lies the key to her creation. While she certainly could have written a straight-forward ethnology that concentrated exclusively on the Indians, she chose to create instead a braided text that incorporates autobiography, ethnology, women's stories, homesteading stories—the panoply of life experiences she had had or heard about—ignoring nearly all the boundaries of race, class, and expectation to write a narrative that cannot be easily categorized. Despite its content and organization, it is not Indian. Neither is it white. It is instead métis, and the very fact that she had the courage to begin, to write a long narrative in her second language to send to her urban, educated, comfortably middle-class employers, bespeaks a self-confidence that is cultural as well as individual, springing not only from history, but also from her giftedness as a raconteur and her knowledge that she had a receptive audience.[100] By refusing to memorialize traditional Indian life as a dying culture for white consumption, by focusing on a vital mixed-race life that drew from two traditions, both important, to create a third, Eliza Morrison reclaimed a bit of the middle ground of shared power and endeavor that had characterized the Great Lakes Indian/French fur trade and the métis world she had known as a child where reciprocity established equality and respect.

THE "MOST DEAREST FRIEND," OR THE muse, to whom she wrote, Kitty Gray, was the wife of a prominent Midwestern intellectual, William Cunningham Gray, who occupied a secure position as the editor of the *Interior*, a religious magazine in which he owned a part interest. It was described at the time as the *Harper's Magazine* of the Midwest, although the *Interior* was quite a bit more religiously doctrinaire than its namesake. The other owner was Nellie McCormick, one of the wealthiest widows in the United States, who also owned a half-interest in the Gray's camp in northern Wisconsin so her sons would have a place to go when they came home from Princeton.[101] W. C. Gray and his wife were no ordinary summer tourist folk. Dr. Gray, as he was called, had left a career in journalism that began in 1850 in Ohio and involved several newspapers to take over direction of the *Interior* at the behest of the McCormicks, who had begun a determined campaign to reform Presbyterian Church doctrine and end the feud between northern and southern branches of the church. Cyrus McCormick had spent $100,000 in 1859 to buy and transplant a seminary to Chicago to influence church policy, and the *Interior* was another salvo fired across the pulpits of ministers who didn't agree with him.[102] But Gray had his own agenda as well, and when he wasn't promulgating McCormick's doctrinaire, business-oriented Calvinism of personal responsibility, he was a Romantic, a believer in that cherished nineteenth-century idea that, as Thoreau wrote, "In wildness is the preservation of the world." In other words, Gray was convinced that spending time in the wilderness, in nature, could reform the evil impulses of society.

William Gray wrote the nostalgic editorials he called "Campfire Musings" about the blessings of nature from a perspective hearkening back to the idea of the American wilderness as Eden first proclaimed by William Cullen Bryant, Henry David Thoreau, Ralph Waldo Emerson, and James Fenimore Cooper, earlier nineteenth-century apostles of the benefits of periodic retreats from civilized life.[103] These writers and many others, beginning with Rousseau, believed in the natural superiority of the Indians before white men came because, so the idea went, the Indians were closer to untouched nature, were unsullied by the corruption of materialism, and had led lives of peaceful simplicity and serenity in the "wilderness," although the land was not a wilderness, or even wild, to the Indians who had lived there. The concept of wilderness was an urban invention. The gospel of nature worship had become an ersatz nineteenth-century religion by the time Gray wrote, despite its scant relationship to reality, particularly where the Chippewa and their hundred year's war with the Dakota was concerned.

Much like the beginnings of the national park system in the 1870s and the fashion for elaborate wilderness "camps" and boy scouting that began a few years later, the philosophy of the retreat to nature and the valorizing of the vanishing Indian, what one scholar calls "playing Indian," were reactions to the perceived loss of wilderness, the disenfranchising and destruction of native peoples, burgeoning immigrant populations, massive cultural changes, and unrestrained industrialization: problems that questioned the idea of what it meant to be American and that had no easy answers.[104] In Wisconsin in 1893, Frederick Jackson Turner delivered his thesis that the end of the frontier was at hand and suggested that the landscape of open possibilities that he believed had shaped American character was no longer available, while outside the building where he spoke the region continued the explosive growth that had begun in the 1840s. As Turner lectured, Gray was praising the old-growth forest a few hundred miles north for its ability to uplift civilization because "trees have souls," a rather desperate rhetorical gambit given that even as he wrote in the woods of northern Wisconsin the entire Midwest was being clear-cut to help support an economy that made possible the business of his mentor and thus his newsprint pulpit. His was a pyrrhic gesture of dissent, wafted at the front lines of nineteenth-century Gilded Age industrial capitalism as if he believed that a little gentle contemplation of nature beside a campfire could tame the ruthless economic savagery that had created the blazing industrial hells of Chicago, Detroit, and Cleveland and left great swathes of clear-cut old-growth forests in smoke and ashes so thick Great Lakes steamboat captains couldn't see to navigate.

*Island Lake Camp*

Although Gray does acknowledge in an editorial that "I am the trespasser.... The Chippewa owned these lands before Columbus. Still it is something to reflect that they obtained them by conquest, driving out the agricultural mound-builders, and allowing the land again to go to waste,"[105] he does not appear to realize that the land at Island Lake he memorialized in his "Campfire Musings" columns was never an agricultural paradise (nor would be), and was available for sale to Mrs. McCormick, and so temporary preservation, because the Chippewa had been forced to cede it by businessmen pressuring Congress, not by losing a war. And treaty negotiations in the western Lake Superior region were seldom examples of a dialogue between equal powers. While the Indians may have agreed with Gray that trees had souls, those souls no longer belonged to them but to the United States and the Chippewa were not necessarily US citizens.

The old St. Croix Trail that ran a stone's throw from the Gray campfire had been created by the Indians, partly in response to the diaspora of native peoples displaced into northern Wisconsin by Indian wars provoked by the fur trade and American territorial aggression, and it may have followed a trail first created by other native peoples who had been farming and hunting in Wisconsin for nearly ten thousand years. The landscape Gray praises was hardly "natural" or a "waste" but had been shaped through burning, gardening, domesticating fruit trees into groves, hunting, and gathering for centuries. Gray was privileged to muse about the benefits of nature in his protected spot not because the Chippewa had allowed it to grow up untended, but because the US government and the fur trading companies convinced Indian leaders from various tribes to make the best of a bad situation and take what they could while they could before the land was overrun with settlers, miners, railroad speculators, and lumbermen that the government had no intention of reining in or keeping out. Their land claims extinguished, most of the Indians of the Lake Superior country were packed off to reservations so whites could move in with dynamite, axes, and two-man cross-cut saws to create a true wasteland.

"Extinguishing" Indian land claims is a legal term used in treaty negotiations, but in the context of Gray's wilderness worship the concept of extinguishment takes on a bitterly ironic twist. Gray seemed blissfully unaware that his benign memories of growing up on a homestead above the Miami River on the Ohio frontier were made possible because the Indians' land claims and hearth fires there had been extinguished despite Tecumseh's gifted diplomacy and military leadership, that Gray's childhood happiness among the "noble forests… still standing" depended upon other children's pain and loss. "Were we happy?" he asks innocently. "No family could be more so. Why shouldn't we be?"[106] Forty years later he kindles another fire at Island Lake, one that will be the symbol of his "Campfire Musings" essays, apparently only mildly concerned that only because the property rights of the ancestors of his hired help had been extinguished by another treaty could he write about the ennobling effects of what he called wilderness.

Ennobling for whom? Certainly not for John Morrison and the "lost tribe" of the St. Croix Indians to whom he was related, who had refused to be removed to the Lac Court Oreilles reservation after the 1854 treaty and so lost their tribal rights, lost the possibility of receiving reservation allotments after passage of the Dawes Act in 1887, and lost the support—such as it was—of the US government. Those trees "with the stars glittering in their tangled hair" over which Gray waxed rhapsodic were board feet ripe for conversion to cash by Eastern lumbermen, and the Indians who insisted on living among them in the woods were, in the words of lumber baron and early Wisconsin historian H. C. Folsom, "an intolerable nuisance."[107]

John Morrison had lived with those "nuisance" Indians and, like them and like his métis relatives, he had become adept at coping with changes he could not always control. He farmed at Spider Lake where he could still hunt and trap; he gave up his dreams of a silver fortune to please his wife, and he helped newcomers like the Grays. He became a model of what the government wanted Indians to be: a self-sufficient farmer. When Eliza writes, "My husband says to me, "Now, wife, we've got through with the old Indian style [of] working. Now we will try the white man's style for a while, that is clearing land and planting potatoes, and so forth,'" she is describing not only John's astute adaptability, but also the common practice of a mixed-race person picking and choosing beliefs and practices from both cultures according to the situation. Unlike the white timber cruisers and railroad men John keeps from starvation,

he is capable of earning a living in the old ways or the new.

Today he might be called a post-modern individual, moving between languages and cultures, capable of continuously learning new skills, ranging freely in a global village, but in the nineteenth century there was no global village, only relentless imperialism. Like Eliza, he would have preferred to continue making journeys—she had interrupted his to the Mesabi Mountains to marry her—but the world of the long journeys of his father, and of his own childhood, had become restricted by treaties, immigration, and resource extrac-

*Kitchen at Island Lake Camp*

tion. When he comes back from St. Croix after their marriage, Eliza's father compliments him on being such a great traveler, able to cover miles of woods a day. But the woods were disappearing, and as the years progress, John's journeys become ever more confined until at the last, as Eliza finishes her history with his help, he settles into a house with a small garden in Odanah.

His is another of the voices readers hear through the lilting rhythm of Eliza's stories. Narrators who cannot write themselves, such as her grandmother and Mrs. Bousky, help create a multi-voiced, or métissage, narrative, and Mrs. Morrison's technique of including direct quotations underscores this. But John Morrison was quite capable of writing his own account, and although his wife says that he is planning on writing a bit himself, no narrative survives except quotations attributed to him, and probably edited, in one of the "Campfire Musings" editorials. The exchange that took place between William Gray and John Morrison one evening around the campfire is telling.

According to William Gray Purcell, John Morrison had come to the Gray's camp to make his "annual midsummer visit to see his wife and daughter," and stayed to join the evening campfire. Mrs. Morrison, her daughter Eunice, and Mrs. Bousky lived at the camp all season, cooking, doing laundry, and cleaning for the Grays and their numerous guests from the city. "These girls," Purcell wrote, "had no regular days off, but could plan ahead and take off an afternoon whenever they wished—which was seldom—or a whole day if needed or once in two years perhaps go home for a part week." In short, they were typical nineteenth-century hired help, being paid for doing the same things they would have

done at home and probably glad to get the cash. John Morrison and his sons made do at their farm a few miles away, although several of the sons also worked for the Grays when they were needed, including acting as hunting guides and carpenters for the growing camp compound. To Purcell, "Eliza Morrison was sincere and patient and utterly dependable. Indeed we looked upon her as nearly an indispensable member of our family. . . ."[108] John, meanwhile, had to farm, hunt, fish, garden, tan skins, and take care of his sons, so William Gray relished the opportunity to interview him. This allowed Gray to act as a devil's advocate for popular white views of degraded Indians and then develop a column for the *Interior* that forwarded his own opinions of Indian-white history in the upper lakes.

"This land of yours, then, is really your lost paradise, in which the life of the Indians was happy and good. A person can see that from your own daily life of only a generation ago. The popular descriptions of Indian life were plainly the work of enemies seeking to justify the cruelties and wrongs inflicted on your people by the white men. . . ."

John is thoughtful for a moment before speaking. His wife turns to look at him. Mrs. Boshky [sic] does not move her eyes from the fire.

"Before the white men came, we were men. Our fathers always did what was right and they punished bad men. . . . We were great warriors and we fought for our own a long time. It was not the white men's arms, but their vices which ruined us. . . .

"What makes you think the old times were so much better? You now have good laws, no wars, and the government won't let you go hungry. Isn't this better than the old precarious and dangerous ways of living?"

John Morrison replied, "We did not go hungry. We had more than we wanted. You can see for yourself what we had from what is left after so much destruction. There was no end to the deer, moose, caribou, beaver, lynx, and all the smaller fur animals, and as for the fish, you said there was no fun catching them when you came here, they were too plenty—trout, bass, pike, pickerel, sturgeon, the waters swarmed with them. Then look at our wild rice, our hazel nuts, blueberries, wild plums. And then we had cornfields, and for smoking the kinnikinik. There were buffalo right in these North Woods here, all along just south of Gitchie Gumme, Lake Superior, you know, when my father was a young man. We had no hard work to do. What we did was mainly sport, while it provided us with food and clothing.

"And then we were free. The freest people in the world, with a whole continent in which to enjoy. We are not now what we were. Our people have become drunkards and beggars and cowards. The white man has destroyed us, along with everything else.

"You have among your photographs the picture of a Chippewa grave. That is the grave of the last of the Five Brothers, the great warriors. The Seven Brothers were Tecumseh's best men. They were known all over the Mississippi Valley, and the Five Brothers who came after them were as good. They adopted me when my father died."[109]

*Chippeway Graves at Gordon, Wisconsin, 1894*

How accurately John Morrison was quoted cannot be known since he left no other record. Only one photograph of him survives, taken years later on the reservation, since he was either unavailable or refused to pose for the young Willie Purcell's camera. But despite the cordial relations between the Morrisons and the Grays, despite the Grays relatively enlightened attitude toward Indians, it would not be surprising if the hypocrisy of William Gray's romanticizing about the landscape that was made possible by the Indians' loss left John Morrison skeptical. He had witnessed a traditional way of life vanish under his feet, and he remembered the kindness and compassion of Indian relatives who had adopted him into their family, including their religion, and taught him the skills of hunting that had kept his wife, children, and various whites alive more than once. He chose to retain his Catholicism, and to leave Indian culture to marry and live a métis life until the move to Odanah, but in his firm refusal to share all his knowledge of Chippewa customs for the Gray's consumption in his wife's narrative, he makes an uncompromising point about respect for elders, for tradition, and for a way of life that was being destroyed. John Morrison came from a famous, perhaps venerated, family of Indian leaders and was a descendant of some of the most powerful fur traders working in the western Great Lakes region; William Gray's leadership in a different realm would not have been cause for deference. John, described as quatre-lingual and bi-cultural, would not "translate" Indian customs so they could be appropriated by whites for curiosity or salvage.

Translation is an appropriate metaphor here, since language, like money, is a type of power. The mixed-race fur traders of the eighteenth and nineteenth centuries who spoke (or could "get by") in several languages were invaluable to the fur companies and, if they could read and write a bit, were usually put in charge of posts like La Pointe. The continuing force of Indian languages was being acknowledged even as Mrs. Morrison wrote, since Indian children sent to boarding schools were forbidden from speaking their native languages in order to attempt to force their acculturation into white society.

Language as an instrument of power, and the knowledge of writing that sometimes accompanies it, has particular relevance in *A Little History of My Forest Life*, since Mrs. Morrison wields all the power of a bi-lingual speaker describing her world to a mono-lingual reader whose understanding is limited. Any information Mrs. Morrison chooses not to describe she can withhold by saying her English is inadequate, a patently false claim borne out by her text itself. When she writes that "my English cannot express it," as she attempts to describe her emotions at seeing her husband after a long absence or when mourning the death of her young son, she may be using the excuse of language to avoid sharing deeply personal emotions, or she may be suggesting that English is less eloquently evocative of emotion than Chippewa, not that she is less fluent. That she was aware of the power of language is obvious. She and John raised their children to be bi-lingual in Chippewa and English, an acknowledgment that they, too, would be acculturated métis, would always move between two cultures, and so would need to be fluent in the languages of both.

That they would be bi-lingual instead of quatre-lingual like their father reflects history. Although the French lost their place in North America when they lost the Seven Years' War in America (the French and Indian War) in 1760, the French language persisted in the fur trading regions until well into the nineteenth century because of the forceful legacy of mixed-race culture. The mixed culture of languages, like the mixed culture of the Great Lakes peoples, implies that although the land may have technically belonged to one or another European power and to then the United States, it really belonged to the only people who knew how to survive in it. Until the turn of the twentieth century when upper lakes Indian peoples were restrained on reservations, they and their métis descendants were the real "Caesars of the wilderness," the masters of place, sustenance, and communication, not the European fur traders with trinkets to trade like Raddison and Groselliers who described themselves as Caesars. The casual ease with which John Morrison negotiates the different demands of sometimes competing cultures and languages attests to this. As Eliza Morrison's father notes, he is "liked by the whites," which was becoming ever more necessary in the nineteenth century, but when John's Indian relatives wish him to join in their Midéwiwin ceremonies he diplomatically smooths over his refusal with a gift of tobacco that acknowledges his traditional responsibility as a nephew even as he chooses not to participate to remain true to his Catholic faith. If he does not speak Chippewa with them, he can communicate in signs, another language still. William Gray, for all his erudition, for all his sympathy toward Indian peoples, is at a disadvantage in the woods of northern Wisconsin. Ultimately his campfire becomes a symbol not of companionship and intellectual light as he intended, but of conflagration, of the fires that burned the slashings left from the old-growth forests of the Great Lakes and extinguished any possibilities for traditional Indian life, complete with sign language marked on trees that left a record of culture, of history. Gray's campfire burns only in one place and his journeys are linear—from the city to the camp in summer—rather than circular, free-ranging, multi-cultural, and multi-lingual as the Indians' and métis' had been.

ELIZA MORRISON DOES NOT END *A Little History of My Forest Life* with detailed incidents of life on the reservation at Odanah, as readers might expect, but with Indian stories, unlike all the stories of her life and the lives of others she has told before, and the temptation is to see them as fulfilling yet-another request from Mrs. Gray or as an afterthought. To understand why this is not so, it is necessary to know how Indian stories functioned in the cultures that created them, which Mrs. Morrison does not tell.

In societies without writing, culture—including history, tradition, behavioral rules, and social concerns—are transmitted by stories, either myths (*auwaetchigum*) which conveyed important cultural and historical information and could be told only in winter when the creatures used as examples, often negatively, were hibernating so could not hear and be offended, or tales (*daebaudjimowin*), chronicles of personal experience which illustrated exemplary personal behaviors or cautioned against evil ones and could be told any time of year. Many storytellers were highly respected older women who expected nothing in return for their wisdom except a comfortable place in the lodge and small gifts in return for sharing their knowledge. Stories were a critical part of religious ceremonies, of war activities, of training for the young, and, in the upper Great Lakes, a way to get through the long winters without social collapse, even when starving. Because Indian stories don't come with copyright dates, it is impossible to know when they were created, and the stories with which Mrs. Morrison ends her narrative may have been told in much the same form as she tells them for hundreds of years.

They may also have been revised, by herself or someone else, to comment upon more recent concerns and to suggest appropriate contemporary behavior. No story is timeless, and healthy cultures adapt their traditional stories to address the social problems faced by the audience that hears them. Suspense becomes less important because everyone has heard the stories before, while listening for changes and trying to figure out what the storyteller means

by them become paramount. In other words, if Mrs. Morrison chose to send a message to her readers in a traditional Indian fashion, she would tell a story and leave it to her readers to reflect upon how the message or point of the story commented upon all she had told before. Rather than being an afterthought, the stories with which Mrs. Morrison ends *A Little History of My Forest Life* are the climax of her narrative and are designed to point to the most important elements in it.

Mrs. Morrison's stories do not appear in *Ojibwa Texts*, the collections the ethnologist William Jones, a protégé of Franz Boas who created the discipline of ethnology, assembled at about the same time and in nearly the same place, so readers cannot compare hers with what others told.[110] That is not particularly surprising. Métis like Mrs. Morrison were not self-described Indians living in a traditional manner; theoretically she would not have been considered an uncorrupted informant. In addition, the choice of which stories are preserved is always function of who is doing the preserving, and her stories are not necessarily ones that would have appealed to male, university-trained ethnologists as significant.

Mrs. Morrison's stories are local, and reflect the distinct landscape of the Apostle Islands which have numerous, small, rocky islands where one could easily be marooned. They are women's stories, not the great myths of cultural foundation that among the Chippewa seldom, if ever, have women characters, but which Mrs. Morrison surely would have known. There are no trickster figures, a staple of American Indian stories, and the *windigo*, the cannibal monster made of ice who stalked the winter camps of the Chippewa, does not appear. Mrs. Morrison's stories, like the narratives of preying males she recounts from Mrs. Bousky, are women's literature, the stories communities of women tell to each other, and although she got them from her uncle, they were the ones she chose to pass down to Kitty Gray. She does not interpret them, since traditional storytellers never did, but ends with the songs connected to them as a traditional teller would have ended them, and then changes the subject. Yet, also in traditional fashion, the stories and songs she relates are a comment, a coda, upon all the relationships between men and women she has described in her narrative.

In the first, the tale of Ningoiou and her quest for revenge on her brother-in-law, Omashkego, the main point is obvious: if the man a woman loves behaves selfishly, he deserves to suffer, but revenge is a dangerous tool. Omashkego ignored cultural tradition and offended the woman he first agreed to marry by chasing after her younger sister and caused mayhem as a result. Ningoiou pays for her revenge with her life, but the suitors from the north shore of Lake Superior are portrayed as treating women like objects and ignoring cultural practices. There are no winners in this complex, troubling tale, but there is an acknowledgment that personal revenge for selfish pride, without the sanction of the community after due deliberation, only causes chaos. It may be that this story arose during the hundred-years war between the Chippewa and the Dakota that affected nearly all Indian lives near the present-day Wisconsin and Minnesota border and that was fueled by revenge. As John Morrison related to the Grays, the beginnings of that war might have been "about a murder. If the dead man's friends took vengeance, then the friends of the man who was accused would take vengeance, and when that was started, it never could stop. There would always be vengeance on both sides."[111] Ningoiou's story may also be a reminder that during a time of rapid, unpredictable change, such as the Chippewa had endured for more than a century, allegiance to tradition is important to preserve culture. Finally, the story may have appealed to Mrs. Morrison because it resonated with her own life. Her older sister caused problems in Eliza's life by abandoning their mother's care to marry, and Eliza faced the dangers of ten pregnancies when childbirth was the leading cause of death for women.

The second story is more positive. When Negauajikua is rescued from the rock, Mrs. Morrison suggests that if a woman chooses the wrong man and is abandoned, a noble man will rescue her, just like her dream said he would. This story is every woman's fantasy of being rescued by the man she was supposed to marry all along. It acknowledges the power of dreams in Indian culture, it rewrites the negative ending of the first story, and it may have had personal resonance for Mrs. Morrison as well. She does not say if she experienced an unhappy romance before John returned from the woods to Bayfield and married her, although she suggests through the comments of others that she had refused offers to marry before John. This story may also be an understated comment on their marriage. She has spent much of *A Little History of My Forest Life* describing that marriage, and she's not always written kindly of John, tallying his mistakes while admitting few of her own. For her to end with a romantic tale of rescue is not only a happily-ever-after fantasy, but a statement that their marriage has worked out well. By placing it at the end of her narrative, she points back to the beginning, for the story is about the beginning of a marriage and her autobiography has been about the life of that marriage over time. She has, once again, inscribed a circular journey, not of place or seasons, but of love over time.

TIME AS CIRCULAR, FOLLOWING THE round of the seasons, rather than time as linear, with history as a progression, is a quintessentially Indian concept. One does not always move forward toward some distant ideal of progress, which white, westernized cultures take for granted, but one begins each year anew, replicating a circle of life that encloses all within it. Mrs. Morrison may write a more-or-less linear narrative of her history, but she encloses it

within a narrative circle that has no beginning and no end, linking a traditional Indian past with a mixed-race present. But for her to end her narrative with a happy story, rather than an extended description of life on the reservation at Bad River, is as much a gesture of hope as William Gray communing with trees while lumbermen waited with their saws at the edge of the woods. In their different fashions, both Eliza Morrison and William Gray memorialize ways of life in a place that was being irrevocably changed, and although the Morrison's landscape and the cultures who lived and journeyed there were different from Gray's, both places were vanishing into the paper on which they would be described. *A Little History of My Forest Life* and the "Campfire Musings" editorials celebrate, even as they mourn, a forested past that could never be recovered and so join the métis woman and the white man, and all the voices that they both employed, in what ultimately becomes the oldest and most enduring American lament: an elegy for a lost paradise.

In the Great Lakes, particularly the pays d'en haut of the western Lake Superior country, that paradise is a palimpsest, like a page from an ancient manuscript that has been repeatedly written upon and erased and written upon anew by different peoples. What Eliza Morrison does not choose to discuss, even so fleetingly as William Gray, is that the land the Chippewa lived on and enjoyed before they were forced to surrender it in treaties to whites had once belonged to the others. The western Lake

Superior country that the Chippewa ceded in treaties was land they had forcibly taken from the Dakota when the Chippewa obtained guns from the French, and the reasons are not hard to find. The region was rich in fur and foodstuffs and, for a boreal climate, the living was relatively easy. In a contest of strength, the Chippewa with their guns and their alliance with the French won, and the Dakota were displaced. They eventually developed a rich and colorful life, one often used as a symbol of American Indian culture with horses and buffalo, but it was not without its seasons of starvation and misery, as their stories attest. When the Dakota received guns as well, the war that ensued lasted for more than a hundred years and was ended only by treaties that deprived both tribes of their contested ancestral lands. That war was only the most recent: the western Great Lakes region, including Mrs. Morrison's beloved La Pointe, had been home to a diaspora of displaced and warring peoples for hundreds of years of written history; before that, the archeological records suggest there were thousands of years of migrations, and so probably contests, over who would control the land.

The trenchant, and troubling, question is when do differences in race or ethnicity or class cease being differences between equals, like the Chippewa-Dakota War, and become exploitation and imperialism? There are no easy answers. The Grays were able to play at living in the wilderness and celebrate its beauty, courtesy of the McCormick's industrial revolution dollars, which came from a process that would eventually destroy that same wilderness. The Grays were tourists, not pioneers, but their tourism also enabled the Morrisons to earn hard cash at a time when they might not have been able to do so easily any other way. The Morrisons were loyal and steadfast employees, but the Gray's kindness to them was more than many employers would have bestowed; it also set in motion a chain of reciprocity that led to a unique, historic manuscript. The Grays may well have taken advantage of Mrs. McCormick's money, but she may have believed that by furnishing a camp for the Grays she was buying the loyalty of an editor who would then write benign essays about the virtues of nature rather than the business practices of industrialists like her deceased husband and, as an added benefit, babysit her sons. Perhaps the Grays thought they were contributing to science by collecting the Morrison's stories. Certainly Mrs. Morrison wrote because times were hard and she felt she needed to oblige for past favors, but she also obviously relished the chance to continue telling stories to an appreciative audience that treasured her narrative and preserved it. Students of multi-cultural writing would describe *A Little History of My Forest Life* as a "post-colonial text," that is, a narrative written by someone from a culture that had been colonized, or controlled, by another ethnic group,[112] and suggest that without the operations of power and class, especially as they pressed upon the Morrisons, there would have been no autoethnography. This type of critical lens would view the Morrisons as examples of a colonized people who didn't comprehend how vulnerable and maligned they actually were. If they did muster the strength to resist, it would need to be cloaked in rhetorical strategies and subterfuge, such as telling stories that reflected badly on powerful white men in a narrative written for a whites.

This is a seductive, politically-correct reading of *A Little History of My Forest Life*, and it is supported by Mrs. Morrison's stories about white, urban men assuming Indian women were theirs for the taking. But the white men fail and look like fools, and she gives equal emphasis to the story of an egotistical Indian woman who murders from selfish revenge. Mrs. Morrison may ignore the more war-like incidents of Chippewa history, and she makes explicit that the fur trade could not have operated without native peoples, particularly women, but she also castigates alcoholism among those same Natives. At the time she wrote the politics and history of the upper Great Lakes had been a maelstrom of conflicting claims and sympathies for centuries; few were blameless.

All contemporary readers can know is that although Mrs. Morrison may have taken orders from William Gray as his cook, her writing asserts unequivocally her intelligence and independence, staking her claim to interpret history the same as his editorials did. Indeed, she appears to assume he would use some of her stories in his essays. As her later letters to Mrs. Gray demonstrate, the women remained cordial

into old age, long after the the Grays ceased regularly using the camp and Mrs. McCormick began selling off the timber. The Grays were educated as the Morrisons were not, but the Morrisons were highly intelligent and, moreover, skilled in ways the Grays were not and needed. Mrs. Morrison was a child of several cultures—Indian, European, American, and métis—and in her métissage narrative's organization, languages, and emphasis, it reflects all the cultural possibilities she inherited. She may have written for someone else, but the power to determine what she wrote and how she wrote it was hers alone and she did not relinquish it. She assumed the editor's chair she had seen occupied by William Gray, but for her the power of that position was compromised because she wrote in a era when race had begun to matter as it never had before.

As historians have pointed out, Indians in the United States are perceived as mainstream culture chooses to perceive them, a vision that has alternated among portraits of bloodthirsty savages, of doomed forest nobility, and, most recently, of environmental prophets. But no narrative written by an Indian or a mixed-race person in the nineteenth century can escape a dual complication: autobiography and autoethnology are slippery forms that owe as much to fiction as they do to fact, and Indian or métis texts cannot escape writing into or against a tradition of white cultural dominance that "invents" Indians as it needs them to be to justify taking land or, as William Gray's interview with John Morrison shows, to critique the prejudices of whites. As one critic succinctly puts it, "The 'self' that is identifiable as Indian, and that has come to signify Indian, is Indian in contact with non-Indian."[113] But to be mixed-race like Mrs. Morrison is to be Indian in contact with non-Indian within the same person, which makes mixed-race narrative a different genre from white autobiography or from the ethnologies of traditional, non-English-speaking Indians that were recorded and edited (sometimes wildly) by anthropologists and ethnologists. According to one mixed-race writer, "mixed bloods actively loosen the seams in the shrouds of identities,"[114] but identity is not always a shroud. Sometimes it is a coat of many colors that suggests the powers of royalty to determine, choose, or confer, and sometimes it is a magic covering like the tent of an Indian conjurer, or *jessikid*, that gives the wearer great power to become whatever is desired and to amuse and confound her audience in the process.

Mrs. Morrison may have been asked to describe Indians by white people who had more money, power, and education, who were her employers, and who were interested in her partly because of her heritage. She may have felt compelled to write to repay them and so to establish a more equitable relationship, to make certain they understood they were not providing charity to her as a benighted minority but entering into a gift exchange. But like many writers she used her task to explore what concerned her as well. Set her tale a hundred years earlier and it might have been about being

Indian and meeting fur traders, about escaping the Dakota-Chippewa Wars, and about raising her children to understand the possibilities and problems of being mixed race, all of which she describes her grandmother relating. Set it a hundred years later and Mrs. Morrison could have documented the disastrous failures of government Indian policies, the bitter legacies of racism, and the politics of legalized gaming. Instead, she writes poised on the threshold between the traditional world of the fur trade and métis life she had observed as a child and the booming, unpredictable, and increasingly racist frontier she and her husband were negotiating every day, looking backward and forward in nearly the same breath, as she attempts to braid together all the strands of her life and history and the voices she knew. For her, writing meant, as it has for so many others, the opportunity to impose some order, however illusory, on the chaos of a rapidly changing present.

If the Grays had hoped for a narrative that not only recorded Indian customs but that also would be a useful example testifying to the positive effects of Protestant missionary work among native peoples, Mrs. Morrison's account may have proved faintly disappointing despite her reports of the efforts she made to attend services. Although she says Indians who are Christian are more evolved than those who are not, and she is careful to note who belongs to which church, she chooses no denominational sides. Her respect for her husband's devotion to Catholicism is clear, particularly when she describes the effort he makes to bury his young son in sacred ground in Bayfield despite the journey. More telling is her reaction when she and her children are faced with fear and hunger the first winter on their homestead. She does not look to God or to her Bible for help in overcoming adversity as a white homesteader caught in the same situation might have, but after quickly noting that she prayed, she relates at great length stories of her grandmother's strength on the journey. She is not comforted by abstract male figures of religious devotion, but by Indian women.

She does not write about her mixed-race mother, whom she seldom mentions after noting her marriage, illness, and death, but always about traditional Chippewa women who, like her grandmother and her friend Mrs. Bousky, were capable of heroic feats of strength and survival. At one point she notes the weight of the pack Mrs. Bousky could carry, then later Mrs. Morrison describes her own fall trip to Ashland and the huge pack she carried returning home to Spider Lake. Whenever she writes about her journeys, she describes her strength and determination, beginning with her story of rowing a large fishing boat by herself across the North Channel for a chance to see John Morrison. While she may be distancing herself from an invalid mother whose care cut short her schooling and took fifteen years from her life, she may also be comparing herself to Indian women to distance herself from the white model of delicate femininity being put forward as an ideal at the end of the nineteenth century, one that she may have observed in Mrs. Gray and Mrs. McCormick at Island Lake camp. Eliza Morrison is taking a subtle swipe at white pressures to acculturate, to live like white farmers and their wives, by noting the strength, and thus the freedom and control, of Indian women, and the model she uses for this is Margarette Bousky, another "pure Chippewa woman" like her grandmother, another of the voices given life through Mrs. Morrison's narrative. In both *A Little History of My Forest Life* and in Purcell's *St. Croix Trail Country*, Mrs. Bousky represents the idea of the exotic, the unacculturated Indian, and so in measuring how different she is from herself, Eliza Morrison can measure the amount of her own acculturation into white values. Or so she makes it seem to the unwary reader. But Purcell thought they were sisters and Mrs. Morrison appears to have done just about everything Mrs. Bousky did, except that Mrs. Morrison did it all while having children as well. In fact, Eliza Morrison has it both ways. She differentiates herself from Mrs. Bousky who doesn't speak English and appears to be traditional, but then she demonstrates how she can do everything Mrs. Bousky does and more besides, and so creates, once again, a mixed-race presence.

Like all autobiographers, Eliza Morrison picks and chooses what she will say to create a persona she wishes to present, and that is of a woman who may be part-Indian and who married someone more Indian-like than she, but who is also fully conversant with what it meant to be considered a competent wife and mother in progressive white fashions of the late nineteenth century, complete with homesteading, farming, and spring cleaning. She is careful to note she can distinguish between moral and immoral behavior, that her children have not grown up uneducated despite the lack of a school nearby and, in case there was any doubt, that race has nothing to do with character. Given the hardening racial stereotypes operating in the latter part of the nineteenth century—caused in part by the necessity of demonizing Indians and métis so whites could avoid guilt at taking their land—separating race from morality is a point she underscores. She fulfills all the conventions of white, female autobiography circa 1895: marriage, children (including a tragic death and her depression), church, nursing elderly parents, morality, and homemaking. She then fulfills many of the requirements of ethnological narrative as well: marriage and mourning customs, food-ways, and racial negotiation. And in combining the two, she has created métis autoethnography. She likes sidewalks; she likes living on wild game in the woods. She is proud of being able to pack loads over a rough forest trail, even though at one point her burden is barely manageable because she had shopped too much. She enjoys going to church in town as any white lady would; she loves camping for weeks at a time to make sugar. She keeps up her birch bark house; she notes doing her spring cleaning in her homestead. She speaks Chippewa; she writes in English. The list could go on, eventually incorporating all the possibilities of Eliza Morrison's mixed-race world. Like her husband, she is a citizen of a new world, and although the physical journeys of that world are different, and sometimes more limited than the others she has described, the other journey she embarked on, that of memory and imagination, knew few boundaries.

When Johann Kohl, another white fascinated with the Indian and mixed-race cultures of the Lake Superior region, interviewed a voyageur in 1855, he asked him where he lived. *"Où je reste? Je ne peux pas te le dire. Je suis Voyageur—je suis Chicot, monsieur. Je rest partout."*[115] ("Where do I live? I can't say. I am a voyageur—I am mixed-blood, sir. I live everywhere.") To become a writer is to set out as a voyager in a different, equally fluid realm, a realm of memory rather than of water, and then to live imaginatively everywhere one chooses, facing the risks and toil required, but also experiencing a freedom many never know. The length and complexity of the story Eliza Morrison made time to write while she attended to all her other responsibilities as well was no less an achievement, no less a journey, than all the journeys made by all the voyageurs she had known. But her journey, unlike the others she relates, including her own, did not end, for it is with us still, a mark of her courage and intelligence.

To her, then, the raven's feather for her cap.

# NOTES

## Notes to "Introduction: Eliza Morrison's World": pages 16-42

1. Johann Kohl, *Kitchi-Gami: Life Among the Lake Superior Ojibway* (1860; reprint, St. Paul: Minnesota Historical Society Press, 1985): 260; Theresa M. Schenck, *"The Voice of the Crane Echoes Afar": The Sociopolitical Organization of the Lake Superior Ojibwa, 1640-1855* (New York: Garland, 1997); Jennifer S. H. Brown, *Strangers in the Blood: Fur Trade Company Families in Indian Country* (1980; reprint, Norman: University of Oklahoma Press, 1996); Jacqueline Peterson and Jennifer S. H. Brown, *The New Peoples: Being and Becoming Métis in North America* (Lincoln: University of Nebraska Press, 1985); Patrick J. Jung, "Forge, Destroy, and Preserve the Bonds of Empire: Euro-Americans, Native Americans, and Métis on the Wisconsin Frontier, 1634-1856" (MA thesis, Marquette University, 1997).

2. The exact definition of "frontier" has been debated since 1893 when Frederick Jackson Turner delivered his famous essay, "The Significance of the Frontier in American History," claiming that the development of the United States was explained by an area of open land for settlement. (The land was hardly open, of course, since the Indians lived there.) The frontier as he defined it was borderland between this "free" land and land already settled by whites, a place where various ethnic, cultural, and national groups met across boundaries and established a transient cultures. The frontier closes when one group, usually an intrusive one, gains complete control. See Jung, "Forge, Destroy, and Preserve."

3. Reginald Horsman, in *Race and Manifest Destiny* (Cambridge: Harvard University Press, 1981), explains how racism and manifest destiny intersected in the nineteenth century. Scientific racism was a decades-long popular theory that attempted to prove, by measuring skulls among other things, that some races were biologically inferior to whites. This is one reason nineteenth-century scientists collected Indian remains. See also Reginald Horsman, "Scientific Racism and the American Indian in the Nineteenth Century," *American Quarterly* 27 (1975): 152-68.

4. Hamilton Nelson Ross, *La Pointe—Village Outpost* (1960; reprint, Madison: State Historical Society of Wisconsin, 2000), 19. Ross points out that Radisson and Groseilliers were refused fur trading licenses because they would not agree to let a priest accompany them. At that time the church controlled ninety percent of the fur trade. The explorers' continuing battle with the authorities eventually propelled them to England where they founded the Hudson's Bay Company. For the debate on who went to Wisconsin and when, see Jung, 40.

5. Rhoda R. Gilman, "Last Days of the Upper Mississippi Fur Trade," in *People and Pelts: Selected Papers of the Second North American Fur Trade Conference*, edited by Malvina Bolus (Winnipeg: Hudson's Bay Company, 1972): 103-133; Jung, "Forge, Destroy, and Preserve"; Brown, *Strangers in The Blood.*

6. Peterson and Brown, *The New Peoples.* The concept of a "middle ground" to describe shared power in the fur trade is the creation of historian Richard White in *The Middle Ground: Indians, Empires, and Republics in the Great Lakes Region, 1650-1815* (New York: Cambridge University Press, 1991).

7. Brown, *Strangers in the Blood*, 24, 44-45

8. For more on Great Lakes métis communities, see Jacqueline Peterson, "Many Roads to Red River: Métis in the Great Lakes Region, 1680-1815," in Peterson and Brown, *The New Peoples,* 37-71.

9. Keith R. Widder, *Battle For The Soul: Métis Children Encounter Evangelical Protestants at Mackinaw Mission, 1823-1837* (East Lansing: Michigan State University Press, 1999). See also Carol Devens, *Countering Colonization: Native American Women and Great Lakes Missions, 1630-1900* (Berkeley: University of California Press, 1992).

10. The Bayfield Press, 14 January 1871.

11. Ross, *La Pointe,* 132.

12. Arlan Helgeson, *Farms in the Cutover: Agricultural Settlement in Northern Wisconsin* (Madison: State Historical Society of Wisconsin, 1962): Chapter One.

13. Personal interviews with John "Doug" Morrison, Ashland, Wisconsin, and Earl "Toby" Morrison, Odanah, Wisconsin, September 2000.

14. State of Wisconsin. *State v. Morrin* 117 N. W. 1006. Robert H. Keller, "An Economic History of Indian Treaties in the Great Lakes Region," *American Indian Journal* 4 (February 1978): 2-20; Ronald Satz, *Chippewa Treaty Rights: The Reserved Rights of Wisconsin's Chippewa Indians in Historical Perspective,* Transactions of the Wisconsin Academy of Sciences, Arts, and Letters 79:1(1991); Steven E. Silvern, "The Geography of Ojibwa Treaty Rights in Northern Wisconsin," in *Wisconsin Land and Life,* edited by Robert C. Ostergren and Thomas R. Vale, (Madison: University of Wisconsin Press, 1997): 489-504; Donald L. Fixico, "Chippewa Hunting and Fishing Rights and the Voight Decision," in *An Anthology of Western Great Lakes Indian History,* edited by Donald L. Fixico (Milwaukee: University of Wisconsin-Milwaukee Press, 1987).

15. One of the best recent books on nineteenth-century Indian life is James Wilson's *The Earth Shall Weep: A History of Native America* (New York: Atlantic Monthly Press, 1998). For Wisconsin Indian history, see Robert Nesbit, *The History of Wisconsin,* vol. III (Madison: State Historical Society of Wisconsin, 1985): 418-435; John D. Buenker, *The History of Wisconsin,* vol IV (Madison: State Historical Society of Wisconsin, 1998): 179-194.

16. Jung, "Forge, Destroy, and Preserve," Chapter 8; Walker D. Wyman, *The Chippewa; A History of the Great Lakes Woodland Tribe Over Three Centuries* (River Falls: University of Wisconsin-River Falls Press, 1993); Keller, "An Economic History of Indian Treaties": 2-20.

17. Edmund Danziger, *The Chippewas of Lake Superior* (Norman: University of Oklahoma Press, 1979).

18. Buenker, *History of Wisconsin,* 179-185.

19. Buenker, *History of Wisconsin,* 192.

20. The concept is Verne Dusenberry's in "Waiting for a Day That Never Comes" in Peterson and Brown, *The New Peoples.*

21. The choice métis people made between white culture and reservation life did not necessarily depend on skin color. It was more likely to be determined by where one's closest relatives lived, particularly mothers. See Jung, 516.

## Notes to A Little History of My Forest Life: pages 49-145

22. The early pages and some middle pages of the manuscript are missing. When that occurs, the version here will be based on a typescript. A note in the text will mark the beginning and end of use of the typescript.

23. The letters are printed out of date sequence here since the two letters of October 29, 1894, were apparently included as introductions to the first long section of manuscript, dated October 23. (All letters by Eliza Morrison are from the Eliza Morrison Correspondence, William Gray Purcell Papers, Northwest Architectural Archives, University of Minnesota, Minneapolis, Minnesota.)

24. The dates may be confused here; either she was 14 at the time or she conflated two trips or she remembered her sister's marriage as taking place in a different year from what church records say, which was 1851. Mrs Morrison could be referring to what is now called the Wisconsin Death March which took place in 1850. Her family may not have gone all the way to Sandy Lake, or they may have stayed with her brother, so they may have been protected from the worst of the disaster. Later in the manuscript she will describe another trip in 1851, which had much the same result, although annuities were paid and the Chippewa did not linger.

25. The La Pointe Mission Church Record for November 10, 1851, states: "Called at the house of Robert Morrin to marry Mr. Ervin Leihy and Miss Angelia [or Angelic, for Angelique] Morrin. She was Angelia Beavier."

26. The roll of mixed-blood claiments to compensation from the 1837 treaty was compiled at La Pointe in the fall of 1839. Joseph Coture, age 13 (b. 1826?), Angelique Coture, age 10 (b. 1829?), and Lenore Coture, age 11 (b. 1828?) were enrolled as mixed bloods by Robert Morin, (one "m"). At the same time, Robert Morrin (two "m's") enrolled Frances, age 32 (b. 1807?), William, age 3 (b. 1836?), and Eliza, age 1 (b. 1838?). The record for the Presbyterian school at La Pointe in 1843 lists among the mixed bloods: Eliza Morrin, Annos Morrin, Caroline Morrin, Mary Morrin, Angelic Morrin, and William Morrin. The La Pointe Mission Church records note that Annor (which could be anglicized to "Lenore" or "Hannah") Morrin made a profession of faith and was baptized in 1844. She married Peter Markman of L'Anse August 20, 1844. Angelic Morrin was baptized the same year and she married Ervin Leihy, November 10, 1851, when she was 22 and when Eliza would have been 14, a little while after she says her sister married and so she had to leave school. The 1860 census of La Pointe lists William, Eliza, Robert, Susan, and Margaret as the children of Robert Moran [sic], age 60, and Frances, age 58.

27. (Transcription from the original manuscript resumes here.) Eliza Morrin and John Morrison were married September 28, 1865. Frances Morrin had died August 18, 1865.

28. James B. Clow, the Chicago plumbing magnate, who hunted and fished in northern Wisconsin and hired the Morrison boys as guides and helpers.

29. This letter is inserted here for two reasons. William Gray Purcell has written "Nov. 1894" on the top of the manuscript page at this point. There is also the mark of a rusted paper clip on the page, suggesting that at one time the letter accompanying this next section of the manuscript was attached here.

30. John means that he will use trails through the woods rather than main roads.

31. Page six of the manuscript is missing; transcription from the typescript begins here.

32. Transcription from the original manuscript resumes here.

33. John is suggesting that Wabanimiki is a priest in the Nativist religious movement known as the Midéwiwin, which is what the long wigwam would be used for. Angering him by refusal to participate in a ceremony might be dangerous, and would also be shirking his duties as a nephew, but giving in and participating would go against John's Christian training. Nephews occupied a special place in the Anishinaabeg family; young men had an especially close relationship to their mother's brothers. In John Morrison's case this relationship would have been even closer, since both his parents were dead and he had been adopted by his mother's family. Wabanimiki is honoring John's relationship to famous relatives here and also attempting to get him to join the Midé ceremonies which might mean leaving the Catholic church.

34. Page missing from manuscript here; transcription from typescript begins here.

35. Transcription from the original manuscript resumes here.

36. Throughout her manuscript Mrs. Morrison will use "fit out" and "out fit" to describe getting equipment ready for work. "Out fit" used in this way is an old fur company term and referred to a group of traders who bought goods on credit from the company in fall, traded these goods to the Indians, and sold the furs back to the company. It also meant a place where these traders would gather, such as the "Northern Outfit," and so eventually came to mean a fur trade post or district.

37. This note is not written on a separate piece of paper, but on the folded-over end of a sheet of manuscript.

38. Frances Densmore, *Uses of Plants by the Chippewa Indians* (1926-1927; reprint, New York: Dover Publications, 1974): 308-313.

39. Robert E. Bieder, *Native American Communities in Wisconsin 1600-1960: A Study of Tradition and Change,* (Madison: University of Wisconsin Press, 1995): 103; Richard White, *The Middle Ground,* 218.

40. Apparently Eliza Morrison and her children who were still in school moved into Iron River during the winters so the children could attend classes. When she says "There is no body up to the farm," she is referring to the Morrison homestead at Spider Lake. "John" would be John Morrison who other years may have stayed with his older sons at the farm during the winter, but as she points out, they are all working on the reservation this year. "Mr Ramsdell" was one of the people employed by the Grays to help at their camp in summer; some years he stayed there in the winter. After this date the manuscript begins with "Page 1" and continues to the end. Earlier pages were not always numbered.

41. John Robert Morrison, born 25 June 1866, died 5 July 1897 after a four-year illness. See the letter from Eliza Morrison to Kitty Gray dated August 23, 1897 in the section "Additional Letters" following *A Little History of My Forest Life.*

42. Densmore, *Uses of Plants by the Chippewa Indians,* 386-390.

43. A shingle bolt was a length of trimmed and shaped log that was used to make roofing shingles.

44. A new page begins here and William Gray Purcell has written at the top "Dec. 30. 94." No accompanying letter has been found.

45. This may have been near "Leihy's Mill" as marked on the map "Bayfield & Ashland Counties."

46. The date is, again, written by William Gray Purcell on the top of the page. The message is on a separate piece of paper inserted in the manuscript at this point.

47. The practice of giving decorative medals arose because the French, British, and Americans needed someone who could negotiate business and treaties. Traditionally, Chippewa leadership had been consensual and confined to the totemic band, where leaders did not have authority beyond their relatives, did not have that for life, and different leaders were elected for different tasks. This drove the Europeans and Americans crazy, so they created "made chiefs," that is men who would have the respect of their people but who could also negotiate treaties for at least several bands. These men where given coats and large medals as marks of their authority. Since this went against Indian tradition, "made chiefs" were not always respected. See Richard White, *The Middle Ground,* 179.

48. Peter William Morrison was born at Odanah on October 24, 1867. (Dies before 1880.)

49. She is referring to *Micipijiu* or Missipeshu, the great horned lynx or underwater lion who controlled food supplies and travel by water.

50. There is a paper clip mark on this page as if at one time a letter or an envelope had been clipped to it.

51. William Gray Purcell's date.

52. The passenger steamer *Keewenaw*, 800 tons, was commissioned in 1866. Navigation season opened on the lower lakes that year on March 2. The date for the opening of navigation on Lake Superior would have been much later.

53. Point Iroquois is named after a 1662 battle when the Chippewa overcame a marauding Iroquois war party and killed them all. The Indian name for the point is *nadoueuigoning*, meaning "place of Iroquois bones."

54. The Morrisons probably offered food and supplies for the teamsters, their passengers, and their horses who traveled between Ashland, Bayfield, and Duluth.

55. Angeline Maggie Charlotte Morrison was born at Souix River on November 11, 1868. (Dies before 1880.) When Mrs. Morrison says "the spring of 68," she is confused. This would be the spring of 1869.

56. On April 26, 1855, Robert Morrin had bought outlot 36 in the village of La Pointe, containing three acres. It was 560 feet deep and 210 feet wide along the shore. This was American Fur Company land that was being sold cheaply to former employees. On April 12, 1870 (recorded date) Robert Morin conveyed to Eliza Morin the same property for $500.00. On May 27, 1879, John and Eliza Morrison sold the property to Antoine Denimie for $150.00. Today the property would probably include lot 36, located south of Chief Buffalo Lane.

57. James A. Clifton, "Wisconsin Death March: Explaining the Extremes in Old Northwest Indian Removal," Transactions of the Wisconsin Academy of Sciences, Arts, and Letters, vol. 75 (Madison, 1987): 1-39; Mark Diedrich, *Ojibway Oratory,* (Rochester, MN: Coyote Books, 1990).

58. George Catlin, *Letters and Notes on the Manners, Customs, and Condition of the North American Indians,* 2 vols. (1841; reprint, New York: Dover 1973): 139, pl. 243.

59. Densmore, *Chippewa Music* (1910, 1913; reprint two volumes in one, Minneapolis: Ross and Haines, 1973): vol. II, 83-117, 293-294; vol. I, 171.

60. A "mash man" is a *mashkikiwinni* or doctor in the Grand Medicine Society or Midéwiwin.

61. Mrs Morrison is using the old name for Madeline Island.

62. A rip saw is a hand saw designed to cut wood with the grain.

63. By this sugar season the Morrisons have had five children and lost two. John, Angeline, and Peter were born before they moved to La Pointe. After they returned to La Pointe full time Ervin Charles was born September 27, 1870; George Joseph was born December 12, 1871; Daniel Russell was born December 18, 1873; Thomas Samuel was born April 29, 1875; Benjamin Allen Morrison born September 19, 1877.

64. Michael Bousky's father (also named Michael, born 1794) and Eliza's mother (Francis, born 1802) were brother and sister. "Bousky" is a corruption of Bousquet or Bosquet (French for grove or thicket), probably the name of Eliza's French fur-trader grandfather.

65. Mrs Morrison is referring to Margarette Bousky, her cousin's wife. She is later described as a full-blood Chippewa. William Gray Purcell lists her birth date as 1837, her death date as 1910, and her parents as Gwegwekob and Bamidjiwanokwe, one of whom he believes was a chief at Odanah. His information undoubtedly came from some of the Morrison children who were living at Bad River when Purcell was writing about Island Lake. The 1880 census for Ashland County, Wisconsin, classed both Margarette (age 42) and her husband Michael (age 57) as Indian. In one place in the manuscript Mrs. Morrison relates that "Bousky" died in 1887 at 67 years of age; later she says he died in 1886. No death record has been found.

66. Thomas Vennum, Jr., *American Indian Lacrosse: Little Brother of War* (Washington, DC: Smithsonian Institution Press, 1994); Frances Densmore, *Chippewa Customs.* Bureau of American Ethnology, Bulletin 86 (1929; reprint, St. Paul: Minnesota Historical Society, 1979): 118-119.

67. She may mean 1879 or 1880. There appear to have been two severe winters when food supplies ran low, but this narrative also appears to be a continuation of the story she began earlier.

68. From an interview with William Cunningham Gray, "Campfire Musings," *Interior* (August, 1895; reprint, William Gray Purcell, "Medicine Talk," *The Northwest Architect* 7: 4 [April 1943]): 6.

69. S. A. Barrett, *The Dream Dance of the Chippewa and Menominee Indians of Northern Wisconsin.* Bulletin of the Public Museum of Milwaukee 1 (Milwaukee: 1911); Thomas Vennum, Jr., *The Ojibwa Dance Drum: Its History and Construction,* Smithsonian Folklife Series 2 (Washington, DC: 1982).

70. *Kitchimedkwe* designates the wife of the mashkikiwinni or doctor in the Midéwiwin or Grand Medicine Society.

71. Eunice Maggie Morrison

72. Melting snow and rain would have made the track impassable mud. In frontier country roads

and trails were only useful during summer (when they were dusty) and winter (when they were deep with snow).

73. "Pine hunters" were men who were surveying timber lands for the timber companies, looking particularly for the valuable, old-growth white pine. Pine was more valuable because it would float and so could be transported down the rivers and over the Great Lakes more easily than hardwoods such as maple or oak, which had to be shipped by rail or ship.

74. There is no note for March 4 in the manuscript. William Gray Purcell marks the date twice: after "taken by surprise" he notes "Mar 1895." At the top of the manuscript page beginning "away she went to a certain pointe" (next paragraph) he marks Mar 30 95, but no letter from March 30 has been discovered.

75. Like John Morrison's father, Michael Bousky was a hivernant, a winterer, that is a trader who spent the winter in the woods trading with the Indians.

76. Even without a severe winter, wild rice is not always a dependable crop.

77. Purcell, *St. Croix Trail Country*, 50-52.

78. Mrs. Bousky's story is not far-fetched. For many years in Northern Wisconsin, Indian women were the only women available to loggers and miners. This was one reason local whites helped the Indians resist removal. See R. N. Current, *The History of Wisconsin*. vol. 2 (Madison: State Historical Society of Wisconsin, 1976): 154.

79. Frances Densmore, *Chippewa Customs* (1929; reprint, Duluth: Minnesota Historical Society Press, 1979) : 154-157.

80. In *St. Croix Trail Country* (116) Purcell gives a slightly different version:
   That morning Grandfather Gray and I had gone down to the ice house on the west side of the Island to cut a roast of venison stowed near the ice under a thick layer of sawdust. There we found Mrs. Bosquet, up to her knees in the lake, her blue gingham skirt wet nearly to the waist. She waved us a cheerful greeting with the bread knife she was using to cut, laboriously, green rushes three or four feet long. Around the campfire we had heard 'the ladies,' as women were collectively called by border men in that gallant day, talking about a project to make rush mats for Grandfather's library cabin. Evidently the project was under way.
   Grandfather called to her, "Hold up, Mrs. Bosquet; we'll help you do that easier. Willie, run across to the boathouse and get down that newest scythe hanging on the rafter log. Watch yourself, don't trip on the blade. And row the scow around here." It took me about fifteen minutes. When I got back Mrs. Bosquet had wrung out her skirt and Grandfather had taken the roast up the hill to the kitchen.
   Grandfather now got into the back of the scow and held the blade of the scythe angled out to one side, close to the bottom. I rowed. Down fell a swath of rushes, two feet wide and fifty feet long. Mrs. Bosquet was on the shore, dancing and laughing.
   Later in the morning Will Bicknell, along with young Will, came down bringing the Scovill view camera. By that time Mrs. Bosquet had the big brass kettle boiling over her fire on the shore and had selected and tied the reeds in bunches of even length. These she dipped in the kettle half a minute, first one end, then the other, and hung them over a clothesline to dry before weaving them into the mats.

81. The sequence of living places is unclear. The log house Mrs. Morrison says John built in 1880 was probably at Spider Lake, and the date here, 1881, is wrong. The Bousky's "shanty" which the Morrisons first shared, may have been at Spider Lake, or it may have been at Pike Lake. The manuscript is not clear, but it does not seem logical that John Morrison would have built two houses.

82. Edward Francis Morrison, who was born in 1879, just before the Morrisons left Ashland.

83. The northern Pennsylvania Railroad line from Duluth to Ashland. See map "Bayfield & Ashland Counties."

84. This would be near the St. Croix River.

85. Warren, *History of the Ojibway People;* Schenck, *"The Voice of the Crane Echoes Afar";* White, *The Middle Ground:* 18.

86. The Morrisons moved in 1879. "Taking the cars" was a nineteenth-century term for riding the train.

87. A fisher is a type of weasel.

88. Joseph N. Nicollet, *Journals.* Translated by André Fertey and edited by Martha Bray. (St. Paul: Minnesota Historical Society, 1970): 266-269; Garrick Mallery, *Picture Writing of the American Indians* (1893; reprint, 2 vols. New York: Dover, 1972).

89. The Chippewa believed that the journey down the road to the afterlife took three days. On the way, the dead person was required to cross a narrow, slippery, swaying bridge. Those who fell into the river below perished forever.

90. Unless there is another child unaccounted for, only five Morrison boys were born at La Pointe.

91. St. Louis was the headquarters of the Western Department of the American Fur Company.

92. She has finished.

93. This would have been her puberty fast. Women were not required to dream as men were, but were considered lucky if they did.

## Notes to "Interpretation: Eliza Morrison's Journeys": pages 149-171

94. Race can indeed be a construction, as Reginald Horsman points out in *Race and Manifest Destiny.* For many years in the nineteenth century, white Americans were considered to be a new and better "race," one that was "mixed" from the other races in Europe and so incorporated the best characteristics of all (Horsman, 2-6). The recent census of the United States demonstrates this concept once again. There are now many more people describing themselves as "Indian" than can be accounted for by birth rate alone, suggesting that as it has become acceptable, even fashionable, to be Indian descent, more people have chosen to identify themselves as this race.

95. Historians use the term métissage to mean the joining of a man and a woman of two different races; their children are métis. Literary critics have redefined métissage to mean a new kind of literature that comes from the blending of different traditions. For an excellent historical overview of mixed-race history in America, see Gary B. Nash, "The Hidden History of Mestizo America," *The Journal of American History* 83:3 (December 1995): 941-964. For literary theories about métissage,

see: François Lionnet, *Autobiographical Voices: Race, Gender, Self-Portraiture* (Ithaca: Cornell University Press, 1989); Chris Bongie, *Islands and Exiles: The Creole Identities of Post/Colonial Literatures* (Stanford: Stanford University Press, 1998); François Vergès, *Monsters and Revolutionaries: Colonial Family Romance and Métissage* (Durham: Duke University Press, 1999).

96. The best historical overview of métis life in the Great Lakes region is Peterson, "Many Roads to Red River." The influence of Great Lakes métis culture on literature is more difficult quantify, but a comparison with western American fiction incorporating métis characters is intriguing.

Marie Vautier's analysis of Amerindian and Métis writings in Quebec suggests that these texts, unlike the writings of western American writers, are not hampered by binary limitations (us/Other), tend to be ambivalent about stereotypes and outcomes, and "offer the possibility of a less confrontational perception of difference" (10). She points out that because ethnologists estimate sixty percent of the Québécois population has "du sang indien," (some Indian blood), the complexities are greater than simple postcolonial theories of "the West and the rest" can explain, particularly when dealing with a text by a writer who is the product of at least two centuries of racial mixing and transculturation in a region where there was always a strong Métis or métis presence. Scholars studying American fiction with mixed-blood characters, however, report writers frequently paint a grim portrait of métis life, particularly in the West, where métis either die or suffer rejection by everyone. The only "mixed-bloods" who escape negative fates are those who are what William Scheick calls "figurative half-blood," that is whites who have taken on the values and skills of Indians but keep a white identity; James Fenimore Cooper's Leather-Stocking is an example.

The difference, I would suggest, can be accounted for by the different patterns of white conquest in the Western US and the Great Lakes. In the West, colonialization took place in decades, rather then centuries, racial mixing occurred in a climate of extreme prejudice fostered by white Americans rather than the more tolerant French, and the Western Indians, having seen what happened to Indians in the East, fought back. There was no "middle ground" of shared economic endeavor. *A Little History of My Forest Life* offers an example, however transitory, of métis peoples before they were compelled to choose assimilation or the reservation. To understand Mrs. Morrison's text it is helpful to avoid critical upstreaming, that is applying contemporary critical theories of post-colonialism, transculturation, and ethnocriticism to a text written in a very different era. Mrs. Morrison may be a "colonized subject" but she evades representing herself as the Grays might wish it. She determines how to repay the Grays; when they ask for more about the Indians, she briefly relates something and then goes back to her own story. Indeed, she seldom relates anything about traditional Indian culture that she has not seen or experienced and when she is faced by a custom she doesn't understand, she notes it briefly and moves on. She is hardly, as Louis Owen suggests of mixed-bloods, "a tragic mirror for Euramerica." Contemporary American Indian novelists, nearly all of whom are mixed-race, may well conceive the mixed-blood as tragic; Mrs. Morrison does not. Tragic mixed-bloods may be a legacy of reservations and racism, and symbolize the failure to adapt to it or the results of resistance. Eliza and John Morrison clearly exemplify masterful adaptation and transculturation.

See: Marie Vautier, "Comparative Postcolonialism and the Amerindian in English-speaking Canada and Quebec," *Canadian Ethnic Studies/Etudes Ethnique au Canada* 28:3(3): 5-15; A. B. McClure, "A Literary Criticism: Mixed-Blood Reading," *Wicazo Sa Review* 11:2 (1995): 79-83; Brian Hubner, "'A Race of Mules': Mixed-Bloods in Western American Fiction," *Canadian Journal of Native Studies* 15:1 (1995): 61-74; Louis Owens, *Mixedblood Messages: Literature, Film, Family, Place* (Norman: University of Oklahoma Press, 1998); Arnold Krupat, "From 'Half-blood to Mixed-blood': Cogewea and the 'Discourse of Indian Blood,'" *Modern Fiction Studies* 45-1 (1999): 120-145; William Scheick, *The Half-Blood: A Cultural Symbol in Nineteenth-Century American Fiction.* Lexington: University Press of Kentucky, 1979.

97. Lionnet, *Race, Gender, Self-Portraiture,* 97-129.

98. Purcell, *St. Croix Trail Country,* 33-34.

99. Vergès, *Monsters and Revolutionaries,* 7.

100. Scholars of women's writing suggest that women who have not written before frequently begin in response to a suggestion or a request from a trusted other. I believe that Mrs. Morrison used Mrs. Gray much as male writers use a muse, that is an ideal audience but not necessarily one personally close. Mrs. Morrison and Mrs. Gray, while fond of each other as employee and employer, were not intimate friends. Moreover, Mrs. Gray clearly believed she belonged to a different class. She was usually accompanied to the camp by Annie Zeigler, whom Purcell describes as her "companion." Writing to her husband about her schedule for returning to Oak Park, Mrs. Gray sighs "I thought by waiting until then I would not have to have another attack of Morrisons coming in." Purcell adds a note to her letter which reads "Poor things they loved to visit!" thus underscoring her snobbishness as well as his own. (Gray Family Correspondence, Gray Family Archives, William Gray Purcell Papers, Northwest Architectural Archives.)

For information on women's autobiographical practices, see *Women, Autobiography, Theory: A Reader,* edited by Sidonie Smith and Julia Watson, (Madison: University of Wisconsin Press, 1998): 17. There is a substantial critical literature on American Indian autobiography; it is useful as background. See: H. David Brumble III, *American Indian Autobiography* (Berkeley: University of California Press, 1988); Hertha Dawn Wong, *Sending My Heart Back Across the Years: Tradition and Innovation in Native American Autobiography* (New York: Oxford University Press, 1992).

101. According to Catherine Gray, who recorded this observation, the McCormicks seldom used the camp, while the Grays stayed there all summer for years. Catherine Gray, "Recollections of the McCormick Family," (Gray Family Archives, Ms B2b2.2, William Gray Purcell Papers, Northwest Architectural Archives, University of Minnesota, Minneapolis).

102. For information about Cyrus McCormick, see Herbert Casson, *Cyrus Hall McCormick* (Chicago: McClurg, 1909); William Hutchinson, *Cyrus Hall McCormick* (New York: The Century Co., 1930); Cyrus McCormick, *The Century of the Reaper* (Boston: Houghton, Mifflin, 1931); Thwaites, Reuben Gold, *Cyrus Hall McCormick and The Reaper* (Madison: State Historical Society of Wisconsin, 1909).

103. The *Interior* was published from 1870 to 1910. William Gray collected selections from his "Campfire Musings" editorials in *Camp-fire Musings: Life and Good Times in the Woods* (New York: A. D. F. Randolph & Co., 1894); *Camp-Fire Musings* (New York: Fleming H. Revell, 1902) was published posthumously. Examining the original editorials is difficult since not all of them have been copied to microfilm; Oberlin College does have a complete run of the paper. Other editorials were collected, and probably edited, by William Gray Purcell in *To William Cunningham Gray* (Minneapolis, MN: Bruce, 1946) and *St. Croix Trail Country.*

104. The most comprehensive statement on the idea of the wilderness is Roderick Nash, *Wilderness and the American Mind,* (New Haven: Yale University Press, 1967). Philip J. Deloria, *Playing Indian* (New Haven: Yale University Press, 1998).

105. William Gray, *Camp-fire Musings,* 209.

106. Interview with William C. Gray, Ph.d., LL.D. *The Oak Park Times* 3 November 1899: page 1.

107. Quoted in *The St. Croix: Midwest Border River* by James Taylor Dunn (New York: Holt, Rinehart and Winston, 1965); 22. Dunn quotes Folsom, and then adds ". . . for years [the Indians on the upper St. Croix] have eked out a miserable existence, still plagued by Folsom's modern-day counterparts and their fatuous attitudes." The St. Croix Band of Chippewa Indians finally received federal recognition in November 28, 1938. Gray's description of trees and stars is from William Gray Purcell, *Dr. Gray...Who Was He?* (Bruce: Minneapolis, 1946): 18.

108. The descriptions of John Morrison's visits did not survive from Purcell's drafts to the final version of *St. Croix Trail Country.* He does use it earlier in "Medicine Talk," *The Northwest Architect* 7:4 (April 1943): 4. In *St. Croix Trail Country* he not only removes the description of John's visit as being prompted by seeing his wife and daughter, he does not include his observations that Mrs. Morrison, Mrs. Bousky, and Eunice seldom took days off. In so doing, he effectively erases a good deal of the class difference between the Grays and the Morrisons, which has the effect of making their relationship more equal than it was in reality. (William Gray Purcell Papers, Box 179, Folder 42 a1 and a5.1, Northwest Architectural Archives.)

Purcell's attitude towards the Morrisons was complicated. While he did not give the other white people who worked for the Grays at Island Lake as much attention or respect as he gave the Morrisons (and he gave the McCormicks hardly any), he also labeled his photograph that begins this essay "Democracy," a title that begs the question. If he had really believed the Island Lake camp was a democracy, why did he need to call attention to it except to congratulate himself and his grandparents for their broad-mindedness? Purcell repeatedly refers to one or the other of the Morrisons boys as "our Indian," and although he peppered Eliza and John's sons for information and photographs to include in his book, he also penned a condescending little note on the corner of a letter to Daniel Morrison that Purcell was passing along to someone else: "To amuse you—A Chippewa Indian lives with his daughter—prosperous 'Americans' sure enough in Mil[waukee]—" Purcell began writing *St. Croix Trail Country* in the 1960s, an era when Indian life-ways were once again becoming fascinating to whites as they had been during his grandfather's time, and despite his fond memories of the Morrisons, he also knew his writing about them would find a ready audience.

Purcell, like his grandfather, seems to have been an equal-opportunity curmudgeon, since he is also condescending in his notes on another letter, this one from James B. Clow, the Chicago plumbing magnate who furnished the photograph of the Morrison's homestead. After snarling at Clow for signing himself "Chairman of the Board" of Clow & Sons on company letterhead ("How they love it—"), Purcell repeatedly spells his name "Clough," as if to underscore the Americanization of an Irish name. (Purcell Papers, Ms A42b1, Box 180, Northwest Architectural Archives.)

109. The text of the interview is reproduced in both "Medicine Talk," and *St. Croix Trail Country.* The versions are not identical. Purcell says the interview was printed in the Interior in August 1895, but the editor has been unable to obtain a copy.

110. William Jones, *Ojibwa Texts*. Edited by Truman Michelson. 2 vols. Publications of the American Ethnological Society 7 (New York: E. J. Brill, 1917, 1919).

111. "Medicine Talk," *The Northwest Architect* 7:4 (April 1943): 5.

112. There is a vast literature on post-coloniality, but it begins with Ashcroft, Griffiths, and Tiffin, *The Empire Writes Back: Theory and Practice in Post-Colonial Literatures* (London: Routledge, 1989). See also Mary Louise Pratt, *Imperial Eyes: Travel Writing and Transculturation* (London, 1992). Métissage is one of the newer formulations of post-colonial theory and Lionnet, quoted above, is a good source for information.

113. Grey Sarris, "American Indian Lives and Others' Selves: The Invention of Indian Selves in Autobiography," in *Thinking Bodies*, edited by Juliet MacCannell and Laura Zakarin (Stanford: Stanford University Press, 1994): 146

114. Gerald Vizenor, quoted in Krupat, "From 'Half-Blood to Mixedblood'": 122.

115. Kohl, *Kitchi-Gami*, 260.

# Glosssary of Chippewa Words and Phrases

Chippewa exists in many different dialects and, like all living languages, changes over time. The Chippewa words and phrases Mrs. Morrison uses are varients of northwestern Wisconsin Chippewa dialect as it was spoken in the nineteenth century. The editor thanks Paul DeMain for his help.

Proper names are capitalized

| | |
|---|---|
| Anishinaabeg | Spontaneous People; the Chippewa/Ojibwe |
| atongamig | still water |
| auwaetchigum | myths |
| awause | catfish |
| | |
| baaga'adowe | plays lacrosse |
| bawitig | rapids; lower end of Lake Superior near Sault Ste. Marie |
| biboon | winter |
| biwabiko sibi | metallic river or iron river |
| daebaudjimowin | non-sacred tale or story |
| deen de sa | blue jay |
| | |
| Edanigishik | Light On Both Sides |
| Equaqsayway | A chief's daughter for whom Madeline Island is named. |
| | |
| gagagiuabikong | rock that stands out of the water; Crow Rock. Probably no longer in existence. |
| gaietaakuendaueuin | old climbing place |
| gigonsi sibiwishen | Fish Creek; also wikwedo sibiwishen |
| gimishoomisinaan | grandfather |
| | |
| jessikid | conjurer; tent or lodge shaker |
| | |
| kabibonaka | Winter Maker; literally, "he who makes winter" |
| kakagan | home of the wall-eyed pike; fish trap of stakes |
| Kakinoacassi | John Morrison's mother |
| kaso | a birch bark vessel with a broad bottom and narrow top |
| kichiakakadebosh | untranslated; alligator? |
| kichimeda | wife of medicine doctor |
| Kijiikueyheyihs | Big Little Girl |
| kijinisajiwan | where the river meets the lake? |
| kijisasijiwanong | great falls of water; great current going at a great speed |
| kinikinic | tobacco |

| | |
|---|---|
| kinondawan | long wigiwam, Midé wigiwam; literally "hears it sounding out" |
| Ma Danse | John Morrison's Indian name |
| Makademikokue | Black Beaver Woman |
| makuk | birch bark container with a broad base |
| manidog | spirit helpers; incorporeal beings |
| mashkikiwinini | doctor in the Grand Medicine Society |
| maskisibing | "swamp river," the Chippewa name for Bad River |
| masinabikaniganing | a man carved out of stone |
| Medueiash | Battle By The Wind |
| Megindebad | Natural Big Head |
| mesabi | giant |
| Metance | John Morrison's father's Indian name |
| michikan | fish fence or rack across the river |
| micipijiu | Missipeshu; water monster or spirit, the Great Lynx |
| minnesagaegun | inland lake with island |
| Moningguanekaning | Yellow Bird Point. Also spelled Moningwunakauning and translated as Golden-Breasted Woodpecker Point. Indian name for Madeline Island |
| | |
| Nabaninaiki | White Thunder |
| nadoueuigoning | place of the Iroquois bones; Iroquois Point |
| Negauajikua | Sand Mountain Woman |
| neiamikang | sugaring and fishing place |
| nimanidominan | under water under earth spirit; my spirits |
| nimidana ashinanogosiuin | how many miles is it |
| ningodopuagan | measuring the time with pipe or acertaining the amount of time according to the custom |
| Ningoiou | the one; the oldest? |
| newissakodesibi | "half-burnt wood point river"; the Brule River |
| | |
| odena | town |
| ododeman | totem |
| Omaskigo | swamp Indian |
| Oshibiigan | writing tool? |
| | |
| pikwabiku sibi | river of iron or metallic river; same as biwabiko sibi |
| | |
| sagigamag | thoroughfare |
| shagawamikong | long island, long shallow place; Chequamegon Point |
| Shang wash | untranslated; a young Indian's name |

| | |
|---|---|
| tegoning | gardens; gitigoning—old gardens |
| Wabanimike | untranslated; chief's name |
| Wabegieah | Flower; Eliza Morrison's mother |
| Wasegishegokue | Very Bright Daylight Woman |
| wemitigoshianamia | a Catholic, literally "men of the waving stick," (priests who carried crosses) |
| wiigiwam | lodge shelter or dwelling of any type |
| wiigwaas | birchbark |
| wiisaakodewininiwag | half-burnt wood; a mixed-race person |
| wikwedosibiwishen | creek at the head of the bay |
| windigo | mythic cannible monster made of ice; spirit of excess |
| wisasagawichigewag | ten day's dance; Midé ceremony |

# GLOSSARY OF PLACES

Definitions of Indian place names are from "Indian Place Names in Wisconsin," by Herbert W. Kuhm, in *The Wisconsin Archeologist 33* (March & June 1952): 1-157.

| | |
|---|---|
| Apostle Islands: | A group of islands off the southern shore of Lake Superior near Ashland, Wisconsin. All are part of the Apostle Islands National Lakeshore except Madeline Island. |
| Ashland, Wisconsin | City on the southern shore of Lake Superior forty miles west of Duluth, Minnesota. |
| atongamig | Still Water; unidentified location on the Bad River that contained carvings or pictographs |
| Bad River: | River emptying into Lake Superior east of Ashland, Wisconsin. The Chippewa called it *maski sibing*, meaning "swamp river." Whites mistranslated *maski* "swamp" as *matchi* "bad." |
| Bad River Falls: | Falls area on the Bad River upstream from Odanah; probably near Leihy's Mill |
| Bad River Flats: | Area at the watershed of the Bad River. |
| Bad River Reservation: | Chippewa Reservation established in 1854 on the Indians' historic farming, gathering, fishing, and ricing lands. |
| Basswood Lake | Lake in the present-day Rainbow Lakes Wilderness Area of the Chequamegon National Forest, southwest of Ashland, Wisconsin. It is southeast of Hart Lake, which has a bay named after the Bouskys: Buskey Bay. |
| bawitig | "Falls"; Indian name for the lower end of Lake Superior near Sault Ste. Marie, Michigan, and Ontario. |
| Bayfield: | Town on the Wisconsin shore opposite Madeline Island. |
| Brule River | Bois Brule River in Douglas County, Wisconsin, part of the old fur |

trading route between Madeline Island and St. Louis. The name comes from the Chippewa *newissakode sibi,* "half-burnt wood point river."

| | |
|---|---|
| Chequamegon | Bay and point of land off present-day Ashland, Wisconsin. The word is sometimes translated as "soft beaver dam," although that meaning relates to an Indian legend describing how the point came to be. More accurate translations suggest the word means "a region of shoal water," or "where there are long breakers." |
| Clay Mountain | Unidentified location on the Bad River near Bad River Falls. |
| Crowkey | Cloquet, MN? a town west of Duluth. |
| Crow Rock | No longer exists; Mrs. Morrison says it was six miles south of Bayfield; Chippewa name was *gagaiwabikong* |
| Fish Creek | Stream at the head of Chequamegon Bay, known to the Chippewa as *gigonsi sibiwishen* or *wikwedo sibiwishen,* meaning "little fish creek" or "creek at the bay." |
| Fonderlac: | Fond du lac. A voyageur term for the end (bottom) of the lake, the area surrounding present-day Duluth. Now an Indian Reservation and a town in Wisconsin. |
| Gaietaakuendaueuin | old climbing place; area on the northeastern end of Madeline Island |
| Gardens | The Gardens or the Old Gardens. Historic Indian gardening area of rich land, ricing flats, and sugar maples in the watershed drained by the Bad and Kakagan Rivers. This became the Reservation of the Bad River Tribe in 1854. Chippewa knew it as gitigoning (old gardens). |
| Great Rock Place | Unidentified place on the Bad River near Bad River Falls which may be the Penokee Gap where the river cuts through various strata of rocks, remnants of ancient mountains. |
| Iron Lake | Lake southwest of present-day Iron River, Wisconsin. |
| Iron River, Wisconsin | Town forty miles west of Ashland, Wisconsin, known as *biwabiko sibi* or *pikwabiku sibi* (metallic or iron river) to the Chippewa. |

| | |
|---|---|
| Iroquois Point | Indian settlement on Lake Superior near Sault Ste. Marie, Michigan, so called because the Chippewa overcame a war party of Iroquois there. |
| John Stewart's Point | Perhaps near present-day section 28 on Madeline Island, facing Bayfield, Wisconsin. |
| Kakagan River | River that runs from the Bad River Indian Reservation north into Lake Superior, famed for its wild ricing grounds. It is frequently translated as "home of the wall-eyed pike," but a truer translation would be "trap of stakes," possibly used for catching sturgeon. |
| La Pointe | Village on Madeline Island in the Apostle Islands of Lake Superior. "La Pointe" was the French designation for the region at the western end of Lake Superior, including Madeline Island. |
| Masinabikaniganing | A man carved out of stone. Perhaps Pictured Rock on the Bad River in Bad River Reservation. |
| Middle Fort | The first French fort in 1693 was located on the south point of Madeline Island, now called Grant's Point, what the Ojibwe called moningwunakauning, meaning place of the golden-breasted wood-pecker or flicker. This fort was abandoned in 1698 when the fur trade collapsed. In 1718 the fur trade revived and the French returned to build a second fort at La Pointe Bay where there was a better harbor. This became known as "Middle Fort," so called because it was mid-way between first and last posts of the American Fur Company. |
| Minnesagaegun | Indian name for Island Lake, Wisconsin |
| Missabay Mountain | The hills of the Mesabi Iron Range, northwest of Duluth, Minnesota. Named after the Chippewa *missabe*, meaning "giant." |
| Mississippi River: | Mississippi is the corrupted form of the Ojibwe mishisibi, meaning "large river." |
| Moningguanekaning | Also spelled moningwunakauning, and meaning place of the golden-breasted woodpecker, or yellow bird point on present-day Madeline Island. Eventually moningwunakauning came to refer to the entire island. |

| | |
|---|---|
| Nadoueuigoning | place of the Iroquois bones; Iroquois Point near Sault Ste. Marie |
| Neiamikang | Point on Madeline Island where Indians made sugar and fished. This is probably at the present-day reservation lands on the northeast tip of the Island. |
| North Channel | The passage between Madeline Island and the eastern shore of Wisconsin where Bayfield is located. |
| Odanah | Chippewa word meaning "village." Now a town on the Bad River Reservation east of Ashland, Wisconsin. |
| Old Indian Trail | Trail near near Fish Creek |
| Pike Lake | Lake southeast of Iron River, Wisconsin where the Bouskys lived. Pike Lake is part of a chain of connected lakes, one of which is named Buskey Bay, undoubtedly after the Bouskys. |
| Portage Lake | Lake that bisects the Keeweenaw Peninsula of Michigan, part of the historic Indian route between Sault Ste. Marie and the western end of Lake Superior. |
| Porcupine Mountains | Range of hills on the western shoreline of the Upper Peninsula of Michigan |
| Quebeck | Quebec. Province of Canada. |
| Red Cliff | Indian Reservation north of Bayfield, Wisconsin. |
| St. Croix Falls | Town in western Wisconsin. |
| St. Croix River | River in western Wisconsin that joins the Mississippi and was part of the old fur trade route between Madeline Island and St. Louis. |
| Sault Ste. Marie | Twin cities on either side of the St. Mary's River which separates the United States and Canada at the eastern end of Lake Superior. |
| Shagawamikong | Long Island, the long sand spit that reaches out into Chequamegon Bay from the Kakagon River Sloughs. Another name for Chequamegon. |

| | |
|---|---|
| South Channel | The passage between Madeline Island and the southern shore of Lake Superior |
| Sioux River | River west of Ashland, Wisconsin |
| Spider Lake | Lake a few miles southeast of Iron River, Wisconsin in sections 29 and 30 of Bayfield County where the Morrisons built their homestead.  There is another Spider Lake nearby, now part of the Moquah Barrens Wildlife Area in the Chequamegon National Forest. |
| Spring Lake | Mrs. Morrison describes it as being "south east of Pike Lake," but the name has been changed since she wrote. There is a Spring Lake northwest of Pike Lake. |
| Yellow River | A river in western Wisconsin near the St. Croix River and near the present-day St. Croix Reservation. |

# Glossary of Proper Names

Names are listed as Mrs. Morrison spelled them or as they appear in captions to William Gray
Purcell's photographs.

| | |
|---|---|
| Bicknell, Will | neighbor of William C. Gray |
| Bousky, Margarette | Chippewa woman who was Michael Bousky's wife and worked for the Grays with Eliza Morrison. The spellings Bousky, Bosky, Busky or others are corruptions of the French "Bousquet" or "Bosquet" meaning grove or thicket. |
| Bousky, Michael | Eliza Morrison's first cousin, son of Michael Bousky, her uncle. |
| Clow, Mr. | Chicago plumbing magnate. |
| Edanigishik | Light On Both Sides; a Chippewa chief at Odanah. |
| Equaqsayway | A chief's daughter for whom Madeline Island is named. |
| Five Brothers | Unidentified; perhaps a warrior society from the southern Great Lakes region. |
| Gray, Catherine (Kitty) | Born Catherine Garns; wife of William C. Gray. |
| Gray, Dorothy | Unidentified relative of William Gray |
| Gray, Jonathon | Unidentified relative of William Gray |
| Gray, Will | Grandson of William Gray; cousin of Willian Gray Purcell |
| Gray, William Cunningham | Eliza Morrison's employer; editor of the *Interior*. |
| Leihy, Ervin | Eliza Morrison's brother-in-law, an area businessman and farmer. |
| Kakinoacassi | John Morrison's mother |
| Kijiikueyheyihs | Big Little Girl |
| Ma Danse | John Morrison's Indian name |
| Madweiash | The youngest of the Five Brothers, Chippewa leaders |
| Makademikokue | Black Beaver Woman. |
| McCormick, Cyrus | Inventor; also the name of his son |
| McCormick, Harold | Son of Cyrus McCormick |
| McCormick, Nettie | Mrs. Cyrus McCormick; part owner of Island Lake camp |
| Medueiash | Battle By The Wind; son of the youngest of the Five Brothers and John Morrison's cousin, called George by whites. |
| Megindebad | Natural Big Head. |
| Metance | John Morrison's father's Indian name |

| | |
|---|---|
| Morrin, Angelique | Eliza Morrison's half-sister, wife of Ervin Leihy |
| Morrin, Frances (Wabegiah) | Eliza Morrison's mother; wife of Robert |
| Morrin, Lenore (Hannah) | Eliza Morrison's half-sister; married to Peter Markman of L'Anse, Michigan, a Methodist minister |
| Morrin, Joseph | Eliza Morrison's brother |
| Morrin, Robert | Eliza Morrison's father |
| Morrin, Robert | Eliza Morrison's brother |
| Morrin, William | Eliza Morrison's brother |
| Morrison, John | Eliza Morrison's husband |
| Morrison, John | John Morrison's father (Metance) |
| Morrison, John | Johny; John and Eliza Morrison's oldest son |
| Morrison, Peter William | John and Eliza Morrison's second child |
| Morrison, Angeline | John and Eliza Morrison's third child |
| Morrison, Ervin Charles | John and Eliza Morrison's fourth child |
| Morrison, George Joseph | John and Eliza Morrison's fifth child |
| Morrison, Daniel Russel | John and Eliza Morrisons sixth child |
| Morrison, Thomas Samuel | John and Eliza Morrison's seventh child |
| Morrison, Benjamin Allen | John and Eliza Morrison's eighth child |
| Morrison, Edward Francis | John and Eliza Morrison's ninth child |
| Morrison, Eunice Maggie (Uni) | John and Eliza Morrison's tenth child |
| Muther, Albert | Unidentified; a guest of the Grays |
| | |
| Nabaninaiki | White Thunder |
| Negauajikua | Sand Mountain Woman |
| Ningoiou | The one; the oldest? |
| Norton, John | Accountant for the *Interior* |
| | |
| Omaskego | Swamp Indian |
| | |
| Mr. Pike | Elisha Pike, who owned a saw mill on what is now called Pike's Creek near Bayfield, Wisconsin. |
| Purcell, C. A. | Father of William Gray Purcell; a Chicago grain broker. |
| Purcell, Ralph | Younger brother of William Gray Purcell |
| Purcell, William Gray | Grandson of William Cunningham Gray; author of *St. Croix Trail Country* |
| | |
| Shang wash | A young Indian |
| Seven Brothers | Unidentified; perhaps a warrior society from the southern Great Lakes region. |
| G. A. Stahl | Gabriel Stahl; a business person in Bayfield who was a brother to Thomas Stahl, a La Pointe resident for sixty years. |

| | |
|---|---|
| Sission, Everett | Neighbor of the Grays in Oak Park, Illinois |
| Vaughn, Mr. | Samual Vaughn; a Bayfield businessman who owned a lumber mill, contracted out mail service, and operated steamboats. |
| | |
| Wabanimike | Chief at the Gardens, Indian settlement, later reservation, near Odanah, Wisconsin. |
| Wabegieah | Flower; Eliza Morrison's Mother |
| Wasegishegokue | Very Bright Daylight Woman |
| Wheeler, Mr. | Leonard Wheeler, missionary to the Chippewa who was instrumental in helping create the Odanah Reservation and so avoid relocation for the tribe. |
| | |
| Young, Gordon | Caretaker at the Gray's camp |
| | |
| Zeigler, Annie | Companion of Catherine Gray |

# ILLUSTRATION CREDITS

Apostle Islands National Lakeshore, National Park Service, Bayfield, Wisconsin
Clarke Historical Library, Mt. Pleasant, Michigan
Detroit Institute of Arts, Detroit, Michigan
Gilcrease Institute of American History and Art, Tulsa, Oklahoma
Historical Collections of the Great Lakes, Bowling Green State University, Bowling Green, Ohio
Milwaukee Public Museum, Milwaukee, Wisconsin
Minnesota Historical Society, St. Paul, Minnesota
National Archives of Canada, Ottawa, Ontario
Northwest Architectural Archives, University of Minnesota Libraries, Minneapolis, Minnesota
St. Louis County Historical Society, Duluth, Minnesota
State Historical Society of Wisconsin, Madison, Wisconsin
Wisconsin Cartographers' Guild

Area Surrounding Pike and Spider Lakes, Editor's Collection
Ball Play of the Dahcota Indians, Seth Eastman, Minnesota Historical Society (AV1991.85.42)
Bear Claw Necklace, Detroit Institute of Arts (81.644)
Bird's Eye View of Ashland, State Historical Society of Wisconsin (Whi(x3)33161)
Bird's-Eye View of Chequamegon Bay and Apostle Islands, State Historical Society of Wisconsin (Whi(x3)53969)
Campfire Gathering, William Gray Purcell, Northwest Architectural Archives (482)
Canoe Shooting the Rapids, Frances A. Hopkins, National Archives of Canada (C-2774)
Catherine "Kitty" Gray, William Gray Purcell, Northwest Architectural Archives
Chippewa Leggings, Detroit Institute of Arts (81.181.1)
Chippewa Yarn Bag, Detroit Institute of Arts, (81.285)
Chippeway Graves at Gordon, Wisconsin, 1894, William Gray Purcell, Northwest Architectural Archives
Cradle Board Carried By Mother, *Chippewa Customs*, Frances Densmore, Clarke Historical Library
Cutting Birch Bark Preparatory to Removing, *Uses of Plants by the Chippewa Indians,* Frances Densmore, Clarke Historical Library
Democracy, William Gray Purcell, Northwest Architectural Archives
Dog Team, Bayfield, Wisconsin, 1900, State Historical Society of Wisconsin Whi(x3)24674
Double Ball and Stick, and Lacrosse Ball and Racket, Milwaukee Public Museum (Cat. No. 426961)
Drum (or Dream) Dance Drum, Milwaukee Public Museum (Cat. No: 421001)
Eliza Morrison about 1894, William Gray Purcell, Northwest Architectural Archives
End and Fringe of Netted Belt, *Chippewa Customs*, Frances Densmore, Clarke Historical Library
Fish Drying Over Fire, *Chippewa Customs*, Frances Densmore, Clarke Historical Library
Fish Skiff and Sled Dogs, Apostle Islands National Lakeshsore, National Park Service
George and Ben or Tom Morrison with Deer, William Gray Purcell, Northwest Architectural Archives

Granulating Trough, Stirring Paddle, Granulating Ladles, and Makuk of Granulated Maple Sugar, *Uses of Plants by the Chippewa Indians,* Frances Densmore, Clarke Historical Library

Indian Dances, *Catlin Sketchbook*, George Catlin, Gilcrease Museum

Indian Sugar Camp, *The American Aboriginal Portfolio*, Seth Eastman, Clarke Historical Library

Indian Women Procuring Fuel, *The American Aboriginal Portfolio*, Seth Eastman, Clarke Historical Library

Island Lake Camp, William Gray Purcell, Northwest Architectural Archives

James Red Sky's Migration Chart, Wisconsin Cartographers' Guild

John and Eliza Morrison with Eunice and Grandchildren, Northwest Architectural Archives

Kitchen at Island Lake Camp, William Gray Purcell, Northwest Architectural Archives

La Pointe in 1852, State Historical Society of Wisconsin (Whi (x3)25367)

Letter Written by Eliza Morrison to Catherine Gray, Northwest Architectural Archives

Mackinac Boats at Manitowoc, Wisconsin, Historical Collections of the Great Lakes

Map: Bayfield & Ashland Counties, State Historical Society of Wisconsin (Whi(x3)53970)

Map: Madeline Island, Editor's Collection

Medicine Dance, *The American Aboriginal Portfolio*, Seth Eastman, Clarke Historical Library

Midéwiwin Bag, Detroit Institute of Arts (81.486)

Midéwiwin Lodge, *Chippewa Music,* Frances Densmore, Clarke Historical Library

Moccasin Made by Eliza Morrison for William Gray Purcell, William Gray Purcell, Northwest Architectural Archives

Morrison Homestead, James B. Clow, Northwest Architectural Archives

Mrs. Bousky Curing Rushes for Mats, William Gray Purcell, Northwest Architectural Archives

Ojibwe Wigwam at Grand Portage, Eastman Johnson, St. Louis County Historical Society

Old Mission Church and Cemetery, State Historical Society of Wisconsin (Whi(x2)20159)

Profile Rock, Apostle Islands National Lakeshore, National Park Service

Purcell's Map of Spider Lake, William Gray Purcell, Northwest Architectural Archives

Snowshoe Dance, at the First Snowfall, George Catlin, Gilcrease Institute

Stacked Dishes and Empty Cones, the Latter to be Filled with Sugar, *Uses of Plants by the Chippewa Indians,* Frances Densmore, Clarke Historical Library

Symbolic Petition of the Chippewa Chiefs, State Historical Society of Wisconsin (Whi(x3)34127)

The Long Journey (map), Editor's Collection

Two Pages from *A Little History of My Forest Life*, Northwest Architectural Archives

Unfinished Reed Mat on Frame, *Chippewa Customs,* Frances Densmore, Clarke Historical Library

William Cunningham Gray, William Gray Purcell, Northwest Architectural Archives

Woman Scraping a Buckskin, Milwaukee Public Museum (Cat. No. 50080-1)

Yarn Bag, front and back views, Detroit Institute of Arts, (81.285)

# Bibliography

Ashcroft, Bill, Gareth Griffiths, and Helen Tiffin. *The Empire Writes Back: Theory and Practice in Post-Colonial Literatures.* London: Routledge, 1989.

Barrett, S. A. *The Dream Dance of the Chippewa and Menominee Indians of Northern Wisconsin.* Bulletin of the Public Museum of the City of Milwaukee, vol. 1, article 4. Milwaukee, Wisconsin, 1911.

Bieder, Robert E. *Native American Communities in Wisconsin 1600-1960: A Study of Tradition and Change.* Madison: University of Wisconsin Press, 1995.

Blackbird, Andrew. *History of the Ottawa and Chippewa Indians of Michigan.* 1887. Reprint Petosky: Little Traverse Regional Historical Society, [n.d.].

Bongie, Chris. *Islands and Exiles: The Creole Identities of Post/Colonial Literature.* Stanford: Stanford University Press, 1998.

Brown, Jennifer S. H. *Strangers in the Blood: Fur Trade Company Families in Indian Country.* 1980. Reprint. Norman: University of Oklahoma Press, 1996.

Brumble, H. David III. *American Indian Autobiography.* Berkeley: University of California Press, 1998.

Buenker, John D. *The History of Wisconsin,* vol. IV. Madison: State Historical Society of Wisconsin, 1998.

Catlin, George. *Letters and Notes on the Manners, Customs, and Condition of the North American Indians,* 2 vols. 1841. Reprint. New York: Dover 1973.

Casson, Herbert. *Cyrus Hall McCormick.* Chicago: McClurg, 1909.

Clifton, James A. "Wisconsin Death March: Explaining the Extremes in Old Northwest Indian Removal." Transactions of the Wisconsin Academy of Sciences, Arts, and Letters 75 (1987): 1-39.

Current, R. N. *The History of Wisconsin.* vol II. Madison: State Historical Society of Wisconsin, 1976.

Danziger, Edmund. *The Chippewas of Lake Superior.* Norman: University of Oklahoma Press, 1979.

Deloria, Philip. *Playing Indian.* New Haven: Yale University Press, 1998.

Densmore, Frances. *Chippewa Music.* 2 vols. 1910-1913. Reprint. Minneapolis: Ross and Haines, 1973.

_____. *Uses of Plants by the Chippewa Indians.* 1926-1927. Reprint. New York: Dover Publications, 1974.

_____. *Chippewa Customs.* 1929. Reprint. Duluth: Minnesota Historical Society Press, 1979.

Devens, Carol. *Countering Colonization: Native American Women and Great Lakes Missions, 1630-1900.* Berkeley: University of California Press, 1992.

Diedrich, Mark. *Ojibway Oratory.* Rochester, MN: Coyote Books, 1990.

Dunn, James Taylor. *The St. Croix: Midwest Border River.* New York: Holt, Rinehart and Winston, 1965.

Dusenberry, Verne. "Waiting for a Day That Never Comes." In *The New Peoples: Being and Becoming Métis in North America.* Edited by Jacqueline Peterson and Jennifer S. H. Brown. Lincoln: University of Nebraska Press, 1985.

Fixico, Donald L. "Chippewa Fishing and Hunting Rights and the Voight Decision." *An Anthology of Western Great Lakes Indian History.* Edited by Donald L. Fixico. Milwaukee: University of Wisconsin-Milwaukee Press, 1987.

Gilman, Rhoda R. "Last Days of the Upper Mississippi Fur Trade." In *People and Pelts: Selected Papers of the Second North American Fur Trade Conference.* Edited by Malvina Bolus. Winnipeg: Hudson's Bay Company, 1972.

Gray, Catherine, "Recollections of the McCormick Family," (Gray Family Archives, Ms B2b2.2, William Gray Purcell Papers, Northwest Architectural Archives, University of Minnesota, Minneapolis).

Gray Family Archives. William Gray Purcell Papers. Northwest Architectural Archives, University of Minnesota, Minneapolis, Minnesota.

Gray, William C. *Camp-fire Musings: Life and Good Times in the Woods.* New York: A. D. F. Randolph & Co., 1894.

_____. *Camp-Fire Musings.* New York: Fleming H. Revell, 1902.

Helgeson, Arlan. *Farms in the Cutover: Agricultural Settlement in Northern Wisconsin.* Madison: State Historical Society of Wisconsin, 1962.

Horseman, Reginald. "Scientific Racism and the American Indian in the Nineteenth Century," *American Quarterly* 27 (1975): 152-68.

_____. *Race and Manifest Destiny; The Origins of American Racial Anglo-Saxonism.* Cambridge: Harvard University Press, 1981.

Hubner, Brian. "'A Race of Mules': Mixed-Bloods in Western American Fiction." *Canadian Journal of Native Studies* 15 (1): 61-74.

Hutchinson, William. *Cyrus Hall McCormick.* New York: The Century Co., 1930.

*Interior*, 1870-1910. Oak Park, Illinois.

Jones, William. *Ojibwa Texts.* Edited by Truman Michelson. 2 vols. Publications of the American Ethonological Society 7 (New York: E. J. Brill, 1917, 1919).

Jung, Patrick J. "Forge, Destroy, and Preserve the Bonds of Empire: Euro-Americans, Native Americans, and Métis on the Wisconsin Frontier, 1634-1856." MA thesis, Marquette University, 1997.

Keller, Robert H. "An Economic History of Indian Treaties in the Great Lakes Region." *American Indian Journal* 4 (February 1978): 2-20.

Kohl, Johann Georg. *Kitchi-Gami: Life Among the Lake Superior Ojibway.* 1860. Reprint. St. Paul:

Minnesota Historical Society Press, 1985.

Krupat, Arnold. "From 'Half-blood' to 'Mixed-blood': *Cogewea* and the 'Discourse of Indian Blood.'" *Modern Fiction Studies* 45.1 (1999): 120-145.

Kuhm, Herbert W. "Indian Place Names in Wisconsin." *The Wisconsin Archeologist* 33 (March & June 1952) 1-157.

La Pointe Mission Church Records. Minnesota Historical Society, Duluth, Minnesota.

Lionnet, Françoise. *Autobiographical Voices: Race, Gender, Self-Portraiture.* Ithaca, NY: Cornell University Press, 1989.

Mallery, Garrick. *Picture Writing of the American Indians.* 1893. Reprint. 2 vols. New York: Dover, 1972.

McCormick, Cyrus. *The Century of the Reaper.* Boston: Houghton, Mifflin, 1931.

McClure, A. B. "A Literary Criticism: Mixed Blood Reading." *Wicazo Sa Review* 11(2): 79-83.

Morrison, Eliza. Correspondence. William Gray Purcell Papers. Northwest Architectural Archives, University of Minnesota Libraries, Minneapolis, Minnesota.

_____. *A Little History of My Forest Life.* Edited by Austin J. McLean. LaCrosse, WI: Sumac Press, 1978.

Morrison, Earl "Toby." Personal Interview. Odanah, WI, September 2000.

Morrison, John "Doug." Personal Interview. Ashland, WI, September 2000.

Nash, Gary B. "The Hidden History of Mestizo America." *The Journal of American History* 83:3 (December 1995): 941-964.

Nash, Roderick. *Wilderness and the American Mind.* New Haven: Yale University Press, 1967.

Nesbit, Robert. *The History of Wisconsin*, vol. III. Madison: State Historical Society of Wisconsin, 1985.

Nicollet, Joseph N. *Journals.* Translated by André Fertey and edited by Martha Bray. St. Paul: Minnesota Historical Society, 1970.

Owens, Louis. *Mixedblood Messages: Literature, Film, Family, Place.* Norman: University of Oklahoma Press, 1998.

Peterson, Jacqueline, and Jennifer S. H. Brown, eds. *The New Peoples: Being and Becoming Métis in North America.* Lincoln: University of Nebraska Press, 1985.

Peterson, Jacqueline. "Many Roads to Red River: Métis Genesis in the Great Lakes Region, 1680-1815." In *The New Peoples: Being and Becoming Métis in North America.* Edited by Jacqueline Peterson and Jennifer S. H. Brown. Lincoln: University of Nebraska Press, 1985.

Pratt, Mary Louise. *Imperial Eyes: Travel Writing and Transculturation.* London: Routledge, 1992.

Purcell, William Gray. "Medicine Talk." *The Northwest Architect* 7:4 (April 1943): 4-6.

_____. Papers. Northwest Architectural Archives, University of Minnesota Libraries, Minneapolis, Minnesota.

_____. *Dr. Gray...Who Was He?* Minneapolis: Bruce, 1946.

_____. *To William Cunningham Gray.* Minneapolis: Bruce, 1946.

_____. *St. Croix Trail Country: Recollections of Wisconsin.* Minneapolis: University of Minnesota Press, 1967.

Ross, Hamilton Nelson. *La Pointe—Village Outpost.* 1960. Reprint. Madison: State Historical Society of Wisconsin, 2000.

Sarris, Greg. "American Indian Lives and Others' Selves: The Invention of Indian Selves in Autobiography." In *Thinking Bodies.* Edited by Juliet MacCannell and Laura Zakarin. Stanford: Stanford University Press, 1994.

Satz, Ronald N. *Chippewa Treaty Rights: The Reserved Rights of Wisconsin's Chippewa Indians in Historical Perspective.* Transactions of the Wisconsin Academy of Sciences, Arts, and Letters, vol. 79, no. 1, 1991.

Scheick, William. *The Half-Blood: A Cultural Symbol in Nineteenth-Century American Fiction.* Lexington: University Press of Kentucky, 1979.

Schenck, Theresa M. *"The Voice of the Crane Echoes Afar": The Sociopolitical Organization of the Lake Superior Ojibwa, 1640-1855.* New York: Garland, 1997.

Silvern, Steven E. "The Geography of Ojibwa Treaty Rights in Northern Wisconsin." In *Wisconsin Land and Life.* Edited by Robert C. Ostergren and Thomas R. Vale. Madison: University of Wisconsin Press, 1997.

Smith, Sidonie, and Julia Watson. *Women, Autobiography, Theory: A Reader.* Madison: University of Wisconsin Press, 1998.

State of Wisconsin. *State v. Morrin.* 117 N. W. 1006.

*The Bayfield Press,* 14 January 1871.

*The Oak Park Times,* 3 November 1899.

Thwaites, Reuben Gold. *Cyrus Hall McCormick and the Reaper.* Madison: State Historical Society of Wisconsin, 1909.

Turner, Frederick Jackson. "The Significance of The Frontier In American History." Address delivered at the forty-first annual meeting of the State Historical Society of Wisconsin, December 14, 1893.

Vautier, Marie. "Comparative Postcolonialism and the Amerindian in English-Speaking Canada and Quebec," *Canadian Ethnic Studies* 28:3 (1996): 4-15.

Vergès, François. *Monsters and Revolutionaries: Colonial Family Romance and Métissage.* (Durham: Duke University Press, 1999).

Vennum, Thomas Jr. *The Ojibwa Dance Drum: Its History and Construction.* Smithsonian Folklife Studies, no. 2. Washington, DC: Smithsonian Institution Press, 1982.

_____. *American Indian Lacrosse; Little Brother of War.* Washington, DC: Smithsonian Institution Press, 1994.

Warren, William W. *History of the Ojibway People.* 1885. Reprint. St. Paul: Minnesota Historical Society Press, 1984.

White, Richard. *The Middle Ground: Indians, Empires, and Republics in the Great Lakes Region, 1650-1815.* New York: Cambridge University Press, 1991.

Widder, Keith R. *Battle For The Soul: Métis Children Encounter Evangelical Protestants at Mackinaw Mission, 1823-1837.* East Lansing: Michigan State University Press, 1999.

Wilson, James. *The Earth Shall Weep: A History of Native America.* New York: Atlantic Monthly Press, 1998.

Wong, Hertha. *Sending My Heart Back Across the Years: Tradition and Innovation in Native American Autobiography.* New York: Oxford University Press, 1992.

Wyman, Walker D. *The Chippewa; A History of the Great Lakes Woodland Tribe Over Three Centuries.* River Falls: University of Wisconsin-River Falls Press, 1993.

# INDEX

See the glossaries beginning on page 185 for detailed listings of Chippewa words and phrases, personal names, and places. See the Bibliography beginning on page 198 for secondary sources.